to firmer ground

John Langmore is the author of *Dealing with America:
the UN, the US and Australia*, and is currently a
Professorial Fellow in the Department of Political
Science at the University of Melbourne. From 1997
to 2002 he was the Director of the UN Division for
Social Policy and Development, and from 1984 to
1996 he served as a Federal Labor MP.

to firmer ground

RESTORING HOPE IN AUSTRALIA

JOHN LANGMORE

UNSW PRESS

A UNSW Press book

Published by
University of New South Wales Press Ltd
University of New South Wales
Sydney NSW 2052
AUSTRALIA
www.unswpress.com.au

© UNSW Press 2007
First published 2007

National Library of Australia
Cataloguing-in-Publication entry

    Langmore, John, 1939– .
    To firmer ground: restoring hope in Australia.

    Bibliography.
    Includes index.
    ISBN 978 086840 847 7.

    1. Quality of life - Australia. 2. Social values -
    Australia. 3. Social action - Australia. 4. Australia -
    Social conditions. I. Title.

    306.0994

Design Josephine Pajor-Markus
Cover photos Di Quick
Printer Griffin Press

This book is printed on chlorine-free paper.

contents

Foreword   *David Yencken*   *vii*

Acknowledgments   *xi*

1   THE STATE OF AUSTRALIA   *1*

2   INDIVIDUAL INCOME OR WELLBEING FOR ALL?   *23*

    Overcoming injustice: Practical and symbolic
    reconciliation for Indigenous Australians
    Nicola Henry   *45*

3   TURNING THE TIDE: SOLUTIONS TO AUSTRALIA'S   *54*
   ENVIRONMENTAL CRISIS   *NICOLA HENRY*

4   HUMAN SECURITY: GUARANTEEING A DECENT LIFE   *87*
   FOR ALL   *ANDREW SCOTT*

5   INVESTING IN THE FUTURE: *121*
   AN ECONOMY WHICH SERVES SOCIETY

    Ireland's economic transformation:
    Strategy and pragmatism   *Roy Green*   *152*

6   ADVANCING GLOBAL SECURITY AND JUSTICE   *156*

7   REVITALISING AUSTRALIAN DEMOCRACY   *179*

8   A WAY FORWARD   *204*

   Notes   *216*

   Index   *239*

History says, Don't hope
On this side of the grave,
But then, once in a lifetime
The longed for tidal wave
Of justice can rise up
And hope and history rhyme.

Seamus Heaney, *The Cure at Troy*, 1990

foreword

The Australian Collaboration encourages the publication of books by prominent Australians. Previous books have included *How Ethical is Australia?: An Examination of Australia's Record as a Global Citizen* by Peter Singer and Tom Gregg and *A Big Fix: Radical Solutions for Australia's Environmental Crisis* by Ian Lowe.

The Collaboration felt that a book reviewing the state of Australian society would be a valuable addition to the material available for a general readership and approached Professor John Langmore to see if he was interested in writing a book of this kind. We thought that he would have an unusual perspective as an economist, former member of the federal Parliament, long-time senior official of the United Nations recently returned to Australia, and Professorial Fellow in the Centre for Public Policy at the University of Melbourne. Subsequently Dr Andrew Scott, senior lecturer at RMIT University, Dr Nicola Henry, researcher at the University of Melbourne, and Professor Roy Green, Dean of the Macquarie Graduate School of Management, joined the team of authors.

The potential span of such a book is huge, so the authors have necessarily been selective in what they have chosen to review and analyse. The book's main themes are: the state of Australian society; the different and often conflicting goals of income maximisation and human wellbeing; the most appropriate responses to Australia's environmental crises; human security and the guarantee of a decent life for all; an economy that invests in the future and serves society; Australia's role in advancing global security and justice; and the revitalising of Australian democracy and multiculturalism. *To Firmer Ground* concludes with a series of recommendations to set Australia on a more thoughtful, balanced and purposeful path.

The book offers many challenges to prevailing policies and orthodoxies. A central theme is the need for a much improved balance between environmental, social and economic policies so that Australia can genuinely set out along a path towards a sustainable society in the broadest interpretation of that term. *To Firmer Ground* gives especial attention to Ireland and the Nordic countries (Sweden, Denmark, Norway and Finland), as countries which have achieved very high economic growth, but also developed more equitable societies and acted more purposefully to combat global and local environmental degradation than Australia has. That they have been able to achieve these social and environmental goals without any diminishment of their economic performance makes them important role models for a productive, fairer and more sustainable world. The book devotes a chapter to global security and justice, arguing strongly that in a globalised world every country should do its utmost to strengthen the United Nations and other international bodies, since more and more problems – such as climate change and global poverty – can only be solved by international action. Australia is roundly criticised for undermining the work of key United Nations bodies such as the Office of the United Nations High Commissioner for Human Rights and for its inadequate support for other international bodies, activities and protocols. Australia's very small, if slowly growing, foreign aid contribution and its practice of including security costs such as the cost of imprisonment of asylum seekers at Nauru in its aid budget are also noted.

The need for a fairer society is a central theme. Much more effective strategies to eliminate poverty and to promote social inclusion are therefore key policy changes proposed. The book argues that justice for Indigenous people is an issue that will continue to haunt Australia unless solutions can be quickly found for Indigenous disadvantage. Australia's economic liberal (economic rationalist) policy orthodoxy is unfavourably compared with the economic policies of countries such as Ireland and the Nordic countries. There is strong support for a multicultural Australia and for multicultural policies that reinforce tolerance and respect for difference, that work to eradicate racism and prejudice, and that seek to help migrants assimilate comfortably into Australian society. Special attention is devoted to recent attacks on democracy and to the diminishment of public accountability in Australia.

Chapter 3 is devoted to growing environmental threats. To allow a more extensive discussion of a limited number of topics, the chapter concentrates on three themes only: climate change; water; and biodiversity loss. The chapter describes the growing scientific evidence of climate change, drawing on the findings of the Intergovernmental Panel for Climate Change in its Fourth Assessment Report, released in early 2007. The inaction, both within Australia and overseas, of the Howard Government during its eleven years of office is noted with deep regret. The section on climate change sets out the steps now required in Australia to tackle climate change with energy and effectiveness. The chapter describes in what ways water and biodiversity loss are important issues in their own right, but are also increasingly linked to climate change.

The Australian Collaboration is an association of seven leading national community organisations: Australian Conservation Foundation; Australian Council of Social Service; Australian Council for International Development; Choice (Australian Consumers Association); Federation of Ethnic Communities' Councils of Australia; National Council of Churches in Australia; and Trust for Young Australians.

The book is an expression of the views of its authors and not of the Australian Collaboration or any of its members. The Collaboration, however, hopes that it will stimulate wide debate. We believe that the issues discussed here are of great significance to Australia.

David Yencken
Chair, Australian Collaboration

acknowledgments

Contributors' Notes

Professor Roy Green is Dean of the Macquarie Graduate School of Management, Sydney. Previously he was Dean and Professor of Management for six years at the Faculty of Commerce, National University of Ireland, Galway.

Dr Nicola Henry is a Lecturer in Legal Studies in the School of Social Sciences at La Trobe University. She is also a researcher for the Australian Collaboration on key social, cultural, political and environmental issues.

Dr Andrew Scott is Senior Lecturer in the School of Global Studies, Social Science and Planning at RMIT University, Melbourne. He is author of two books and many other publications, a former national policy adviser to the Labor Opposition on employment and training, and was a visiting researcher in Sweden at the beginning of 2007.

This book has been a cooperative venture. It was commissioned by David Yencken, Chair of the Australian Collaboration. Though the task would have been impossible without the analysis and policy proposals of the councils which are members of the Collaboration, the book is not a summary of their views and member organisations are not responsible for the content.

Australian Policy Online (APO) was also an invaluable source of information about proposals being made by many people and organisations in relation to all the issues discussed. Reading the weekly lists from APO was like having a brilliant and highly efficient research assistant who drew attention to all substantial papers, speeches, analyses and reports.

The task was so substantial and the time limit so tight that it was essential to seek help. Dr Nicola Henry agreed to write the chapter on environmental crises and the section on justice for Indigenous Australians. Dr Andrew Scott was also able to assist by writing the chapter on social issues and the case study on Nordic countries. As well, both Nicola and Andrew participated in discussion about the rest of the book and contributed to the editing and polishing of the manuscript. Roy Green responded immediately to a request for a note on lessons from the Irish experience and this enriches the proposals.

I would like to thank the following poets for permission to quote from their work: Bruce Dawe for 'Doctor to Patient', published in *Sometimes Gladness: Collected Poems* (several editions, Pearson Longman, Melbourne), and Chris Wallace-Crabbe for 'Joy on the Very Edge of History', in Les Murray (ed.) *The Best Australian Poems 2005* (Black Inc, Melbourne, 2005). I am grateful too to *HarperCollins* Publishers for permission to quote Judith Wright's 'Child and Wattle Tree' from *Collected Poems 1942–1985*, and to Faber and Faber for permission to quote Seamus Heaney's 'The Cure at Troy' from *Open Ground: Selected Poems 1966-1996*.

I am deeply grateful for professional editing and thoughtful comments by Stewart Firth, Katie Langmore and Jenny Little. For a second time my daughter Katie Langmore thought of a well-judged title for a book I have written. David Yencken's comments were tough and detailed and contributed to the ordering of priorities and to the rigour and accessibility of the writing. I also greatly appreciated comments on various sections by Graeme Garrett, Naomi Langmore and Stuart Macintyre, and by John Nevile and other participants at a colloquium organised by Geoff Dow and held at the University of New South Wales in December 2006 at which the economic recommendations were presented.

The Centre for Public Policy at the University of Melbourne was the perfect place to be based while drafting, and I thank Mark Considine, Ann Capling, Dennis Muller and Lauren Rosewarne. Two conferences inspired and organised by Brian Howe and Lauren Rosewarne through the Centre – *Transitions and Risk: New Directions in Social Policy*, held in February 2005, and *From Welfare to Social Investment: Re-imagining Social Policy for the Life Course* in February 2007 – were especially stimulating. A day seminar to discuss Hugh Stretton's book *Australia Fair* was most valuable, and I am grateful to the speakers Belinda Probert, Tony Dalton, Jenny Lewis, Ralph Willis, Peter Christoff and to Hugh Stretton himself.

During the preparation and writing, my wife Wendy Langmore gave constant encouragement, wise counsel, constructive suggestions and much pertinent comment, and I am profoundly grateful for her loving support and engagement in the project.

Andrew Scott thanks his wife Lily D'Ambrosio and their daughters Eleanor and Madeleine for support and also Brian Howe for being a good office neighbour and supporter.

Nicola Henry would like to thank Peta Malins, James Hannan, Adele Henry, Michael Henry, Lia Kent, Kirsty Duncanson, Antonia Quadara, Don Henry, Peter Christoff and Alex Gordon for their helpful comments on the 'Turning the tide' chapter; and Brent Collett for his kindness, patience and love.

While all of these people made important contributions to improving the quality of analysis and prescription, not all their advice was taken and I alone have responsibility for the final manuscript.

chapter 1

the state of australia

For most Australians there is delight in our country. To poet Chris Wallace-Crabbe, Australia is the 'Great Good Place':

Windows give onto sheer pastoral, soothing paddocks

of beige pigmentation and fretwork foliage.

Clouds and drizzle have given over completely.

Over the dark wine we laugh like immortals.

This table is Olympus with a teapot;

while those rainbow lorikeets whistle over,

not bothering at all with orchestration:

it has become the Great Good Place.[1]

A qualitative study of 'Generation Y' (people aged 16 to 24 years) found that:

To young people Australia is the desirable land. It is beautiful, spacious, full of sunlight and beckoning beaches and it is free. Australian society is 'laid back' which, to young people, is a very attractive attribute. It is a society where one can do what one wants and reap the rewards, particularly if one's expectations are not too high and one does not want too much.[2]

The Great Prayer of Thanksgiving used by the Australian Uniting Church as part of its Eucharistic service includes the stanza:

We bless you for this wide, red land,

for its rugged beauty,

its changing seasons,

for its diverse peoples

and for all that lives upon this fragile earth.

Australia's social norms include kindness, fairness and decency. Journalist Pamela Bone wrote in her last article before retiring because of cancer that the principal lesson she had learnt during her illness was:

That there is an amazing degree of kindness around. I have been overwhelmed by kindness: the kindness of family, of friends, of work colleagues, the kindness of people in shops and cafes … of doctors and nurses … There simply is a great instinct for kindness in most people.[3]

Many Australians consider this to be the best country in the world. They wouldn't want their children or grandchildren to grow up anywhere else.

Representative democracy is firmly established at the centre of the Australian political system, and Australian federal and state governments have in the past led the world with their initiatives. There is a long history of political experimentation in the Australian electoral system. Civil liberties have seemed firmly entrenched – until recently.

While early European settlers were predominantly Anglo-Celtic, and British and Irish culture still dominates, continuing high levels of migration from many countries keep on enriching our diverse population. Though there has always been some subdued antagonism between ethnic groups and occasionally there have been outbreaks of hostility, the principal characteristic of Australian community relations has been acceptance of diversity. Since the 1970s, and until recently, official support for multiculturalism has generally facilitated absorption of migrants with little friction.

For the last half century, assessments of national living standards have been based on income. Comparisons of Australia's position in the world conventionally begin with income, and real net national disposable income averaged $37,200 per person in 2005–06.[4] Using comparisons of purchasing power, Australia's average income is much the same as that of several other developed countries, such as the Netherlands, Japan, Germany, the United Kingdom, Sweden and France.[5] Norway, the United States and Ireland have significantly higher incomes, but all other countries have average incomes classified as lower, much lower, or impoverished. However, average income is a misleading indicator because it is inflated by high income earners. The median or middle income in the spread of Australian's incomes was about $26,000 in 2005, far below the average.[6]

The last 15 years have been an unprecedented period of sustained growth of Gross Domestic Product (GDP). Between the mid 1990s and 2005–06, real net national disposable income per head grew by close to 3 per cent a year, appreciably faster than during the previous two decades.[7] However, as Dennis Trewin, the Australian Statistician, acknowledges, 'around the world a consensus is growing that countries and governments need to develop a more comprehensive view of progress, rather than focusing mainly on economic indicators such as Gross Domestic Product'.[8] One such measure is the UN Development Programme's Human Development Index, which includes life expectancy and educational attainment as well as average income. On this measure, Australia had the third highest ranking, after Norway and Iceland, and was followed by Canada, Sweden, Switzerland, Ireland and the United States (in that order).

Employment has been growing strongly – by 1.9 million between 1996 and 2006. The number of officially measured unemployed fell from 770,000 in 1996 (8.2 per cent of the workforce) to 550,000 people 10 years later (4.6 per cent).[9] Sixty-nine per cent of working age Australians were employed in 2003, well above the same year's average for Organization for Economic Cooperation and Development countries (the OECD is the club of developed countries), which was 65 per cent.[10]

Australians are now amongst the most long-lived people in the world. In 2005, life expectancy at birth was 79 years for males and 83 years for females.[11] The male life expectancy rate was exceeded only by Iceland and Hong Kong and the female rate by Japan and Hong Kong. In Australia, deaths due to heart disease and stroke have fallen dramatically during the last decade, and even deaths due to cancer have fallen significantly. These major improvements lie behind the remarkable increase in life expectancy since the start of the 1970s – 10 years for men and 8.5 years for women.

Another dimension of privilege is home ownership: 70 per cent of Australian households own their own home outright or with a mortgage, although housing affordability has fallen in recent years due to skyrocketing house prices, compounded more recently by rising interest rates. In 2005, 67 per cent of households had a computer and 56 per cent were connected to the internet. Very few dwellings in Australia are without running water, a toilet and an adequate kitchen.

None of these indicators is adequate to describe comprehensively what most of us regard as the principal determinants of our wellbeing and happiness. There are many other dimensions of life which are important to most people, including the quality of relationships, economic security, satisfaction with work, health, the comfort of accommodation, the fulfilment of leisure and social harmony. When the Australian Bureau of Statistics (ABS) asked adults how they felt about their lives as a whole in 2001, 76 per cent said that they were delighted, pleased or mostly satisfied, and less than 6 per cent felt mostly dissatisfied, unhappy or terrible.[12] Most people who experience personal difficulties such as loss of income or sickness manage to maintain their sense of wellbeing, but chronic stress, pain or failed personal relationships can undermine people's sense of wellbeing. Australian life satisfaction scores compare favourably with those of other countries with high incomes; they are about the same as those of the United Kingdom, New Zealand and the United States, though below those of Denmark and Switzerland.[13]

It is sometimes argued that the number of Australian residents who choose to live overseas is evidence of social, cultural or political discontent. However, the proportion of Australians residing in other OECD countries, for example, is well below that of most comparable countries. The ratio of Australian expatriates in developed countries per 100 of the population living in Australia is 2.8. For Canada it is 5.8, for the United Kingdom 7.6 and for New Zealand 19.3. Only for the United States and Japan is expatriation considerably lower – the ratio for both is 0.5.

International travel illustrates to Australians our relative affluence and the quality of our human services, and also another dimension which many of us take for granted – space. Not only are our regional neighbours (such as Indonesia, China and India) far more densely populated, but also Australia has the lowest population density among developed countries: 2 people per square kilometre, compared with 29 in the United States, 242 in the United Kingdom and 385 in the Netherlands.[14] Australia has 0.3 per cent of global population and occupies 5.6 per cent of the world's land mass. It also has an even higher proportion of global mineral reserves. Of course most Australian land is arid or has low fertility, but that is also true of Canada, where population density is 50 per cent higher. Australia's spaciousness allows quarter acre (1012m²) blocks for urban housing; in most cities of the world people have to live in multi-storey blocks or shanties.

Australia's national security is strengthened by isolation. Rather than tyrannising us as it has in the past, distance makes us safer. Australians are also unique in being the only people who have unified control of a continent. John Hooker writes accurately but acidly:

> All in all I have lived a charmed life ... I have never been shot at, napalmed, tortured, been assessed as Stateless, or pushed a handcart in the company of thousands of other refugees ... In this century, Darfur and Iraq are reminders of the conditions faced by well over half the human race. But in Australia, we see these unpleasant things at a remove. We are 'girt by sea' ... We have never had our houses burnt to the ground, or seen people hanging in the main street. In our splendid isolation, the world has passed us by.[15]

Whether or not we have a high ranking on this or that standard, it would be difficult to argue that we are not a privileged people. And there are so many natural beauties in the Australian landscape. Judith Wright is only one of many eloquent poets who have celebrated innumerable aspects of Australia's natural loveliness:

> Round as a sun is the golden tree.
> Its honey dust sits down among the light
> to cover me and my hot blood
> and my heart hiding like a sad bird
> among its birds and shadows.[16]

Australians' appreciation of our natural heritage has grown, and so too has the strength of our motivation for preserving it. We are also proud of the achievements of our sports men and women; of the success of Australian films, actors and directors; of our scientists, musicians, writers and artists. We have many reasons to feel privileged and secure. Migration scholar James Jupp writes that, 'By many measures Australia is the most stable, united and self-satisfied society on earth.'[17] Former

Governor-General Sir William Deane describes Australia's situation with his usual honesty and wisdom:

> Let us rejoice and be grateful for all the achievements of our past. At the same time, let us be honest and courageous about the failures and flaws which mar those achievements. The damage we have done to the land, its rivers and coasts, notwithstanding our love of its beauty, the unacceptable gap between the haves and the have-nots, in this land of the 'fair go' for all. How far we still have to travel on our journey towards genuine reconciliation between indigenous peoples and the nation of which they form such a vital part. Together we can overcome these flaws and look forward to a fairer Australia.

Challenges

1. SHORT-SIGHTEDNESS

Australia's privilege conceals neglect of many issues of overwhelming importance. Within our own society we see environmental destruction, inequity, social and economic injustice, under-employment, exclusion, violence, anxiety (both as a widespread feeling and as a clinical condition), depression, obesity and addiction; and globally we see a future threatened by climate change, the breakdown of multilateral cooperation, escalation in the spread and sophistication of nuclear weapons, the risk of pandemics and the impoverishment of half of humankind, compounded by the erosion of international standards relating to the conduct of war and treatment of prisoners.

In relation to climate change, Australia has the highest net greenhouse gas emissions per person in any OECD country, a third more than in the United States and double the average for OECD countries. Yet though Australia signed the Kyoto Protocol (which sets targets for reductions of greenhouse gas [GHG] emissions) in 1997, the Commonwealth Government is one of two signatories which have failed to ratify the treaty. Tipping points are being reached in factors causing global climate change. Glaciers are melting, the Greenland icecap is slipping, Arctic sea ice is retreating, and ice-shelves in Antarctica are disintegrating. Vast areas of melting permafrost in Russia directly release methane. 'We used to think that it would take 10,000 years for melting at the surface of an ice-sheet to penetrate down to the bottom. Now we know it takes 10 seconds,' says one climate scientist.[18] The conventional view used to be that sea levels would rise very gradually as atmospheric warming worked its way slowly through ice-sheets several kilometres thick, but crevasses were forgotten. When surface ice melts in Greenland and Antarctica, the water drains down to the base, lubricating the interface between ice and rock and enabling the whole ice-sheet to slip towards the sea. Sea levels, which were rising by 2mm a year in the early 1990s, are already rising by 3mm a year. American environmentalist Bill McKibben writes powerfully that:

> The regular reader of *Science* or *Nature* is treated to an almost weekly load of apocalyptic data, virtually all of it showing results at the very upper end of the ranges predicted by climate models, or beyond them altogether. Compared with the original models of a few years ago, ice is melting faster; forest soils are giving up more carbon as they warm; [and] storms are increasing much more quickly in number and size.[19]

Scientists are therefore becoming alarmed about the speed with which climate change is occurring, yet they have self-censored their comments to the public through fear of being branded scare-mongers. CSIRO researcher Dr Barrie Pittock writes that some scientists are reluctant to speak out for fear that doing so could jeopardise their jobs.[20] He is concerned that those who report that the speed of global warming is escalating risk being perceived as exaggerating the dangers and labelled as unreliable and biased, when in fact they are simply reporting the results of their research. Ian Lowe, National President of the Australian Conservation Foundation (ACF), also reports that the Commonwealth Government has been so reluctant to receive information about climate change that the ACF and other experts have been cut off from access to ministers and advisory bodies.[21] This is one of many examples of the national government repressing non-government organisations (NGOs) and researchers who have views different from its own (see Chapter 7).

Another example of short-sightedness is the threat to Australian biodiversity. Between 1990 and 2000 Australia was one of only four OECD countries where harvesting and clearance of forest exceeded growth. From 1995 to 2005, the number of bird and mammal species listed in Australia as extinct, endangered or vulnerable rose from 120 to 169.[22] Short-sightedness has also been evident during the severe drought at the start of the 21st century – there has been no effective water management regime, and the over-allocation of water has continued unabated. Australian rivers and wetlands have been negatively affected by altered hydrological flows, increased nutrient loads, soil erosion, land clearing, dryland salinity, habitat destruction and the continuing spread of introduced invasive species. Such environmental damage clearly has high economic as well as environmental costs.

Short-sightedness is also clearly evident in public investment in education, training, research and infrastructure. Participation in education is growing, but Australia still performs relatively poorly in relation to comparable OECD nations (see Chapter 4). The rate of completion of upper secondary education in 2003 of 62 per cent was regrettably well below the OECD average of 66 per cent. Australia has tended to coast on the long commodity boom instead of innovating, and encouraging entrepreneurship. The consequences of under-resourced schools and overstretched and underfunded vocational education and training (VET) and tertiary education are skill shortages and hasty importation of skilled migrants, and high Australian unemployment and underemployment (see Chapter 4). For example, economists Chandra Shah and Gerald Burke conclude that, 'At current levels of supply, there will be a shortfall of 240,000 people with VET qualifications over the ten years to 2016.'[23] Other examples of social short-sightedness are discussed later.

The annual application of a so-called efficiency dividend (through which the government arbitrarily cuts expenditure by 1 or 2 per cent each year on the presumption that efficiency is improving) to Commonwealth research institutes and libraries, amongst many other agencies, means that there has been a continuous erosion of research funding during the last decade (see Chapter 5). The most striking example is that between

1996–97 and 2004–05 the number of people employed full-time by Commonwealth organisations on research and development (R&D) was cut from 10,400 to 9,300 – and this was during a decade in which real national income rose 44 per cent.[24] In 2005 the Commonwealth spent a total of $1.57 billion on R&D through its research organisations, considerably less than the increase in annual defence expenditure of $2 billion announced in the 2006 budget.

There have been many reports of the seriousness of Australia's infrastructure crisis. Anecdotal evidence includes road and port congestion, public transport breakdowns, electricity blackouts and longer and longer waiting lists for public housing, elective surgery and child care. The Business Council of Australia claims that the country needs to invest $50 billion in road, rail and water assets, and $40 billion in the electricity sector, if it is to sustain growth rates of around 4 per cent, which is what is needed to maintain our current productivity and prosperity (see Chapter 5).[25] Neglect of infrastructure adds to production costs and so to prices and reduction of exports, and so to the high current account deficit (5.6 per cent of national income in 2005–06) and the rising level of Australian foreign debt (currently 53 per cent of GDP).

2. UNFAIRNESS

Although many Australians maintain an egalitarian image of our society, class distinctions are growing. The wealthy feel a sense of entitlement while the poor despair. 'Contemporary Australia is marked by a series of sharp contrasts – between confident, cheerful affluence and "the working poor", between the city and the bush and between those who feel they belong and those on the margins,' observes social analyst Hugh Mackay.[26] Yet many Australians would agree with the British Commission on Urban Life and Faith that, 'Countering social inequality, and trying to reduce it, is the litmus test of a society's moral adequacy.'[27]

One of the clearest indicators of unfairness is that despite the growth of employment, many people who want more paid work cannot get it. At the end of 2006, about half a million people were unemployed and the average duration of unemployment – that is, for people actively looking for work – was still 40 weeks. The astonishingly misleading definition of employment as anyone who works for one hour or more a week, paid or unpaid, means that many people classified as employed actually want additional work. In September 2005, as well as the 547,000 unemployed, 567,000 of those working part-time would have preferred to work more hours, another 51,000 people were actively looking for work and available to start within a month and 60,000 discouraged job seekers would have sought employment if they believed there were opportunities. The Dusseldorp Skills Forum reports that 540,000 young Australians were not in full-time learning or work in 2006.[28] The ABS reports that 11.4 per cent of the labour force is underutilised.[29] This means that over 1.2 million people are unable to find all the paid work they want. Many mature-age workers are concentrated in regions of high unemployment, do not have decent job prospects and are relying on allowances or pensions for survival. This injustice involves a terrible rejection of people who want more work, who want to increase their incomes, fulfil their potential and make a fuller contribution to the community. Such waste squanders much available energy and talent and destroys dignity. Poet Bruce Dawe describes the situation with empathy in his poem 'Doctor to Patient':

> Please sit down. I'm afraid I have some
> rather bad news for you: you are now seventeen
> and you have contracted an occupational disease called
> unemployment. Like others similarly afflicted
> you will experience feelings of
> shock, disbelief, injustice, guilt, apathy, and aggression
> (although not necessarily in that order) …
> However, you will discover, as time passes,
> that your presence in itself will make others
> obviously uncomfortable …

The Productivity Commission suggests another perspective on this, arguing that 600,000 people could be added to the workforce if government policies were changed so that workforce participation rates could lift to match those in other developed countries.[30]

Eminent former senior Commonwealth economist Fred Argy shows that equality of opportunity is being eroded.[31] Substantive equality of opportunity is a situation in which everyone is able to develop their full potential, irrespective of the circumstances of their birth and childhood. This involves ensuring that educational, training and employment opportunities are readily accessible to all. Argy shows that:

> the interaction of market forces and policy developments in Australia
> is creating a two-tier society in employment, health, education,
> housing and public transport, as well as wide regional disparities
> in opportunities and growing poverty traps ... For the more
> disadvantaged in our community, the new policy environment will
> mean *less* choice and *less* scope for upward income mobility.[32]

Yet a 2006 Roy Morgan survey found that 91 per cent of respondents believe a fair go is important.[33]

Difficult though it is to reach agreement on a definition of poverty, and on how to measure it, a review by Saunders and Bradbury concludes that during the decade to 2002–03, relative poverty (relative to a percentage of average wages) increased slightly, by just over 1 per cent, with most of the increase taking place between 1995–96 and 1999–2000.[34] This is extremely disappointing given the growth in average income during this period. One measurable indicator of poverty is financial stress, symptoms of which include inability to pay bills on time or going without food or heating because of a shortage of money. In 2003–04, 13 per cent of the population lived in households with high financial stress;[35] 22 per cent of people lived in households in which pensions or allowances were the principal source of income – in many cases, these pensions or allowances left these people below the poverty line. For example, a single adult on an allowance received just over $250 a week in March 2006, when the weekly poverty line for an adult living alone was $330.[36] Struggling single mothers were being pressured to find jobs, under threat of loss of their benefit payments. The Welfare to Work Program introduced in mid 2006 cruelly reduced payments to single mothers, people with disabilities, refugees and asylum seekers.

A study mapping social disadvantage across Australia, by Professor Tony Vinson for Jesuit Social Services and Catholic Social Services Australia, found that:

> despite our nation's recent strong economic growth, some communities remain caught in a spiral of low school attainment, high unemployment, poor health, high imprisonment rates and child abuse … Pockets of concentrated and severe social disadvantage have become entrenched across rural and remote as well as suburban Australia.[37]

The report concludes that the major factors that cause poverty to be passed on from one generation to the next include low income, early school leaving, limited computer and internet access, physical and mental disabilities, long-term unemployment, prison admissions and child maltreatment.

The distribution of income in Australia is very unequal by international standards. The Luxembourg Income Study found that Australia was amongst the half dozen most inequitable countries in the OECD. The Gini coefficient (a measure of income inequality) for Australia was 43 per cent higher than for Sweden, the most equitable country.[38] The Luxembourg Study, which is regarded as the best quality international assessment of income distribution, has also calculated that inequality grew in Australia between 1995 and 2003 (the most recent year so far assessed).[39]

The official data conceal the explosive growth of top incomes. Eminent Oxford economist Tony Atkinson and Andrew Leigh of the Australian National University (ANU) conclude that, 'At the start of the twenty-first century, the income share of the richest 1 per cent of Australians was higher than it had been at any point since 1951.'[40] The gap between CEO pay and average pay is steadily widening. In 1992, the remuneration of a typical executive in Australia's top 50 companies was 27 times the wage of the average worker, yet only 10 years later, by 2002, it had risen to 98 times.[41] By 2005, median annual pay for the top 20 company CEOs was $6.8 million; for CEOs in companies ranked between 20 and 50, it was $4 million; and CEOs in the next 50, it was $2.3 million.[42] The Australian Council of Superannuation Investors (ACSI), which represents the industry superannuation funds, has also found that the bonus portion of executives' pay has no correlation with company profitability![43] The growing economic power of this plutocracy foments resentment, suspicion of conspiracies and distrust in the possibility of social justice and threatens to change the very character of Australian society. As the families of the very rich grow up, they may well become a new class of propertied Australians living on inherited wealth and without the need to work, creating a permanently and profoundly unequal society. Even the US Senate is taking some action to limit the extent of tax-free payouts to corporate executives by setting a cap on the amount of compensation they can defer until retirement.

The proportions of wages and profits in our national income are increasingly inequitable. The wages share of national income has been trending down from about 56 per cent in 1996–97 to 53.6 per cent in 2005–06; the profit share rose during the same period from about 22.5 per cent to nearly 27 per cent.[44] One consequence of the growth of the profit share of national income is that average income – the national income divided by the number of adults – is a less and less reliable indicator of personal income.

Wealth and power are even more unevenly distributed. In 2003–04 the wealthiest 20 per cent of households, with an average net worth of $1.4 million, owned 59 per cent of total household wealth and the 20 per cent with the lowest assets, averaging $23,000 per household, had only 1 per cent.[45] This means that the richest one and a half million people own assets averaging 60 times as much as the poorest one and a half million. Of course one of the most influential determinants of wealth is age: young people have little, and most people accumulate wealth through their life cycle, but this doesn't account for much of the inequality in the distribution of wealth. The clearest example of the growing concentration of power is the media industry, in which the increasing proportion of ownership by a few mega-wealthy proprietors is repressing public discourse (see Chapter 7).

Some symptoms of deprivation and injustice are entrenched. Life expectancy for Indigenous Australians is estimated to be 59 years for males and 65 years for females. This is 17 years less than the equivalent averages for the whole Australian population. At all ages under 75, Indigenous death rates are at least twice those of the non-Indigenous population. School retention rates to Year 12 for Indigenous Australians are also well below those of other Australians, even though they rose from 31 per cent in 1995 to 40 per cent in 2005.

3. INSECURITY

Many Australians are feeling more insecure and anxious. Households owe more than ever in personal debt and mortgages, and their economic security is being undermined by the abolition of employment rights and protections. In fact nothing characterises the present situation of Australian employees more than a loss of the working conditions that once gave them security, predictability and the chance to have a full family life. Part-time workers in particular are increasingly at the beck and call of their employers.

Rising interest rates are a major source of anxiety for mortgagees, small businesses and lower income earners. People save less and owe more. The continuing reductions in household savings and increases in debts are causing rising household interest payments (10.7 per cent of household disposable income in the March quarter of 2006).[46] Household debts are now so large that a higher proportion of household incomes are being spent on servicing mortgages and other debts than in the early 1990s recession when the official interest rate was much higher.[47] Personal debt for tertiary education is multiplying. Total household debt in 2006 exceeded $1 trillion, which is seven times the amount owed in 1988 (when these calculations were first made).[48] Such debts, combined with growing casualisation of work, and reduced protections for consumers, are increasing risk and insecurity.

Anxiety and fear are also being exacerbated by exaggeration of the dangers of terrorism, asylum seekers, crime, ethnic conflict and social disintegration. As in the United States, this pretence has been picked up and amplified by sections of the Australian media, which 'is saturated with apocalyptic warnings' about threats to our way of life, writes MP Carmen Lawrence:

> Such unrelenting bombardment is enough to make even the most
> fearless start to wonder if they might not be in denial and that
> Armageddon is truly imminent. In reality, the developed world has
> never been safer … I ask whether we have lost our sense of proportion
> when measuring prudence and fear, and whether we are sacrificing
> tangible freedoms for a spectral safety.[49]

Some symptoms of social and psychological insecurity are increasing. The proportion of the whole Australian population reporting a long-term mental or behavioural problem increased from 5.9 per cent in 1995 to 11.0 per cent in 2004–05, though this probably reflects in part an increased willingness to report mental health issues.[50] Twenty per cent of Australians have a disability – a physical, emotional or nervous impairment lasting for six months or more which limits activities and restricts participation. The proportion of risky and high risk drinkers has grown from 10 to 15 per cent during the last decade. Fifty-eight per cent of males and 40 per cent of females are overweight or obese; this is a substantial increase in only one decade. Close to half of all adults have a low intake of fresh fruit and a third have less than the recommended minimum amount of exercise. Smoking is declining, but only very slowly. In 2004–05 only 10 per cent of men and 13 per cent of women reported that they had none of four lifestyle risk factors which contribute to heart disease and strokes – smoking, high alcohol consumption, being overweight and having little exercise.

A careful survey of challenges facing youth conducted for the Brotherhood of St Laurence concluded that:

> There are improvements in some areas, such as youth suicide rates,
> cigarette smoking or youth unemployment, yet these promising trends
> … do not apply [generally] to Indigenous youth, who remain the
> most disadvantaged group. Young refugees face particular challenges
> regarding their mental health, access to education and pathways into
> employment. Youth from low-income families also experience a high

level of disadvantage, particularly in the areas of physical and mental
health, literacy, numeracy, school achievement and housing, but also
in accessing resources such as textbooks or computers that are vital for
their participation in education and leisure activities.[51]

Australia has long had a dark underbelly. Australia's foundation as a
convict settlement established traditions of stratification, exploitation
and brutality, especially of Indigenous people, which have not been
obliterated by two centuries of political and cultural development.
The White Australia policy and the exclusion of Indigenous peoples
from the rights of citizenship until 1967 are only the most publicised
examples of past Australian racism. The death of Mulrunji Doomadgee
within less than an hour of being taken into custody on Palm Island in
2004 and the refusal of the Queensland public prosecutor to charge the
police sergeant who was alleged to have kicked him to death appeared
to be yet another example of more than two centuries of repression of
Indigenous peoples. Fortunately, on the advice of Sir Laurence Street, the
Queensland Government overrode the public prosecutor and charged
the arresting police sergeant. Corruption also breeds insecurity. The
Australian Wheat Board's (AWB's) cavalier bribery of Saddam Hussein's
underlings in direct contravention of UN Security Council rules, and
the AWB management's attempted mockery of the Cole Inquiry in
2006 by claiming amnesia about the corruption, was not only unethical
but also illegal, and treacherous of Australia's interests.

Gang murders in Melbourne can also be seen as symptoms of
entrenched criminal activity and a struggle for illegal power. The
ABS reports that the incidence of violent crime in Australia dropped
significantly between 1996 and 2005. Nevertheless, in this apparently
relatively peaceful country, 5.8 per cent of women and 11 per cent of
men still experienced an incident of violence in the 12 months before
the ABS's 2005 survey. This violence was concentrated among the
young, though since violence against women at home is under-reported,
total incidence is impossible to know.[52] Forty per cent of adult women
and 50 per cent of adult men report experiencing violence during their
lifetime. The incidence of household crimes such as attempted break-ins
and motor vehicle theft also fell sharply between 1998 and 2005, from

about 9 per cent to 6.2 per cent.[53] Imprisonment rates have increased during the last decade, though, from 129 to 163 people per 100,000, and this latter rate is higher than in most years of the last century. The imprisonment rate of Indigenous people is 12 times that of the non-Indigenous population.

4. SOCIAL DISHARMONY

Australians seemed to have accepted multiculturalism as the best way to integrate new communities into Australian society – until about 10 years ago. Since then some political leaders have gradually undermined people's faith in the idea. Leading the pack was Pauline Hanson and her One Nation Party, which called for an end to immigration. The Howard Government (Liberal/National Coalition) then adopted some of Hanson's proposals, such as the temporary protection visa, and routinely depicted refugees as a security threat. The Cronulla riots of 2006, when groups of Ocker and Lebanese Australians fought in the streets of a Sydney beach suburb, suggested a further erosion of popular support for multiculturalism, though much has since been done in Cronulla to repair the damage. Howard's Treasurer, Peter Costello, spoke early in 2006 of 'mushy, misguided multiculturalism'. The Howard Government dropped the phrase 'Multicultural Affairs' from the name of the Department of Immigration and Multicultural Affairs in 2007, replacing it with 'Citizenship'.

Although 95 per cent of people living in Australia are Australian citizens, we have the highest percentage, amongst OECD countries, of the population born overseas: 23 per cent in 2001.[54] As an immigrant society with a dominant Anglo-Irish culture, Australia has long been faced with the issue of how to support the settlement of migrants from non-English speaking countries. The Whitlam Government (Australian Labor Party [ALP] 1972–75) introduced multiculturalism to 'extend rights and privileges to immigrants which were already enjoyed by the native born, without requiring the abandonment of cultures, languages and religions not derived from Britain or developed in colonial Australia'.[55] All official policies on the issue have stressed the supremacy of existing institutions and of the English language. Multiculturalism was continued by the Fraser Government (Lib./Nat. 1975–83), which defined it as 'not a oneness, but a unity, not a similarity, but a composite, not a melting pot but a voluntary bond of dissimilar people sharing a common political and institutional structure'.[56] The idea of 'productive diversity' moved the debate on to the contribution which people with a variety of cultures could make to Australia.

The Hawke Government (ALP 1983–91) made the first severe cuts in the adult migrant education program in 1986, and the Keating Government (ALP 1991–96) introduced mandatory detention of asylum seekers in 1991. Both of these policies created political space for subsequent governments to make further counterproductive cuts in integration services for migrants – and to introduce more brutal detention policies during the *Tampa* crisis in 2001, when Australia prevented more than 400 rescued refugees on board a Norwegian container ship from landing on Australian soil. These policies had the support of both major parties, but they dismayed a large minority of the community and evoked outspoken criticism from a minority of parliamentarians from all parties.

The parliamentary critics were representing the trenchant condemnation coming from many community organisations as well as their own values: detention does not reflect Australian hospitality. Our common practice has been to welcome visitors. 'Probably your greatest asset is the friendliness and helpfulness of your people', wrote one international visitor recently.[57] The hospitality offered to those attending the Olympic Games in Sydney was a particularly fine example. Australians were proud and pleased by the comments and publicity both here and overseas about how well the Olympic Games were organised and how kind we had been, as hosts, to our visitors. The Howard Government's response to the *Tampa* affair, and the support it received from the Kim Beazley-led Opposition, was a direct repudiation of this tradition. Astonishingly, our national leaders refused to assist refugees from Afghanistan (where Australia did not have a migration office) or Iraq (which ministers were condemning as a dictatorship) who were attempting to seek safety in Australia. Our international reputation for well-organised settlement procedures and multiculturalism was shattered. Author Caroline Moorehead writes:

> In recent years, a continent born of immigrants ... has effectively
> redefined itself as the most excluding nation in the world toward
> refugees and asylum seekers ... No other country, in fact not even the
> United States in the wake of September 11, has treated those fleeing
> persecution with such callousness.[58]

The treatment of asylum seekers and the denial of their civil rights has brought shame to secular, Judeo-Christian, Muslim, Buddhist and Hindu Australians alike. Australian governments have slowly and insidiously abandoned the kindliness on which the nation prided itself. In a letter critical of our cruelty to asylum seekers, theologian the Rev. Dr Norman Young wrote to *The Age*, 'One of the most deep-rooted biblical traditions is the requirement to offer hospitality to the stranger, sanctuary to the oppressed, and care for the widow and the orphan.' Current policy on asylum seekers is the antithesis of one a humane government could support, and our government claims that most of its members are Christians. The perception of a White Australia policy has re-formed in Asia and also in North America and Europe. A comment by Indonesian analyst Jusuf Wanandi in the *Jakarta Post* about the Australian elections in 2001 illustrates justifiable Asian responses:

> Following an ugly political campaign in which racism, xenophobia
> and bigotry became the main tactics to win the federal election,
> Australia's status regionally and internationally has been reduced to a
> pariah.[59]

Australia's security would be served better by adopting policies consistent with international law. Indefinite detention without trial before a properly constituted and independent tribunal breaches provisions of the UN Universal Declaration of Human Rights such as Article 14: 'Everyone has the right to seek and to enjoy in other countries asylum from persecution.' Article 31 of the UN Convention on the Status of Refugees states that a refugee should not be penalised for an unlawful mode of arrival, yet that is what happens through the so-called Pacific solution. The UN High Commission for Refugees has said it was 'concerned about the detention of refugees on Nauru and Manus Island. We consider such detention inconsistent with the provisions of the Refugee Convention.' While Australia refuses to apply international human rights law itself (or to advocate for a fair trial from the Americans for David Hicks) it has little moral authority to advocate for Indonesia's honouring of human rights in the provinces of Papua, for example.

Australian's unease about migration has softened in recent years.[60] Since 1996, the proportion of respondents to an attitudes survey who want less migration has fallen from more than 60 per cent to less than 40 per cent at the same time as the net annual intake of migrants has risen from around 70,000 to about 120,000. Factors in changing attitudes are likely to have included falling unemployment and increasing awareness of the economic benefits of immigration. Perhaps this augurs well for improving social harmony.

In short, while Australia remains fortunate and successful, many citizens are uneasy about the failure to tackle climate change, the neglect of education, growing inequity, insecurity, and the reversal of multiculturalism. This book reviews Australia's current situation, identifies major contemporary challenges to Australian society and discusses ways of making our country more secure, sustainable, fair and vibrant. The purpose of the book is to sharpen analysis about Australians' concerns and interests, to clarify ways in which they are inadequately expressed in current policies, and to explore feasible alternatives and priorities.

Later chapters also discuss other national challenges, including the Americanisation of domestic and foreign policy, media concentration, and the growing centralisation of political power. High priority areas requiring immediate attention include preschool services, public school infrastructure, and vocational education and universities; employment opportunities for all; industrial relations; health services; and housing accessibility (Chapter 4). Many long-term issues have been receiving too little attention in current public policy. Four long-term challenges which require immediate decisive action are: climate change (Chapter

3); investing in economic security (Chapter 5); advancing global security and justice (Chapter 6); and the revitalisation of Australian politics (Chapter 7).

The next chapter discusses underlying influences, an alternative paradigm for addressing them, and the particularly pressing needs of Indigenous Australians.

chapter 2

individual income or wellbeing for all?

In spite of many signs of personal optimism and buoyancy, there is growing concern about the state of Australian society: rougher, tougher, more competitive, less compassionate. This produces stress, edginess and a feeling of personal vulnerability. In our struggle to keep up with an ever-accelerating pace of change, we are sacrificing many of our traditional courtesies and values.

Hugh Mackay, 2005[1]

Social surveys show that the majority of Australians are paradoxically both relatively comfortable with the national situation and also unsure about some policies and longer term prospects. In 2006 Hugh Mackay identified self-absorption and escapism as characterising the national mood: 'Consumers are looking … for some light relief and for some distraction from a troubled world.'[2] There have been 15 years of relatively rapid economic growth, for which there is widespread appreciation. Yet the high levels of personal debt, plus rising interest rates and high petrol prices during 2005 and 2006 increased anxiety.[3] So though the majority have a general sense of material wellbeing, at the same time there are widespread insecurities and fears.

The Australian National University (ANU) Survey of Social Attitudes, which was first conducted in 2003, provides authoritative findings on what Australians feel about major social, economic and political issues.[4] The 2003 survey showed that family is central to Australians' identity. Three-quarters of all respondents listed their family as being among the three most important groups influencing their identity, the other two being occupation and Australian nationality. Maintenance of economic growth and of a stable economy are the highest national priorities of over half of respondents. Unsurprisingly, 'most people value economic and physical security and quality of life and self-expression'. Many Australians are worried about job security: one in eight respondents said they thought they were 'very likely' or 'fairly likely' to lose their job in the next year, and half of all respondents thought that it would not be easy to find another job with the same income and conditions.

The survey confirmed the findings of other opinion polls, which have consistently shown that the proportion of Australians who prefer higher public spending on health and education to lower taxes has been rising steadily since 1990, and was a substantial majority in 2003.[5] Services for which a majority of respondents are willing to pay 'quite a bit more tax' or 'a little more tax' are health and Medicare, primary and secondary education, environmental protection, and defence.[6] It is therefore an amateurish electoral misjudgment for some politicians to claim that tax cuts are the highest political priority. Advocacy of further tax cuts demonstrates ignorance of voters' preferences, or readiness to succumb to the 'constant clarion call from the rich and privileged for the last two decades' for tax reductions.[7]

Most respondents tend to support a fairer redistribution of income across the community, but the majority are also 'ungenerous' to those they think are not making an effort to find work. Support for some forms of welfare is weak: most respondents believe that most unemployed could find a job if they really wanted to. The great majority of people support universal provision of services: 83 per cent of respondents think that governments are best suited to deliver education and 80 per cent consider this to be the case with health services too. Many people are concerned to strengthen justice for Indigenous people, restore hospitality to Australia's treatment of asylum seekers, enhance human and environmental health and wellbeing; and for Australia to adopt a more autonomous foreign policy.

While most Australians are optimistic about their personal future, their confidence in the future quality of life is declining. Research Fellow Richard Eckersley writes that polls in 1988 and 2005 found that the proportion of respondents saying they believed the quality of life in this country would improve fell from 30 per cent to 23 per cent, while the proportion believing it would worsen rose from 40 to 46 per cent – not a great difference, but surprising given 15 years of economic expansion.[8] There was a considerable difference between what respondents thought would happen and the future they would prefer. They were asked to compare a 'growth-oriented' scenario focused on individual wealth, economic growth and enjoying the 'good life', with a 'greener' scenario focused on community, family, equity and harmony with the environment. The proportion *expecting* the growth scenario increased from 63 per cent in 1995 to 77 per cent in 2005, and the proportion *preferring* the green scenario increased from 81 to 89 per cent. So the divergence between the direction of Australia's society and its expressed preferences is increasing. Hugh Mackay identifies 'an underlying, rather wistful concern that "the Australian way of life" is under threat – from commercial pressure, materialism, drugs (legal and illegal) and a steady decline in manners and morals'.[9]

Public discourse stirred during 2006 and 2007. Complaints about the low level of public debate became increasingly common – as the level of debate started to rise. Unease about Australia's values and direction grew. The so-called WorkChoices Act generated insecurity and anger and motivated hundreds of thousands to attend protest rallies in cities in all states and territories. Climate change took off as a general public concern. Revulsion at the slaughter in Iraq strengthened. Many people who had been sceptical of climate change or supported the invasion of Iraq changed their minds. Critics began to receive more attention. There were packed audiences for public lectures, conferences on ideas and literary festivals. There was more debate within the Coalition about policy issues. Following the election of Kevin Rudd as leader, the Labor Party contested more issues with greater vigour and began proposing more alternatives. The Greens maintained their focus on Australia's ever-growing environmental problems.

MISGUIDED ECONOMIC POLICY

One underlying cause of unease is the current economic ideology, sometimes misnamed 'economic rationalism' and often described internationally as neo-liberalism or the Washington consensus. Supporters of the ideology generally believe that it makes good sense and argue like Margaret Thatcher – that There Is No Alternative (TINA). Since this ideology is a direct descendent of 19th century liberalism, it is both accurate and acceptable to supporters to use the descriptive term 'economic liberalism'.[10] At the extreme, however, economic liberalism can and does become market fundamentalism, which involves making marketisation an end in itself rather than a means to other economic and social goals. For the last quarter century both major party groupings have adopted the ideology of economic liberalism, and though politicians have continued to take note of community attitudes, their perceptions have been skewed by the dominant ideology. The economic liberal fog has obscured politicians' view of voters' preferences.

Liberal economists have been so preoccupied with maximising individual income that other aspects of wellbeing have been excluded.

Their principal recommendations for achieving growth of individual income have been minimising the role of the state by reducing public expenditure and taxation, privatisation of public enterprises, and deregulating the financial and corporate sectors. Many have been so obsessed with efficiency that effectiveness, harmony, social justice and environmental responsibility have been forgotten entirely. Liberal economists argue for reduction of inflation as the principal goal of macroeconomic policy, rather than seeking growth of employment simultaneously. There have been artificial attempts to deliver public services such as health and education through markets. To economic liberals, freedom for economic actors – principally corporations – has mattered more than human rights of individuals and social groups, such as freedom of expression. At the peak of the influence of liberal economics, in the 1980s and 1990s, market fundamentalists claimed that the market was a more authentic guide for public policy than were political processes. They argued that politics was so corrupted by special interests that the way money was used was a clearer guide to people's preferences.

After a quarter century of liberal economic dominance, under both Labor and Liberal governments, it is time for Australians to examine its consequences – both good and bad – identify lessons, and think about whether any re-evaluation of national goals and public policy could be beneficial. Two of the clearest outcomes of the economic liberal ascendancy set up a striking dichotomy: while the strategy has been associated with a long period of economic growth, market fundamentalists have actually made no progress at all towards their principal goal of reducing public expenditure and taxation. Public expenditure and taxation, as proportions of national income, are now higher than ever. Economic growth has been achieved by abandoning the main economic liberal goal. This in itself seems a clear reason for moving on.

One feature of economic liberalism is its obsession with individual income maximisation, to the exclusion of other dimensions of wellbeing. National public policy still focuses on growth of GDP and devalues many policies which would contribute to human wellbeing and equality of opportunity. This is not simply an expression of ideology, however; it also reflects the interests of the powerful rather than those of the whole population.[11]

Not only is economic liberalism preoccupied with maximising income and so with individual acquisitiveness, but policies adopted by its supporters have sometimes contributed to market failure. Market fundamentalists have a utopian view about markets and tend to neglect evidence of the extent of market failure. Markets commonly fail to generate efficient outcomes because of monopolies and the concentration of ownership; because of consequences (externalities) that are not expressed in prices – such as the impact of greenhouse gas (GHG) emissions on climate, which has costs for the nation which the emitters do not have to pay; because of the failure of prices to reflect future scarcities, causing less than optimal investment decisions; and because of incomplete information. And markets give far more power to the wealthy than to others, and so reinforce inequity. Government intervention is therefore essential for a society that wishes to increase both efficiency and equity. Public intervention can also be counterproductive, though, so governments must continually aim to increase the effectiveness of intervention. Two major consequences of over-reliance on markets are increasing inequity in the distribution of income and increasing economic insecurity (see Chapters 4 and 5). Australia is becoming a more unfair and a meaner society. The preoccupation with personal income maximisation can also lead to unprincipled opportunism, the erosion of ethical boundaries and the growth of white collar and corporate crime.

While economic liberalism has been so strongly entrenched, rigorous evaluation of the wider consequences of the policy has been downplayed, not given the same publicity as the policy itself, or its so-called successes. The economically successful proclaim the benefits of the dominant ideology while the sceptics become disillusioned and resigned. Together with the Howard Government's repression of public discourse and dissent (see Chapter 7), this political atmosphere has caused a sense of powerlessness – and its corollary, political passivity. The ascendency of liberal economics has meant that big political issues such as economic strategy, income distribution, social and environmental policy and provision of public services appeared to have been settled, leaving only technical and marginal issues for discussion. As former Labor minister Barry Jones said at the launch of his autobiography, 'The politics has dropped out of politics.' A major consequence of this marginalisation of politics is that other issues of principle and morality are marginalised too. Jones writes, 'By 2006, "Liberty! Equality! Fraternity!" had been displaced by "Materialism! Self-interest! Exclusion!".'[12] Monash University political science professor James Walter argued powerfully a decade ago that:

> A real commitment to politics, as the ground for mediating between the social and economic spheres, is now more important than ever. Yet such politics requires ideas, imagination and genuine competition between coherent alternatives and this is what the triumph of the liberal ideal (in its current incarnation) denies us. Where there is only one idea, as Fukuyama points out, 'idealism will be replaced by economic calculation, the endless solving of technical problems' ... the greatest problem is that once we abandon politics for economics, we abandon the capacity to imagine new solutions.[13]

The quality of both personal and public life has been undermined by preoccupation with individual income and accumulation of material goods, and neglect of broader concerns. Acquisitiveness has stimulated the growth of individualism and commercialisation in Australia just as it has in America. Constant emphasis on material goals and denigration of generosity and cooperation have damaged the quality of Australian community life. The successful have a growing sense of entitlement which undermines mutual responsibility, and lower income earners have been marginalised.

In the rest of the English-speaking world people have reacted against the extremes of market fundamentalism. In the largely social democratic developed countries of the European Union (EU) the ideology has never been dominant. Australian public policy has yet to catch up with the defeat of the market fundamentalist advocates in Britain and America (see Chapter 5), but criticism of economic liberalism is increasing. Eminent economist and former Governor of the Reserve Bank Dr H.C. Coombs wrote, over a decade ago:

> The intellectual and moral basis of Australian society is being
> corrupted by the subordination of its institutions to the demands
> of the owners and entrepreneurs of 'the economy'. The economy
> has become a system simply for making profits for people who own
> things.[14]

Dean Drayton, in his farewell speech as President of the Uniting Church
of Australia in July 2006, said:

> [F]or too many of our politicians the market is God. Budget after
> budget of this government has had a preference for the rich. At least
> 10 per cent of our population is trapped in poverty and millions if
> not billions elsewhere in the world are sacrificed on the altar of this
> market economy. What we are blind about is the way we are allowing
> economic rationalism and the free market to control our country.[15]

Most of us know intuitively that there is much more to life than
possessions and consumption, and this has caused some reaction
against assertive materialism. Richard Eckersley quotes one survey
which found that 75 per cent of respondents thought that 'too much
emphasis is put on improving the economy and too little on creating
a better society'.[16] Allowing the intermediate goal of economic growth
to dominate national life has been a major misjudgement of this era.
There is widespread and growing recognition that wellbeing depends
on many factors as well as income. Quality of life is more than the
standard of living. Our happiness depends on such things as loving and
being loved, security, autonomy, productive work, enjoyable leisure,
achievements and harmony. The goal of economic security has a vital
place in any framework for public policy, but so do seeking to improve
the quality of life and the common good – they are core public policy
goals, for they put economic growth in a wider perspective. If we could
put these larger goals front and centre, attention would be focused on
the quality of economic development being sought and on the social
and environmental elements of national progress.

Over half the respondents to a survey of attitudes about
contemporary economic policy in 2003 felt that too much attention

was being given to consumerism and that there was too much pressure and stress.[17] Many of us continue to sense a lack of balance, which we would like to improve by reducing work pressure and thus building our capacity (and increasing the time we have available) for relationships, cultural vitality, sport and other relaxations. In Australia as in Europe there is an increasing search for a reorientation which would improve the quality of life. Why not recognise that Australians work the longest average hours of any OECD country and gradually reduce standard working hours rather than increasing pay as part of the reward for growing productivity? This would also enable a more equitable sharing of available work by increasing total employment. Growing numbers of people are consciously downshifting – adopting 'sea-change' or 'tree-change' lifestyles – and accepting lower income as a key to a more balanced and fulfilling life.

VALUES AND IDENTITY

There has been a lot of talk about Australian values lately. In September 2006 a reporter from *The Sunday Age* visited a town outside Melbourne in search of opinion. He writes that he arrived too early in the day for tea, so crossed the road to the pub and asked Jenny the barmaid about values. 'Geez, that's a bit deep for this time of day,' she said. The reporter wrote, 'This in itself could be a clue for new Aussies: keep it light until lunchtime.'[18]

The process of identifying values can be important in itself, for clarification of values and goals is a direct way of reducing uncertainty about national identity and the meaning of Australian nationality. A number of attempts have been made in recent years to articulate the shared values and principles that guide Australian society. In 2000, the Australian Citizenship Council proposed seven civic principles:

⇨ respect and care for the land;
⇨ maintenance of the rule of law;
⇨ a fair society supported by equality under the law;
⇨ strengthening representative liberal democracy;

⇨ a tolerant, inclusive and multicultural society;

⇨ devoted to the wellbeing of all; and

⇨ valuing the unique status of Aboriginal and Torres
    Strait Islander people.

The Brotherhood of St Laurence commissioned an investigation in 2002 which found that shared values included democracy, justice, caring for others, equality, a less selfish society, loyalty, and self-determination.

The Australian Ministerial Council of Education, Employment, Training and Youth Affairs started a study in 2002 to provide the basis for values education in Australian schools. A set of nine common Australian values were identified:

⇨ care and compassion;

⇨ doing your best;

⇨ fair go;

⇨ freedom;

⇨ honesty and trustworthiness;

⇨ integrity;

⇨ respect;

⇨ responsibility; and

⇨ understanding, tolerance and inclusion.

When asked about these, Jenny the barmaid said: *Care and compassion* 'Rates high'; *Doing your best* 'What's your best? It's an open question.' But is *freedom* really a value? 'Too right it is. Who are you to decide what I can and can't do?' *Honesty and trustworthiness, integrity, respect, responsibility, tolerance, inclusion*: Jenny sees them all as good. 'Everyone has a right to feel they belong.'

Australians have often been described as undemonstrative, and sceptical of pretension, arrogance or inflated patriotism. We commonly avoid making a fuss about things that displease us. Australians have also been seen as suspicious of doctrine. Australian tradition includes both being generous and being self-seeking. The majority do not want our country to be globally famous as the nation that treats asylum seekers more brutally than any other; in which human rights conventions are systematically neglected; in which Indigenous people have a life expectancy 17 years shorter than the population average; or in which the Prime Minister will not act to discourage racism or apologise to Aboriginal people for terrible injustices. All policy should reflect such fundamental values as kindness, decency and fairness and be expressed with honesty – and to say so is neither superficial nor sentimental. We do want our country to be recognised as welcoming to visitors, and generous to those struck by disaster, as millions of Australians were in response to the tsunami.[19]

Yet the emphasis on material prosperity has undermined these traditional Australian values. Leaders who emphasise only prosperity reinforce materialism and acquisitiveness. Hugh Mackay reports that, 'Under Howard we have become less compassionate, less tolerant and more uninhibited in the expression of ethnic and religious prejudice.'[20] Despite the strong Australian tradition of egalitarianism, the strength of support for fairness has apparently fallen, even though the great majority of survey respondents still say that a fair go is important. US research comparing attitudes of economics students before they began their courses and after they finished showed that they became more narrowly self-interested and uncooperative while studying liberal economics. The same effect seems to occur amongst Australian economics students.[21] During the last quarter century Australian public policy has been dominated by graduates in economics.

Studies of values suggest that there is widespread unease about the state of Australian ethics and morality. Many people wish for a society in which generosity, fairness, environmental responsibility and peacefulness are celebrated. Is it possible that such concern could generate a more active search for means of strengthening social solidarity and the justice of Australian society?

WELLBEING AND HAPPINESS

While the preoccupation with income maximisation and acquisitiveness persists, a growing number of analysts, commentators, scholars and concerned community organisations are suggesting that happiness is a more complete indicator of wellbeing than income. A new science of happiness is developing, and Harvard University's currently most popular class is reported to be in happiness or 'positive psychology'.[22] Most people recognise that it is better to enjoy life than to suffer, and though not everyone accepts the utilitarian view that happiness is the ultimate value, the desirability of happiness is undisputed. What makes for happiness differs – it can include contentment, joy, acceptance of suffering and much more. Happiness is certainly a preferable state to misery, and one which we instinctively seek. British economist Richard Layard, who wrote a seminal book on happiness, is probably correct in declaring that happiness:

> is our overall motivational device. We seek to feel good and to avoid pain ... For what makes us feel good (sex, food, love, friendship, and so on) is also generally good for our survival ... The search for good feeling is the mechanism that has preserved and multiplied the human race ... it is impossible to explain human action and human survival except by the desire to feel good.[23]

Research in many countries has led to the conclusion that personal happiness depends principally on seven factors:

⇨   family relationships;
⇨   financial situation;
⇨   work;
⇨   community and friends;
⇨   health;
⇨   personal freedom; and
⇨   personal values.[24]

The Australian Social Attitudes Survey confirms that family relationships are the most important basis of happiness for most Australians. Strong relationships have been shown to improve the functioning of the immune system, extend life, speed recovery from surgery and reduce the risk of depression.

Philosophers and religious leaders have broadly believed that happiness or contentment depends on leading a virtuous and ultimately satisfying good life and that happiness is the reward for a life well lived. Paraphrasing Jesus, cartoonist Michael Leunig writes, '"Love one another and you will be happy." It's as simple and as difficult as that. There is no other way.'[25] Many philosophers consider happiness a paradox, something that can only be found by seeking something else.[26] Many religious and moral leaders have talked of the principle of reciprocity, of doing to others as you would have them do to you. Recent research confirms the importance of this ethic, for people who care about others are on average happier than those who are preoccupied with themselves. Many have argued, and researchers have concluded, that having a purpose and making progress towards it are key elements of happiness.[27] For those with a purpose and a framework of beliefs and values, happiness results from living them.

Described in these ways, wellbeing can sound rather individualistic, so it is important to emphasise the imperative of the associated goal of common wellbeing, that is, seeking the wellbeing of all, or the common good. The Anglican Book of Common Prayer includes in the weekly service the prayer to 'Guide the people of this land, and of all nations, in the ways of justice and peace; that we may honour one another and serve the common good.' Working for the common good is a fundamental aspiration of those seeking happiness and wellbeing for all. 'The central purpose of a nation should be to improve the quality of life of its people,' writes Richard Eckersley.[28] He defines quality of life as 'the degree to which people enjoy the conditions of life – social, economic, cultural and environmental – that are conducive to total wellbeing: physical, mental, social and spiritual'.

Some social scientists agree with the 19th century political philosopher Jeremy Bentham that the goal of maximising the general level of happiness is the best guide to public policy. Endorsing an earlier philosopher, Bentham wrote the famous lines which are the basis for utilitarian philosophy: 'The greatest happiness of the greatest number is the foundation of morals and legislation.'[29] Utilitarianism is a prosaic and unfamiliar name for ideas and assumptions which Australians have taken for granted for most of our history. As international relations scholar and Master of Ormond College Hugh Collins writes,

Australians have been like Bentham in searching for 'the institutional means for achieving that public good which maximises private interest'.[30] Australians have tended to be pragmatists, less interested in visions and philosophies than in the practical policies which improve the general quality of life and opportunities for the individual. Collins illuminates Australian political history by showing that utilitarianism was the prevailing philosophy in Britain when Australian foundations were being laid in the 19th century and has been influential ever since. Historian Keith Hancock wrote in 1930 that, 'Australian democracy has come to look upon the State as a vast public utility, whose duty it is to provide the greatest happiness for the greatest number.'[31] This utilitarian orientation was still powerful in the 20th century. For example, Prime Minister Robert Menzies offered a utilitarian program of national development as a basis for individual interests. Market fundamentalism has been a deviation from the tradition of pragmatic utilitarianism, for it displaces the goals of happiness and wellbeing with obsessive preoccupation with markets and efficiency, which leads to relative neglect of the social dimensions of life.

Increasing happiness and wellbeing have been criticised as goals for government because of their complexity and the difficulty of measuring them.[32] Both criticisms have a superficial validity. Some dimensions of happiness are factors which government can do only a little to influence – the quality of family relationships, for instance – but others, such as economic security, health and personal freedom, are strongly influenced by government. Measures of happiness and wellbeing vary little over time, so they are of little use as indicators of policy success. However, even the critics recognise that, 'It is entirely reasonable to want to live in a society not totally dominated by commercial or material concerns.'[33] So as a description of an overarching orientation for public policy, improvement of the opportunities for happiness and wellbeing makes sense. The way to put such an orientation into practice is by adopting goals for society that contribute towards those ends – such as access to education and health services, opportunities for paid work for all who want it, adequate income support for those who cannot work, stable climate, gender equality, equity in the distribution of income and so on. These sorts of explicit objectives evolve as circumstances, preferences, human insight and measurement capacity change.

A NEW SOCIAL AND ECONOMIC SETTLEMENT

Seeking wellbeing for all and the common good can be interpreted in many ways, but if they are sought rigorously, national strategy will evolve substantially. Bringing economic, social and environmental policy together is a central challenge for public policy. Improving wellbeing has social, economic and environmental dimensions, and requires a comprehensive strategy for strengthening Australian performance, including by improving the availability and quality of education and training; increasing support for research and innovation; investment in other social as well as physical infrastructure; and policies for environmental sustainability. These policies can be integrated and mutually supportive – there are strategies which improve efficiency, equity and sustainability simultaneously.[34]

Focusing public policy on improving wellbeing and the common good would be readily operational. There would be many implications for a government which explicitly included improving wellbeing amongst its goals for the nation. Increasing workplace security rather than undermining it would be a necessity. So would improving opportunities for balancing work, family life and caring. This would involve recognising the important transitions – between education, child-bearing and care, sickness and retirement – that occur over the life course.[35] Extending the range of policies which help anticipate and manage risk would be valuable. Increasing the incomes of low earners would do far more to increase their happiness than equivalent increases for high income earners, so equitable income policies rather than tax cuts for the wealthy would be another high priority. Opportunities for lifelong education and training would encourage people to increase their capacity for enjoyment as well as for productive work. Reducing social exclusion through readily available English language training and active community development programs would be valuable. Policies for reducing the misery caused by, for example, unemployment and mental illness, would be vital. Such policies are not utopian; they would be welcomed by voters.

There are many examples of such strategies. One recently published is Hugh Stretton's book *Australia Fair*. Most of the analysis and proposals in this book are consistent with Stretton's views, but concentrate on priorities for the next couple of parliamentary terms rather than for the longer term. Another set of examples are policies proposed at a ground-breaking conference in February 2007 organised by former Deputy Prime Minister Brian Howe on the theme 'From Welfare to Social Investment: Re-imagining social policy for the life course'. He called for 'a new social settlement' in which the economy is driven by a social purpose. The background paper for the conference argued for social policy 'that aims to build capability, recognise difference and encourage participation while also promoting citizenship rights and addressing issues of poverty and inequality'.[36] In Howe's view, the recognition that social policy is often a form of social investment would lift the priority which it should receive in Budgets and other decisions about public policy. This is in sharp contrast to the liberal economic view, which seeks to minimise public social expenditure and therefore increases exclusion from income support, services and housing.

Brian Howe's conference was opened by Professor Sir Anthony Atkinson, who described his proposal for a minimum income to encourage participation and reduce exclusion as well as reducing poverty, which he calls a Participation Income (details in Chapter 5). One aim of a Participation Income is to acknowledge and support parents and carers who contribute fundamentally important services to social wellbeing. People need to be able to choose not to work when responsibility for family care requires that.

Another source of examples is the experience of countries where economic and social policy are integrated – industrial and antipoverty policy in Ireland, research, innovation and human services in Finland, and industrial development and energy conservation in Germany, for instance. Social democracy, particularly as practised in the Nordic countries and the Netherlands, is among the strategies which continue to offer relevant examples of alternatives to Australia. A brief comparative overview of the Nordic nations ends Chapter 4, and one on Irish economic strategy concludes Chapter 5.

Atkinson cited the European Union as a whole as an example of a major entity attempting to integrate economic, social and environmental strategy. At the meeting of Heads of State and Government in Lisbon in March 2000, the EU adopted the strategic goal of becoming 'the most competitive and dynamic knowledge-based economy ... with more and better jobs and greater social cohesion'.[37] The EU is engaging in economic competition with the United States and Asia, but the inclusion of social cohesion amongst its goals is also reinvigorating social policy. The aim is 'a social Europe in the global economy'. Four strategic pillars have been adopted: growth, employment, social inclusion and sustainable development.

A Shortlist of Fourteen Structural Indicators has been created to enable an objective assessment to be made of Member States' progress (see below). The Shortlist covers six domains:

⇨   economic development;
⇨   employment;
⇨   innovation and research;
⇨   economic reform;
⇨   social cohesion; and
⇨   the environment.

The concrete indicators in the table suggest possible areas on which Australian policy too could be constructively concentrated. The EU has set a target of growth in employment to 70 per cent for men of working age and 60 per cent for women by 2010. Particular attention is being focused on raising the employment rate of men and women aged 55–64 to 50 per cent by 2010. Social inclusion is measured by indicators of exclusion, which are not so precise. They encompass financial poverty, income inequality, regional variation in employment rates, long-term unemployment, joblessness, low educational qualifications, low life expectancy and poor health. There have not, however, been any substantive EU-wide policy initiatives to help Member States achieve these goals. Each country sets its own specific targets for reducing unemployment, poverty and social exclusion and prepares its own two-year action plans. A peer review process helps countries learn from each other.

This strategy has not been in operation for long enough to make a major impact, but there has been some progress. Between 1999 and 2005, the employment rate for the enlarged EU rose from 61.9 per cent to 63.8 per cent, and the long-term unemployment rate fell slightly.

However, the risk of poverty has not been significantly reduced so far. Nevertheless, in relation to poverty, Europe as a whole performs substantially better than the United States. Atkinson shows that if the United States had the same poverty rate as Europe – 15 per cent rather than 24 per cent – the number of poor in the United States would be reduced by 27 million.[38]

An example of the EU's commitment to integrated policy is its environmental policy. The EU has been a global leader in efforts to protect the environment.

The European Union's environmental policy is based on the conviction that economic growth, social progress and environmental protection all help improve our quality of life. What is more, they are interlinked. A careful balance must be struck between them if development around the world is to be sustainable – in other words, if future generations are also to enjoy a better quality of life. The major challenges for the environment today are climate change, the decline in biodiversity, the threat to our health from pollution, the way in which we use natural resources and the production of too much waste. The EU is addressing these challenges by setting high environmental standards, and by promoting new ways of working and cleaner technologies. New environment-friendly technologies developed in Europe could also make our economy more competitive and so contribute to increasing exports, reducing imports and thus creating jobs.[39]

Much opinion on these issues is more fully developed in other countries than in Australia. The UN World Summit for Social Development held in Copenhagen in March 1995 adopted the goals of the eradication of poverty, the achievement of full employment and the fostering of secure, stable, inclusive and just societies. These goals were expressed and expanded through ten commitments in the Summit Declaration, which included:

⇨ creating an economic, political, social, cultural and legal environment that would enable people to achieve social development;

⇨ eradicating absolute poverty in the world through decisive national actions and international cooperation by a target date to be set by each country;

⇨ promoting the goal of full employment as a basic policy goal;

⇨ promoting social integration based on the enhancement and protection of all human rights;

⇨ achieving equality between women and men;

⇨ attaining universal and equitable access to education and primary health care; and

⇨ increasing resources allocated to social development.

The five chapters of the Summit's Programme of Action described a detailed strategy for working towards those commitments.

These are extraordinarily ambitious goals and programs, and yet they were adopted by the largest meeting of national leaders ever held up to that time. Just the holding of the Social Summit was a triumph, for it was the clearest and most authoritative statement that a reaction against the extremes of economic liberalism was beginning, that priorities were changing and that social goals could have greater weight. The Summit Declaration was the start of a global campaign to end desperate poverty, a campaign equivalent to that for the ending of slavery. It could be argued that words don't matter, but the intensity of the negotiating sessions showed that this would be a superficial assessment. The outcome was the result of preparatory meetings at which every word was discussed in detail and carefully negotiated. There were strong

SHORTLIST OF EU STRUCTURAL INDICATORS

INDICATOR NUMBER		CLASSIFICATION
1	GDP per capita measured in common purchasing power	Growth
2	Labour productivity per person employed	Growth
3	Employment rate of persons aged 15–64*	Employment
4	Employment rate of older workers (aged 55–64)*	Employment
5	Youth educational attainment (% aged 20–24 having completed at least upper secondary education)*	Social Inclusion
6	Expenditure on research and development as % GDP	Innovation
7	Comparative price levels	Growth
8	Gross fixed capital formation as % GDP	Growth
9	At risk of poverty rate after social transfers (% of persons with equivalised disposable income below 60% of national median)*	Social Inclusion
10	Long-term unemployment rate (those unemployed 12 months or more as % total active population)*	Social Inclusion
11	Regional cohesion (coefficient of variation of employment rates across regions within countries)	Social Inclusion
12	Index of total greenhouse gas emissions, compared to Kyoto base year	Environmental
13	Gross inland consumption of energy divided by GDP	Environmental
14	Index of inland freight transport volume relative to GDP, indexed to 1995 = 100	Environmental

* disaggregated by gender

source Tony Atkinson, 'EU social policy, the Lisbon Agenda and re-imagining social policy', *Henderson Oration,* presented to the conference 'From Welfare to Social Investment', Centre for Public Policy, University of Melbourne, 21 February 2007.

disagreements about many issues, resolution of which required making difficult compromises.

Following the Social Summit, many countries and international organisations attempted to implement the commitments and programs. In 2000, 110 countries reported taking some action. For example, China announced that it was attempting to eradicate the most severe forms of poverty. About 30 countries set themselves time-bound poverty reduction targets and 78 issued poverty reduction plans or included chapters on poverty reduction in national economic and social strategies. Many countries gave more attention to employment than they had five years before, including the Member States of the EU, as has just been described. Many countries lifted the priority given to education, health, housing and social protection.

After the Summit, fewer countries deliberately adopted economic policies which directly increased unemployment or other forms of deprivation. Some governments and institutions ignored or acted inconsistently with the Social Summit commitments and recommendations, including Australia and the United States, and the policies of the International Monetary Fund (IMF) were little affected. Yet the Summit consensus reflected the agreed position of those who spoke for their governments at the time.

The Social Summit outcomes did not, of course, reduce the complexity of practical policy choices. Yet agreeing on shared goals and indicators was a major step, for greater clarity about objectives allows a sharper and more cost-effective focus for programs. The momentum on these issues was carried forward at a Special Session of the UN General Assembly which was held in Geneva in June 2000, and which was organised by my Division for Social Policy and Development. Yet the Australian Government showed its contempt for this meeting and for these issues by being the only developed country (other than Japan, where an election campaign was in progress) which did not send a delegation headed by a minister. Australia did not even send senior public servants – all other countries did. The Special Session adopted 40 additional policy commitments or innovations aimed at more effective movement towards the goals. One of the most notable was setting the first global target for poverty reduction: to reduce by half the proportion of people in the world living in extreme poverty by 2015. This was adopted by the Millennium Assembly held in New York in September 2000, and became the first of the Millennium Development Goals (MDGs) prepared from the Millennium Assembly declaration. Australia continues to be alone in failing to adopt the MDGs as the basis for its aid program.

Towards the end of 2006 the results of a national survey of the attitudes of Australians to happiness and social wellbeing by Ipsos Mackay were published by the Australia Institute.[40] The survey results confirm the conclusions of this chapter. When respondents were read eight alternatives and asked, 'Which one is most important to you with regard to your own happiness and wellbeing?', 59 per cent said partner/spouse and family relationships, followed by 18 per cent who said health, 8 per cent community and friends, 5 per cent religious/ spiritual life, 4 per cent money and financial situation, 2 per cent a nice place to live, and work fulfilment, and 1 per cent didn't know. When asked about 'the overall quality of life of people in Australia, taking into account social, economic and environmental conditions and trends', and whether 'life in Australia is getting better, worse, or staying about the same', 25 per cent replied a lot or a little better, 34 per cent said about the same and 39 per cent said a lot or a little worse. When read the statement, 'A government's prime objective should be achieving the greatest happiness of the people, not the greatest wealth' and asked whether they agreed or disagreed, 77 per cent said they agreed, 16 per cent disagreed and 7 per cent didn't know.

The President of the Australian Conservation Foundation, Professor Ian Lowe, has suggested that our vision should be of 'an Australia that is ecologically sustainable, economically viable, socially just and fun to live in'.[41] A small meeting in March 2005 of people experienced in public policy suggested a set of national goals for Australia: 'an equitable, inclusive and secure society within a strong and sustainable economy, characterised by mutual care, social justice, creativity, trust and environmental responsibility, and with a democratic and accountable government that values national independence and contributes to global security, peace and justice'. These are attractive visions. The question is whether credible policies based on them could be sufficiently appealing and persuasive to a majority of citizens. That is the subject of the next four chapters.

Indigenous people have experienced prolonged and severe injustices, and their wellbeing deserves particular attention. This chapter therefore concludes with a section on the implications of this orientation for justice and reconciliation for Indigenous Australians.

Overcoming injustice: Practical and symbolic reconciliation for Indigenous Australians

Nicola Henry

The removal of Indigenous people from their land, the forcible removal of children from their families, and the ensuing legacy of dispossession, racism and deprivation represents a shameful blight on the Australian nation. While over the years there have been some landmark legal cases and successes in cultural and political recognition of the extensive inequalities emanating from centuries of injustice, Law Professor Larissa Behrendt argues that a psychological *terra nullius* ('land belonging to no one') continues to pervade contemporary Australia in both mythology and policy.[42] The Australian Government's response to reconciliation has been largely ad hoc and reactive. Governments have not only failed to achieve measurable improvements in the health and wellbeing of Indigenous people (practical reconciliation), but they have also failed to adequately acknowledge injustice (symbolic reconciliation). The Howard Government has refused to issue a formal apology to the Stolen Generation; nor has it embraced an adequate policy framework for self-determination. A renewed reconciliation policy that is guided by both practical and symbolic measures to overcome the economic and social exclusion faced by Indigenous Australians is of paramount importance if self-determination, social justice and cultural autonomy for Indigenous Australians are to become realities.

Reconciliation entails justice, equality, recognition and healing. The aim of reconciliation in Australia must be to repair the cultural divisions between Indigenous and non-Indigenous Australians and to promote cooperation, harmony, tolerance and respect. The Council for Aboriginal Reconciliation (CAR) defined the main goal of reconciliation as: 'To bring about, through education, a greater level of awareness of Aboriginal history, cultures, dispossession, continuing disadvantage and the need to redress disadvantage. In short, we must come to terms honestly with our history as a nation.'[43] Although 'reconciliation' has a number of interpretations, some practical and symbolic goals may be identified: first, to promote Indigenous leadership, governance and self-determination (the management of local government, land and community centres, road maintenance, and education in schools, for example); second, to foster economic independence; third, to improve the lives of Indigenous people through housing, health, education and employment programs and services; and fourth, to build a learning space for Indigenous history, culture and society that recognises the Aboriginal and Torres Strait Islander people as the first Australians and acknowledges the disadvantage caused by colonisation.

In 2001, CAR presented the Federal Government with a National Strategy to Sustain the Reconciliation Process. This was a roadmap for the practical, cultural and spiritual dimensions of reconciliation, aiming to promote recognition of Aboriginal and Torres Islander rights, overcome relative disadvantage and foster economic independence within Indigenous communities. Some of their recommendations are discussed below.

PRACTICAL MEASURES

The marginalisation and deprivation of Indigenous Australians is evident in the standard social indicators. According to a recent report published by Oxfam Australia and the National Aboriginal Community Controlled Health Organisation (NACCHO), Australia ranks bottom in the league table of first-world nations working to improve the health and life expectancy of Indigenous people.[44] Life expectancy at birth for Indigenous Australians is 17 years less than for all Australians (as noted above) and infant mortality is about three times the rate of the non-Indigenous population. According to the report, these health indicators are 'not only a national scandal: they are an international scandal when compared to recent health advances in Indigenous populations in other first-world countries'.[45] In New Zealand, Canada and the United States, for example, the life expectancy gap is seven years. The large gap between Indigenous and non-Indigenous life expectancy in Australia reflects deeply entrenched social and political inequalities in health, education, housing and employment. These statistical measures are not just arbitrary numbers. As Indigenous leader Professor Mick Dodson has noted:

> The statistics of infant and perinatal mortality are our babies and
> children who die in our arms … The statistics of shortened life
> expectancy are our mothers and fathers, uncles, aunties and elders
> who live diminished lives and die before their gifts of knowledge and
> experience are passed on. We die silently under these statistics …[46]

Completion of schooling is much lower for Indigenous people than for non-Indigenous people in Australia. In 2006, 21 per cent of 15-year-old Indigenous children were not participating in secondary education, and Indigenous students were only 50 per cent as likely as non-Indigenous students to continue to Year 12. The differences in these figures for remote Indigenous communities are even more stark. In 2002, 45 per cent of the Indigenous population over 18 years of age had not completed Year 10. Employment figures also reflect the wide gulf between Indigenous and non-Indigenous Australians. Currently, about 17 per cent of the Indigenous population is unemployed, compared with 4.6 per cent of the non-Indigenous population. (Note that if this estimate did not take into account Indigenous people 'employed' on the Community Development and Employment Program, the Indigenous unemployment rate would be about 40 per cent.) Indigenous people are also over-represented in the criminal justice system as both victims and perpetrators of crime, with Aboriginal women in remote communities

45 times more likely to have been the victims of abuse than non-Indigenous women.[47]

The debilitating effects of alcohol and substance abuse within Indigenous communities are widely documented. The National Drug Research Institute, for example, recently reported that alcohol causes the death of an Indigenous Australian every 38 hours.[48] Sexual abuse and family violence in remote Indigenous communities has also been the focus of much attention, although it has been wrongly suggested that abuse is intrinsic to Indigenous culture. As Mark Leibler, the co-chair of Reconciliation Australia, stated:

> To suggest that rape and paedophilia are part of Aboriginal culture is defamation. Whether it's used as an excuse by perpetrators or a cop-out by non-Indigenous Australians who find this explanation easier than facing up to their own responsibilities, it is slanderous and it is wrong.[49]

In 2004–05, the Federal Government abolished the Aboriginal and Torres Strait Islander Commission (ATSIC), a government body through which Indigenous Australians could advise governments on Indigenous issues, advocate recognition of rights and deliver and monitor specific Indigenous programs and services. The policy and coordination of Indigenous matters is now under the control of the Office of Indigenous Policy Coordination (OIPC) within the Department of Families, Community Services and Indigenous Affairs (FaCSIA). Since the abolition of ATSIC, government policy on Indigenous issues has been carried by mainstream departments. This reflects the government's 'whole-of-government approach', which is based on the principle that successful solutions require shared responsibility between governments and Indigenous communities. The approach was designed to coordinate policies across departments, but to date these new policies have failed to deliver any significant improvement to Indigenous wellbeing.[50] For example, Shared Responsibility Agreements (SRAs) are agreements between governments and Indigenous communities based on 'mutual obligation'. Critics argue that SRAs place coercive conditions on Indigenous funding and that power imbalances during the consultation stage privilege the interests of the state.[51] Under the new approach, Indigenous groups are required to offer commitments in return for government funding. In the first publicised SRA, in December 2004, community leaders in Muland in the east Kimberley were required to ensure the following: that children shower daily and wash their faces twice a day (to reduce the incidence of trachoma); that rubbish bins at every house be emptied twice a week; that pest control be undertaken four times a year, as well as other commitments such as school attendance and anti-petrol sniffing measures. In return, the community was given a new petrol bowser and regular health checks for children.

According to social epidemiologist Michael Morrissey, SRAs have cast 'the government in the role of a benevolent patriarch', for they not only imply that remote Indigenous communities are to blame for their situation, but they are also in 'flagrant contradiction to the continuing rhetoric of equal treatment' since they have been formed solely in Aboriginal settlements.[52] In addition, only 1 per cent of total government expenditure has been invested in this scheme.[53]

There was some improvement in the 2007–08 Commonwealth Budget. There were 26 initiatives – in remote housing, early childhood, education, health and economic independence – totalling $815.7 million of new and extended funding for over five years. In particular, $374 million was set aside for home visits by health professionals to Aboriginal chlidren in outer regional and remote areas. However, Gary Highland, national director of Australians for Native Title and Reconciliation (ANTaR), has stated that the modest increase of around $30 million in Aborigianl health was well below what is needed to address Indigenous health inequities.[54]

A systematic review of government policies and programs is required so that programs that are not working are replaced by creative and innovative programs that will work to reduce Indigenous disadvantage. Above all, a huge investment of resources is required to dramatically reduce the vast social inequalities that divide Indigenous and non-Indigenous Australians. The third-world standards of Indigenous health, education, employment and housing should not be tolerated in a country that is ranked third in the world in terms of human wellbeing.

Australia must emulate and go beyond the standards that are being set by other first-world nations and begin closing the disgraceful gap between Indigenous and non-Indigenous Australians.

Native title and land rights also require greater attention at the policy level in order to increase their social, economic and cultural benefits for Indigenous communities. In the famous 1992 *Mabo* Case, the High Court of Australia ruled that the legal concept of *terra nullius* was invalid and that native title over land before European colonisation is recognised in common law. The decision led to the enactment of legislation recognising the rights of the Indigenous people to possession of their traditional lands in accordance with their customs and traditions. Aboriginal groups have since gained greater control over large areas of land through several pieces of native title legislation. Between 18–20 per cent of Australia is currently under Indigenous control, but most of this land has little commercial value and is in remote and desert locations. In order to foster economic development, particularly in regional and remote communities, Australian governments must design economic development strategies to underwrite Indigenous development.[55] Professor Jon Altman, Director of the Centre for Aboriginal Economic Policy Research, suggests that a hybrid economy with three sectors – the customary, market and state – is essential to 'charting development pathways in modern Australia that accord with local and regional aspirations in all their diversity'.[56] Indigenous visual art is an important example of productive activity mostly located in remote communities, founded on customary practice, and tailored for the market (the Indigenous visual art sector is currently worth approximately $100 million per annum).[57]

In the mineral sector, land rights deliver some commercial benefits to Indigenous communities who have been granted 'de facto mineral rights', but some critics have pointed out that the Native Title Act puts Aboriginal people in a weak negotiating position and land use agreements between Indigenous communities, mining companies and governments have been poorly constructed. For instance, at the end of a six-month negotiating period, if the Aboriginal people have not reached an agreement with the mining company, the company can go to the National Native Title Tribunal and request that the mining lease be issued so that the project can go ahead. In the last ten years, this has happened on 16 occasions. Amendments to the Native Title Act currently being debated in the House of Representatives could increase the powers of the Minister for Indigenous Affairs and the Native Title Tribunal and erode the native title rights of Indigenous people.[58] Professor Ciaran O'Faircheallaigh argues that only one-quarter of agreements deliver 'very substantial outcomes', and that about half have 'little by way of substantial benefits'.[59]

SYMBOLIC MEASURES

The Australian Government declares that 'reconciliation will not become a reality until Aboriginal and Torres Strait Islander disadvantage has been eliminated'. While it is incontestable that social, economic and political disadvantage must be overcome in Australia, the government holds a particularly narrow view that fails to recognise reconciliation as a complex, multi-dimensional, lifelong process with inseparable symbolic and practical goals. The government's approach has been to reject the symbolic aspects of reconciliation, such as an apology, recognition, and self-determination.[60] This makes reconciliation untenable. Australia needs a major shift in governmental policy which recognises that reconciliation will not become a practical reality until *both* disadvantage is eliminated and formal recognition of grave injustices is given.

In their roadmap for reconciliation, Reconciliation Australia made a number of recommendations for governments, organisations and communities that would promote symbolic reconciliation. The following recommendations deserve strong support: changing the date of Australia Day to a date that is inclusive of all Australians; Native Title policy reform (incuding compensation, recognition, development and self-determination); changing Commonwealth legislation to ensure that policies and practices comply with Australia's international human rights obligations; giving state and territory governments greater discretion to take into account customary laws (consistent with human rights standards) in criminal justice sentencing; and constitutional reform, including the addition of a preamble to the Constitution which recognises the Indigenous people as the first people of Australia, a treaty, and a national bill of rights.

Political representation is another issue to be explored. The abolition of ATSIC left a gaping hole in Indigenous political representation. At the national level, some have suggested creating seats in the House of Representatives for election by Indigenous people. All parties have failed to nominate sufficient Indigenous candidates to ensure that Indigenous people are fairly represented in Parliament. (This may be compared with New Zealand, where there are 7 Maori seats.) At around 2.5 per cent of the total Australian population, if Indigenous people could choose to enrol and vote on an Indigenous electoral roll, and the seats represented the same average numbers of electors as other electorates, there would be three or four Indigenous seats. Although such a reform raises many issues, it could be a major step towards greater political engagement and political power for Indigenous Australians.

In addition to all these measures, it could be argued that the single most important step is the formal acknowledgment of injustice. Reconciliation between the powerful and the powerless, writes Robert Manne, Professor of Politics at La Trobe University, 'requires the powerful to acknowledge, without equivocation, that grave injustices have been committed. It requires, however, from the powerless, only that they accept the sincerity of the apology, the appropriateness of the acts of reparation, and that they can find it in their hearts to forgive.'[61] An apology does not remove disadvantage, or wipe any slate clean, but it would be a step towards mutual respect and tolerance, signifying a new pathway for relations between Indigenous and non-Indigenous Australians. In countries such as New Zealand, Canada and the United States, government leaders have issued formal apologies to their Indigenous populations for past injustices. It is time Australia did the same.

In his 2006 Australia Day address, Prime Minister John Howard spoke in glowing terms of Australia's dominant culture: 'In Australia's case, [the] dominant pattern comprises Judeo-Christian ethics, the progressive spirit of the Enlightenment and the institutions and values of British political culture. Its democratic and egalitarian temper also bears the imprint of distinct Irish and non-conformist traditions.'[62] The 'dominant cultural paradigm' is a deeply entrenched ideology that privileges European 'progressivism' while also promoting social exclusionism. The treatment of Indigenous people in Australia – in both a historical and contemporary context – contradicts that vision of freedom, democracy and egalitarianism. The injustice towards minority groups, be they Indigenous people or other communities, exposes a dominant culture that is not demonstrating the values it so proudly proclaims.

The on-again-off-again journey towards reconciliation in Australia has been seen by many as a farce. The Howard Government's reconciliation agenda is failing to deliver measurable improvements to the socio-economic wellbeing of Indigenous lives. Its policy has also failed to provide formal and symbolic recognition of the long legacy of social, economic and political injustice bequeathed by non-Indigenous Australians to the Indigenous people of this country. The dispossession of Indigenous people from their land and culture need not, however, entail a narrative only of defeat. The pains and deprivations cannot be erased, but a renewed commitment to reconciliation has the capacity, one would hope, to foster empowerment and reconnection within Indigenous communities. It could also begin to address systemic injustice, and foster greater harmony, tolerance and respect between Indigenous and non-Indigenous Australians. As Nelson Mandela proclaimed, 'the greatest glory in living lies not in never falling, but in rising every time we fall'. This is the challenge of reconciliation for all Australians.

chapter 3

turning the tide: solutions to australia's environmental crisis

Nicola Henry

We stand now where two roads diverge … The road we have long been travelling is deceptively easy, a smooth superhighway on which we progress with great speed, but at its end lies disaster. The other fork of the road – the one 'less travelled by' – offers our last, our only chance to reach a destination that assures the preservation of the earth.

Rachel Carson, *Silent Spring*

What will·they tell their children if their increasingly large houses, four-wheel drives and refusal to ratify Kyoto cost them the nation's foremost natural jewels?

Tim Flannery, *The Weathermakers*

With a maze of coral reefs and scattered islands stretching for 2600km off the coast of northeast Australia, the Great Barrier Reef has been described as the single largest living organism on Earth. The reef is a tropical haven for diverse marine wildlife, including dugongs, sea turtles, dolphins, whales, fish, sea snakes, molluscs and birds. Due to the effects of global warming, the Great Barrier Reef's vast but delicate ecosystem is under increasing threat. As sea surface temperatures rise, spectacularly coloured forests of coral polyps are transformed into deserts of calcium carbonate skeletons. This is known as 'coral bleaching', a phenomenon that can lead to the death of majestic coral communities. Alongside the degradation of a national and international treasure, coral bleaching leads to the decline of marine biodiversity, the outbreak of coral reef predators, and the loss of billions of tourism dollars.

Global warming is the greatest challenge of our time. World-renowned geneticist and biophysicist Dr Mae-Wan Ho has described global warming as 'the greatest tragedy the human species has ever enacted'.[1] Future weather patterns are likely to be more intense and unpredictable, with far-reaching environmental, economic and social consequences. Rising sea levels, crop failure and declining water supplies could threaten humanity with crippling economic downturn, massive population displacement, violent conflict, widespread starvation and disease. Global warming could also result in the extinction of a million species by the end of the century, including the transformation of the sumptuous Amazonian rainforest into a barren desert or, at best, a 'sparse cover of semi-desert plants'.[2]

This chapter addresses the interconnected array of environmental issues currently facing Australia. The first part of the chapter examines global warming, its implications for Australia and the long-term strategies required to dramatically reduce greenhouse gas emissions. The second deals with drought and the national water crisis. The third and fourth parts focus on biodiversity loss and land degradation. (Space limitations prevent full discussion of some other very important environmental issues – notably human settlements and estuarine and marine environments – but these issues are mentioned in other contexts throughout the chapter.)

On thin ice:
The challenge of climate change

Climate change is the variation of weather patterns over time due to natural processes, such as solar radiation, and human (anthropogenic) activities. The atmospheric accumulation of carbon dioxide, methane, nitrous oxide and water vapour keeps our planet much warmer than if there were no greenhouse gases or clouds in the atmosphere. Radiant energy from the sun enters the atmosphere and is absorbed by the surface of the Earth. This energy reradiates into the atmosphere as infrared radiation or 'heat', which is absorbed by active greenhouse gases. When too much heat becomes trapped in the atmosphere, it causes a net global warming, which puts pressure on the Earth's climate system, leading to climate change.[3] In recent times, climate change is most commonly referred to as 'global warming', which is the rise in average global surface temperatures.

While the Earth's climate is constantly changing over time, the rapid increase in atmospheric greenhouse gases, and therefore also in surface air and water temperatures, has noticeably altered weather patterns in recent decades. The scientific evidence of global warming is now overwhelming. In February 2007, the United Nations Intergovernmental Panel on Climate Change (IPCC) released its report from Working Group I, which concluded that the average surface temperature of the globe increased over the 20th century by at least 0.7°C.[4] Based on six alternative scenarios, IPCC projections indicate that during the 21st century, global temperatures will rise between 1.1°C and 6.4°C above levels at the end of the 20th century. Temperatures are projected to rise by about 0.2°C per decade for the next 20 years.[5]

Scientists have demonstrated that most of the global warming observed over the last 50 years is attributable to human activity: land clearing, agricultural activities and the burning of fossil fuels for electricity generation and transportation. Based on analysis of extracted air bubbles trapped in ancient ice, scientists have shown that atmospheric levels of carbon dioxide are now higher than they have been at any point in the last 650,000 years.[6] As early as 1995, the IPCC concluded that 'the balance of evidence suggests a discernible human influence on global climate'.[7] In 2001, the IPCC strengthened its position, stating, 'there is new and stronger evidence that most of the warming observed over the last 50 years is attributable to human activities'.[8] With heightened confidence, the IPCC announced in 2007 that '[m]ost of the observed increase in globally averaged temperatures since the mid-20th century is *very likely* due to the observed increase in anthropogenic greenhouse gas concentrations' (emphasis in original).[9] When the IPCC says 'very likely', it means there is higher than 90 per cent certainty. And still this is a conservative conclusion. The IPCC draws on the meticulous work of experts from over 130 countries. Thousands of experts are involved in a two-stage scientific and technical review process before the report is presented to the plenary for acceptance. As Tim Flannery, well-known scientist and Australian of the Year, has remarked, 'If the IPCC says something, you had better believe it – and then allow for the likelihood that things are far worse than it says they are.'[10] Indeed many scientists believe that the diminishing capacity of lands and oceans to absorb carbon, in conjunction with rising sea levels, time lags, climate inertia and global dimming,[11] suggest that global warming could be far worse than the IPCC has predicted.

A PERIOD OF CONSEQUENCES

The impact of rapidly increasing global temperatures is far-reaching. Geological studies based on the analysis of ice core samples reveal that prehistoric global warming of about 5°C dramatically transformed Earth, resulting in wildlife extinction, the disappearance of ice sheets and a sea level rise of about 120 metres.[12] During the last ice age, global temperatures were only 5°C cooler than temperatures today – this is a stark reminder of the sensitivity of ecosystems and living creatures to changes in climate. The early consequences of modern-day climate change are already upon us: retreating alpine and continental glaciers, melting polar ice sheets, rising sea levels, as well as regional changes in rainfall and cloud cover, and extreme temperature events. One tragic and iconic symbol of climate change is the polar bear. Camouflaged in thick cream fur, the polar bear uses the snowbound lands and ice floes to hunt for food. The disappearance of the polar bear's ice habitat could, sadly, lead to the extinction of the species by the end of the century.

Climate change is projected to have a staggering impact on human security, public health and living conditions. According to the World Health Organization (WHO), due to an increase in regional temperatures and the frequency and intensity of heatwaves, it is estimated that climate change already contributes to more than 150,000 deaths and 5 million illnesses each year; this is a toll that could double by 2030.[13] Changes in the transmission zones of diseases such as dengue, malaria, and yellow fever, known for their sensitivity to temperature, will contribute to deteriorating living conditions across the globe. By 2080, it is predicted that between 1.1 billon and 3.2 billion people will be suffering from severe water scarcity, and between 200 and 600 million people will be facing devastating food shortages.[14]

Sea level rise due to thermal expansion and the melting of glaciers, ice and snow caps will cause flooding, which will in turn cause a population displacement of 150 million 'climate refugees' by 2050.[15] While coastal cities in the rich, developed world, such as New York, Florida, London and Tokyo, could be partly submerged by sea level rise by the end of this century, it is low-lying countries such as Tuvalu, the Maldives, the Cook Islands, Bangladesh, Indonesia, the Philippines, China, Egypt, Thailand and Vietnam that will be the first to disappear. Saufatu Sopoanga, Tuvalu's prime minister, described global warming as no different from 'a slow and insidious form of terrorism'.[16] Global warming will exacerbate competition for fresh water, energy and food, potentially reigniting ethnic and social tensions, and heightening the possibility of war and terrorism. It will also require unprecedented levels of humanitarian and financial aid to accommodate environmental refugees and to assist those countries seriously affected by climate change.[17]

Indeed, if all countries in the world fail to dramatically cut carbon dioxide emissions, we may reach a 'tipping point' – a point of irreversible damage.

CHANGING AWARENESS

One very positive recent change has been the discernible shift in attitudes to climate change. This has been due in large part to the release and wide distribution of former US Vice-President Al Gore's film *An Inconvenient Truth*, the groundbreaking Stern Review and the release of the IPCC's Fourth Assessment Report (in February 2007). There is now widespread public awareness of the changes in our global climate and growing dissatisfaction with climate change policy. The Stern Review, written by world-renowned economist Sir Nicholas Stern, has had a particularly significant impact. It declared that climate change presents 'very serious global risks', and 'demands an urgent global response'.[18] Stern described climate change as the greatest market failure ever seen, arguing that 'those who produce greenhouse-gas emissions are bringing about climate change, thereby imposing costs on the world and on future generations, but they do not face the full consequences of their actions themselves'.[19]

The Stern report clearly demonstrates the high environmental, social and economic costs of delay and the likelihood of higher mitigation and adaptation costs and more climate change if action is undertaken at a later date. While some politicians (including Australia's Prime Minister, John Howard) continue to position the environment in opposition to the economy, the Stern Review argues convincingly that this is a false dichotomy: it states that stabilising greenhouse emissions at acceptable levels would cost on average 1 per cent of annual global GDP by 2050, while not acting, or continuing with 'business as usual', would cost between 5 per cent and 20 per cent of global GDP.[20]

Soon after the release of the IPCC's Fourth Assessment Report, allegations surfaced that scientists and economists were being offered thousands of dollars from lobby groups funded by Exxon Mobil to undermine the report's findings.[21] In 2006, similar tactics were employed. Fossil fuel companies funded research to dispute climate change science,[22] scientists were gagged by their employers and governments so that they could not publicly discuss the effects of climate change, and a few political leaders continued to discount global warming as the over-exaggerated and scare-mongering tactics of a few delusional scientists.[23] Although now persuaded that the threat of global warming is very real, Australian and US political leaders have been extremely slow to take action. Robert Manne has eloquently captured these failures:

> One of the most dismaying political puzzles of contemporary times is how two of the three leaders who supported the invasion of Iraq, on the basis of exaggerated or falsified intelligence reports about the danger to the world supposedly offered by Saddam Hussein, managed to convince themselves that, despite the near-universal consensus of the relevant scientists, the threat of global warming was not real.[24]

The challenge ahead lies in taking immediate action in order to avoid the most catastrophic consequences of unabated climate change. There is much disagreement, however, over the extent of emissions reductions, and the mechanisms and technologies that are required to achieve these reductions. There are heated debates around the viability of nuclear power, 'clean' coal technologies and renewable energy sources. Equally contested are issues surrounding carbon taxes and emissions trading schemes, as well as whether Australia should ratify the world's only international climate change treaty – the Kyoto Protocol. Australia, and indeed every nation on the planet, is faced with a choice. As marine biologist and nature writer Rachel Carson has said, we can take the 'easy' road to death and extinction, or we can take the road 'less travelled' and save our planet for all species.

RENEWING AUSTRALIA'S FUTURE: LONG-TERM RESPONSES TO CLIMATE CHANGE

Australia has the highest per capita greenhouse gas emissions in the developed world, with the fastest growing emissions in the last decade of any OECD country. The World Resources Institute (WRI) figures show that in 2000, Australia emitted 25.6 tonnes of greenhouse pollution per person, compared with the United States (24.5 tonnes), the United Kingdom (11.1 tonnes), China (3.9 tonnes) and India (1.9 tonnes).[25]

Australia's average surface air temperature has risen 0.7°C over the last century, with 2005 being the hottest year on record.[26] Using global climate model simulations, the Commonwealth Scientific and Industrial Research Organisation (CSIRO) projections indicate average temperature increases in Australia of between 0.4°C and 2.0°C by 2030, and between 1.0°C and 6.0°C by 2070 (relative to 1990 levels).[27] Scientists warn that by 2030 there will be an increase in the number of days over 35°C, a decrease in the number of extremely cold days, a decrease in the incidence of frosts, and an increase in the frequency of tropical cyclones and floods. This means an overall drying trend for large regions of Australia – particularly in the southeast – due to decreased rainfall and increases in temperature and evaporation.[28] The CSIRO reported that although drought is part of normal weather patterns in Australia, it is intensified by climate change.[29] In Australia, climate change could have wide-ranging environmental, economic and social effects, including the loss of Australian national treasures such as the Great Barrier Reef and the Kakadu coastal wetlands, as well as thousands of unique flora and fauna species. These irreversible consequences may result from only a small increase in temperature.

In April 2007, the IPCC released its Working Group II report on impacts, vulnerabilities and adaptations to climate change. This report found that all continents and most oceans are experiencing the effects of climate change, with 89 per cent of 75 studies showing changes consistent with those predicted as a result of global warming. In terms of climate change in Australia, the report's findings confirmed the CSIRO's alarming predictions: water shortages in southern and eastern Australia; significant biodiversity loss in the Great Barrier Reef, the Queensland wet tropics, Kakadu, alpine areas and the sub-Antarctic islands; coastal flooding; extreme weather events; and decreasing agricultural productivity due to drought and fire across much of southern and eastern Australia.[30]

Drawing on the recommendations of leading environmental and economic policy experts, the following nine-point coordinated action plan is proposed for tackling climate change.

ACTION 1: RATIFY KYOTO

The Kyoto Protocol to the United Nations Framework Convention on Climate Change (UNFCCC) assigns mandatory targets to signatory industrialised nations for the reduction of greenhouse gas (GHG) emissions.[31] The Protocol came into force on 16 February 2005 and has been ratified by 169 countries. Signatories are divided into two general categories: developed countries that have accepted GHG emission reduction obligations and developing countries that have no absolute GHG emission reduction obligations in the first phase of the treaty. Developed countries may increase their carbon emissions by purchasing GHG emission reductions from elsewhere. For example, developing countries that implement GHG projects receive carbon credits which may be sold to the developed countries. During the Kyoto negotiations, Australia was permitted an 8 per cent increase from 1990 levels over the period 2008–12, while nearly every other developed country was assigned a mandatory target for *reduction* of emissions. Despite this exceedingly generous concession, the Howard Government has refused to ratify the Protocol. As a consequence, Australia is missing out on the benefits of access to international emissions trading.[32]

The Australian Government argues that the Kyoto Protocol targets are too low to make significant reductions in global emissions and that there is no 'comprehensive or environmentally effective long-term response to climate change'. [33] It also argues that such protocols are valueless until developing countries such as India or China are also required to reduce their emissions. However, developed countries are in a very different situation from developing nations. First, they share responsibility for the bulk of the past and current GHG emissions, and second, they have the economic capacity to make reductions and help developing countries do the same. Melbourne University academic Robin Eckersley has argued that Australia is in contravention of the United Nations Framework Convention on Climate Change.[34] The Convention, which Australia signed and ratified in 1992, states:

> The Parties should protect the climate system for the benefit of present and future generations of humankind, on the basis of equity and in

accordance with their common but differentiated responsibilities and respective capabilities. Accordingly, the developed country Parties should take the lead in combating climate change and the adverse effects thereof.[35]

Australia should be at the forefront of global action on climate change because of our vulnerability to global warming impacts, our natural abundance of renewable energy sources, our heavy per capita carbon footprint, and our responsibility as a rich nation to lead by example and to help developing countries to follow suit. Australia should therefore ratify the Kyoto Protocol as a first step. The next step is to work with other nations to develop a more effective global response to climate change when the first Kyoto commitment period ends, in 2012.

ACTION 2: COMMITMENTS AND BINDING TARGETS

Greenhouse gas emissions are on the rise in Australia. The Australian Greenhouse Office announced in its National Greenhouse Gas Inventory that Australia's net greenhouse gas (GHG) emissions from all sectors increased by 2.3 per cent between 1990 and 2004.[36] It is projected that by 2020, emissions will have reached 127 per cent of 1990 levels because of ongoing growth in emissions from the fossil fuel energy sector.[37] A recent study by the Climate Institute of Australia says that Australia's GHG emissions have increased by 23 million tonnes over the last three years. This, they say, is equivalent to adding more than five million cars to Australia's roads. Given the urgency of addressing climate change, it is essential that state and federal governments act decisively on significantly reducing emissions.

One step towards achieving major reductions and ensuring a healthy economy is to set effective interim and long-term mitigation targets. This would encourage technological change, mobilise society and promote industry participation.[38] A major reduction in greenhouse gases would thus be achieved by: legislating against an increase in emissions; setting interim targets for emission reductions until 2050; and setting binding targets for renewable energy. The IPCC's Working

Group III report, released on 4 May 2007, concluded that a reduction of between 50 and 85 per cent of emissions and the stabilisation of greenhouse gas concentrations between 445ppm and 535ppm will help avoid dangerous climate change, and would cost less than 3 per cent of global GDP.[39]

Australia should follow the example set by other countries and regions. Nine US states, for example, have legislated targets to reduce emissions to 1990 levels by 2009. California, the world's fifth largest economy, has announced a target of 80 per cent emissions reduction from 1990 levels by 2050. In January 2007, the European Commission announced its new energy strategy, calling on EU states to cut emissions by at least 20 per cent from 1990 levels by 2020, and up to 30 per cent given equivalent global efforts. In March 2007, the UK Government unveiled a plan to make Britain the first nation in the world with legally binding carbon reduction targets – to slash emissions by 60 per cent (from 1990 levels) by 2050. This is a great leap above its Kyoto target of 12.5 per cent by 2012. In February 2007, New Zealand set itself an ambitious goal: to become the world's first greenhouse gas neutral country. This will start with big emission cuts in government, and compulsory targets for biofuel use to replace gasoline. In June 2007, the Leaders of the Group of Eight club of wealthy nations (G8) agreed to the goal of cutting emissions by at least half by 2050 in a landmark pact.

ACTION 3: PUTTING A PRICE ON CARBON

In Australia, electricity prices are amongst the lowest in the world, but the price of carbon-based energy does not reflect its true cost once environmental effects have been factored in. The low cost of Australia's coal-based energy means there is little price incentive to seek out low-emission energy options. To offset this market anomaly and to reach any sort of ambitious long-term targets, the Australian Government must put a price on carbon. This would penalise the polluting parties and reward emissions reducers, and thus encourage business to use (and research) low-emission technologies.

As well as its environmental benefits, a price on carbon would generate additional revenue, which could be used as a substitute for other taxes or to increase support for other emission-reducing outlays, such as public transport. Paul Anderson, CEO of Duke Energy and former CEO of Australian mining company BHP Billiton, argues that a carbon tax is a way to evenly distribute the costs of reducing GHG emissions across all sectors of the economy. It would also set up a smooth transition to an emissions trading scheme.

Under an emissions trading scheme, a limit is set on the amount of carbon dioxide that can be emitted. Companies that exceed their limits are required to purchase or trade permits with other companies which have lower emissions. The ACF argues that a national emissions trading scheme (NETS) needs to meet three key tests:

1. a legislated target range of 60–90 per cent reduction below 1990 levels;

2. a short-term cap of 30 per cent by 2020 to put us on the path towards deep cuts; and

3. the adoption of prices that are sufficient to drive low-emissions technologies.[40]

On 31 May 2007, the final report of the Prime Ministerial Task Group on Emissions Trading was released.[41] The group recommended that Australia should adopt a 'cap and trade'-style emissions scheme with the capacity to link to international trading schemes. The report also recommended that revenue from such a scheme could be reinvested in low-emission technologies (such as nuclear, clean coal and renewable sources). Unfortunately, the group did not set an emissions target; the Prime Minister has pledged to announce this in 2008.

International carbon trading is already occurring through the so-called flexibility mechanisms of the Kyoto Protocol and the EU Emissions Trading Scheme. Under these schemes, nations set caps on carbon emissions but have the opportunity to trade permits on the international market and invest in emission-reducing projects in developing countries (under Kyoto this is called the Clean

Development Mechanism [CDM]). Critics have argued that carbon trading is economically driven as opposed to community oriented and that it draws attention away from the widespread systemic change that is needed to tackle the climate change challenge. Problems with implementation and accounting have also been documented. However, while carbon trading will not solve the global warming crisis, it has the potential to be one of the most cost-effective ways of reducing greenhouse gas emissions.

Another variation on trading is a carbon quota system which would operate at the individual consumer level, giving every person a 'carbon allowance', or a 'right to pollute' which would be tradeable as a commodity or a 'currency'. For example, if you reduced your carbon emissions below your quota because you didn't drive a car, you would then be able to sell your leftover credits to someone who is willing to pay for greater emissions. Each year, the quota would decrease in line with the levels agreed upon by governments (60 per cent reduction by 2020, for example). Before a scheme such as this can be introduced in Australia, however, problems such as threats to equity and civil liberties need to be addressed.

ACTION 4: AN ENERGY EFFICIENCY FRAMEWORK

Energy efficiency also means a reduction in GHG emissions and brings economic benefits through energy savings to consumers, as well as industry. In December 2002, the Australian Government adopted a National Framework for Energy Efficiency (NFEE). The NFEE aims to assess the potential of different technologies and processes to enhance energy efficiency and reduce demand for energy. The Federal Government's 2004 White Paper, *Securing Australia's Energy Future*, allocated $17 million over five years to assist in the introduction of mandatory energy efficiency assessments for large energy users and the extension of minimum energy performance standards for buildings and appliances.[42] However, although these strategies deserve support, they 'consist principally of (a) an inquiry to examine the potential economic and environmental benefits of improving energy efficiency and (b) an in-principle statement of support for reforms to energy markets to remove disincentives to energy efficiency'.[43]

Compared with other developed countries, Australia's energy efficiency performance has been very weak. Minimum energy standards could be applied to plant and equipment, appliances, vehicles and fuels, and all buildings. A positive step would be, for example, a mandatory 5-star energy performance standard in the Building Code of Australia for all new and substantially renovated commercial, residential and other buildings. It could be backed by tax incentives. This could decrease water use by 25 per cent and energy use by 50 per cent. Victoria's 5-star standard is a good example of an effective energy efficiency measure. Already, the implementation of this standard has achieved the greenhouse pollution equivalent of taking 150,000 cars off the road over five years. Financial incentives for improving energy efficiency, plus innovative financing mechanisms, including subsidies, private sector rebates or discounts and levies on energy use, are also useful strategies. It is important that governments introduce energy efficiency targets, such as national binding standards on home insulation and thermostat settings. Overall, governments will have to work in partnership with energy utilities to coordinate efforts to use less energy and reduce energy bills through energy efficiency.

ACTION 5: TRANSFORMING THE TRANSPORT SECTOR

In Australia, emissions from the transport sector are increasing rapidly, and now account for approximately 13 per cent of total emissions. Projections indicate that by the end of the century, transport emissions will have increased by 40 per cent from 1990 levels despite the current range of measures to reduce emissions from the transport sector.[44] Fuel consumption labelling, vehicle rating systems and a range of projects have also been introduced since 2001 to reduce GHG emissions in the transport sector. However, much more needs to be done.

Personal car ownership presents a major problem. In order to slash carbon dioxide emissions, forms of transport that are less polluting must be introduced and people must find alternative means of transportation. Tighter car fuel efficiency and emissions standards are essential, including the regulation of new cars, incentives for getting rid of old cars, the reduction of fuel concessions for aviation fuel, and the abolition of fringe benefits on company cars. This would not only curb transport emissions, but would also help develop and support alternative fuel systems. The Federal Government should aim to have Australian-made hybrid cars on the market by the end of the decade. It should also dramatically expand the public transport system, create more cycle lanes in and around urban areas, and introduce subsidies for the purchase of fuel-efficient cars. Although air travel accounts for less than 5 per cent of carbon dioxide emissions, it too requires greenhouse reform, including: further research into fuel efficiency technologies; ensuring full flight capacity; inclusion in emissions trading; and an environmental tax on each plane journey to adhere to the 'polluter pays' principle.

ACTION 6: PHASING OUT A NATURAL DISADVANTAGE

Coal is the largest single source of fuel worldwide for the generation of electricity. Because of its relative abundance in Australia, coal accounts for 79 per cent of all electricity generation. At $24.4 billion (12.4 per cent) of export revenue, Australia is the world's largest exporter of black coal. It is not difficult to understand why Australia's fossil fuel industry has enjoyed 'unrivalled political influence'[45] and why renewable technologies continue to play a marginal role in the Australian energy market. Australia's energy policy at the national level has long been dominated by the belief that large quantities of cheap energy and resource exports are the key to Australia's future. As the Finance Minister, Nick Minchin, told the ABC in November 2006, 'One of Australia's great strengths is our access to reliable cheap sources of power from coal electricity – it gives this country enormous competitive advantages ... We would be crazy to wantonly or carelessly throw away that advantage.'[46] Ironically, this so-called advantage is the source of the problem Australia (and the world) is now seeking to address. Coal constitutes the largest source of GHG emissions in

Australia. In addition to emitting carbon dioxide and contributing dangerously to global warming, coal is also responsible for harmful air and water pollution, the over-consumption of water, land degradation and occupational health and safety hazards.

The main 'solution' to dirty coal put forward by the Federal Government has been 'clean' coal technology; that is, investment in technologies which enable coal-energy to be produced with fewer GHG emissions. COAL21, a partnership between the coal and electricity industries and federal and state governments, is currently seeking to discover ways to eliminate GHG emissions from coal-based electricity. COAL21 is evaluating two key technologies: Carbon Capture and Storage (CCS) (also known as geosequestration) and the Integrated Gasification Combined Cycle (IGCC). Geosequestration involves capturing carbon dioxide and storing it deep underground. On 23 November 2006, the Australian Government announced a $60 million program to support the world's largest CCS project, in Western Australia. IGCC technology, on the other hand, involves the conversion of coal to gas for direct firing of gas turbines in power stations.

The economic costs of implementing cleaner coal technologies are high. The International Energy Agency (IEA) estimates that the cost of producing power from clean-coal plants will be around three times that of conventional plants. As well as their high costs, carbon capture technologies require entirely new coal-fired plants, which use up large amounts of energy to construct, resulting in increased levels of GHG pollution. There are also major uncertainties regarding the efficacy of such technologies, and major environmental issues regarding the indefinite or long-term storage of carbon dioxide (leakage, for instance). These technological solutions are unproven, and they would not be available for many years. This means it is vital that Australia turns towards technologies that are clean, available and renewable in order to dramatically reduce emissions quickly. Phasing out coal will require sensitivity to coal industry workers and a major transition to renewable energy in order to ensure the creation of large numbers of jobs within this sector.

ACTION 7: HARNESSING NATURAL ABUNDANCE

Centuries ago, human beings found ways of harnessing energy from the natural elements, from burning wood, to inventing sailing boats and windmills, to architectural design that allows the sun to heat indoor spaces. During the Industrial Revolution the potential of fossil fuels to generate energy was unlocked and renewable energy was set aside, in the fallacious belief that the supply of fossil fuels was inexhaustible – and in ignorance of their harmful effects. Today, however, the renewable energy sector is rapidly expanding in response to the greenhouse crisis. Renewable energy sources broadly cover wind, hydro, ocean, solar, and geothermal power, as well as a range of biofuels. Wind is currently the renewable energy source whose use is growing fastest across the world. Renewable energy alternatives have close to zero emissions, require low maintenance and cost after installation, and are available now. Governments must do more to assist industry development, by setting targets for reducing GHG emissions, removing barriers to the national electricity market, introducing taxes, regulations and organisational structures, and increasing funding for infrastructure, education, information, training and export development.[47]

Australia has an abundance of sun, wind and other renewable energy sources such as geothermal and ocean energy. Despite this, renewable sources constituted a mere 4.7 per cent of energy consumption and 5 per cent of electricity production in Australia during 2004–05.[48] In recent times there have been some improvements in the Australian Government's approach to boosting the renewable energy sector. The $75 million Solar Cities project, for example, which involves demonstrating and trialling solar technology in four Australian locations, is a positive step. The 2004 White Paper, *Securing Australia's Energy Future*, also contained some positive developments, including the establishment of the Low Emissions Technology Demonstration Fund, which provides $500 million for commercial technologies that produce large-scale GHG emissions reductions in the energy sector (the first funding round was completed in 2006–07). Other initiatives include rebates for photovoltaic installations and funding to renewable energy companies for research and development.[49]

Although these developments are steps in the right direction, the Federal Government has to date failed to stimulate innovation and development in the renewable energy sector. First, renewable energy projects must compete with cleaner coal projects in order to secure funding via the low emissions fund. This is problematic because renewable energy is not on an even playing field with coal (clean or otherwise), which enjoys the full support of the Federal Government. Second, the Mandatory Renewable Energy Target (MRET) represents a mere 9500 MWh – around 1 per cent increase in renewable energy production – by 2010. And third, renewable energy technology enterprises and skilled personnel are being lured offshore, which is limiting the growth of the renewable energy sector. The Climate Action Network (CAN) in Australia, an alliance of over 30 environmental, health, community development and research groups, has called upon the Federal Government to amend the *Renewable Energy (Electricity) Act 2000* to increase the MRET to 12 per cent of total energy production by 2012, 15 per cent by 2015 and 25 per cent by 2020.[50] The Federal Government should follow the examples set by the state governments in adopting appropriate renewable energy targets[51] as well as ensuring the implementation of a carbon price and introducing subsidies and rebates (for solar installation, for example) in order to make renewable sources more competitive with fossil fuel energy. In some European countries, such as Denmark and Germany, over 20 per cent of the electricity grid is already supplied by renewable energy sources.

Renewable energy is not the silver bullet that will on its own solve the global warming crisis. Disadvantages include the difficulty in generating large quantities of electricity, reliability of supply (of sunshine, wind, water, for instance) and cost. However, using a combination of renewable energy sources has the potential to replace coal-fired electricity in the medium to long term and thereby dramatically reduce Australia's carbon emissions.[52]

ACTION 8: COSTING THE EARTH:
SAYING NO TO NUCLEAR

Fifty years ago, the United Kingdom became the first country to use nuclear energy to generate electricity for civilian use. Today there are over 400 nuclear reactors operating throughout the world, supplying about 17 per cent of the world's electricity. While some developed countries, such as Germany, Sweden and Spain, are phasing out nuclear power, others – including Australia – are contemplating the possibility of a nuclear future. However, only in Finland is a nuclear generator actually under construction. On 21 November 2006, the Australian Government's nuclear taskforce, headed by former Telstra chief Ziggy Switkowski, released its draft report. The report recommended that nuclear power could be introduced in Australia to help reduce carbon dioxide emissions if the Federal Government imposed a price on carbon.[53]

Using nuclear power raises a number of issues. First is the issue of cost. The Switkowski report argues that nuclear power would be 20–50 per cent more expensive than coal, but with carbon pricing used to increase the price of fossil fuel energy, nuclear power could be made competitive. The report concedes, however, that this would only be possible with 'additional measures to kick-start the industry', which presumably means that government subsidies would also be necessary.[54] The report fails to factor in hidden costs such as construction, insurance, decommissioning, waste management and terrorism harm-minimisation strategies. The second problem with nuclear power is the storage of waste and the risk of exposing human and animal life to radiation. The report argues that Australia has suitable locations for deep underground repositories for waste. However, there is no adequate solution for the disposal of high-level radioactive waste anywhere in the world. The third issue is safety. Although the Three Mile Island disaster and Chernobyl may be exceptional examples of nuclear accidents, safety concerns should not be downplayed. Fourth, nuclear power generation heightens the risk of nuclear weapons proliferation because fissile material from a nuclear power plant could be used to produce nuclear weapons, which of course pose a threat to global survival.

Two additional factors must also be taken into account when considering the nuclear power option in Australia. First, the process of building (and later decommissioning) a nuclear power station means high GHG emissions: it involves construction, testing, and uranium mining. Second, it is too late for nuclear power in Australia. The Switkowski report revealed that even if we started now, it would be another 10–15 years before the first commercial nuclear power plant would be operational in Australia; some experts believe it would be much longer. As Nicholas Stern pointed out, the task of addressing climate change is urgent: 'Delaying action, even by a decade or two, will take us into dangerous territory. We must not let this window of opportunity close.'[55]

ACTION 9: STOP LAND CLEARING

When bushland, forests and other vegetation are destroyed, stored carbon is released into the atmosphere, contributing to the stock of GHG emissions. Trees and plants absorb carbon dioxide through the process of photosynthesis, so deforestation also reduces carbon storage capacity, as well as disrupting water cycles, contributing to soil erosion and causing habitat and biodiversity loss. While much attention has been devoted to economic and engineering solutions to tackling climate change, changes in land use that would reduce greenhouse pollution are often overlooked. On 29 March 2007, Australia's Prime Minister announced a $200 million plan to plant trees in Southeast Asia in order to curb the effects of deforestation and cut GHG emissions in the region. Although this is a positive step, all Australian governments need to do much more. Ideally, their actions would include reducing land clearing in general, as well as preventing soil degradation and supporting extensive reforestation in Australia.

OUR HOPE FOR ACTION ON CLIMATE CHANGE

A 2006 editorial in *The Age* stated: 'In just 12 months, the changing environment has gone from being a peripheral issue to something at the very heart of public debate and personal concern, involving not just those sympathetic to sustainability but every individual living under the sheltering, shifting skies of climate change.'[56] If we are to solve our environmental problems, Australians must remain committed to reducing GHG emissions through reduced energy and water consumption and energy efficiency measures. Governments need to actively encourage action at the individual and household level through increased education in schools and communities about both the potentially catastrophic consequences of climate change for us and for future generations and what we can all do, as individuals, households, communities and a country, to reduce our environmental footprint. It is time for governments to rethink their fossil fuel ideology and take immediate action on climate change. A coherent, consistent, and equitable climate change policy requires, above all, effective leadership, ideas and vision. Australia has the opportunity to move from laggard to leader in climate change policy. Maybe we can hope to save the nation's natural treasures not merely for ourselves, but for other species and for future generations.

The drying continent:
Water, drought and Australia

Of all the inhabited continents, Australia has the lowest percentage of rainfall as run-off, the lowest volume of water in riverine environments, and the smallest area of permanent wetland. Due to a combination of factors, including climate change, drought and the over-allocation of water for irrigated agricultural and urban use, Australia's inland water systems are under considerable stress. Clearly, we need to invest more resources in monitoring, preserving and protecting our precious aquatic reserves. This requires the adoption of a 'diverse portfolio of initiatives'[57] as well as visionary leadership and innovation at all levels of government.

The over-extraction and allocation of water for irrigation over the years has led to the decline of many rivers and ecosystems in

Australia. Australian rivers and wetlands have been affected by altered hydrological flows, increased nutrient loads, soil erosion, land clearing, dryland salinity, habitat destruction, and the introduction of invasive species. In 2002, the National Land and Water Resources Audit (NLWRA) examined the sustainability of 90 per cent of Australian rivers. The NLWRA estimated that 66 per cent of our total river length was moderately modified, 19 per cent substantially modified, and 1 per cent severely modified, and that 23 per cent of rivers were significantly impaired, 6 per cent severely impaired, and 2 per cent extremely impaired.[58]

There have been some significant improvements over the past five years, including increased allocations of water to the environment, greater habitat restoration, invasive species control programs, improved irrigation practices, and greater cooperation between federal, state and territory governments. In 2003, the Murray-Darling Basin Water Agreement was signed by the premiers of New South Wales, Victoria and South Australia and the Chief Minister of the Australian Capital Territory. The Agreement allocates $500 million over five years to address the over-allocation of water and the declining health of the river system. The Murray-Darling Basin 'Living Murray' Programme is, for example, set to recover 500 billion litres of water for the Murray River environment through a range of member state targets to reduce water consumption and reallocate water to environmental flows.

In 2003, the Council of Australian Governments (COAG) agreed on a national blueprint for water reform in Australia called the National Water Initiative (NWI). The NWI represents an innovative shift in water resource policy, and over the coming years it will completely alter the way water is owned, used and reused in Australia. Objectives include: ensuring ecosystem health in rivers; improving water planning, pricing and accounting; addressing over-allocation in agriculture; and conservation in urban regions to develop more efficient water management regimes (such as better use of stormwater and recycled water). In order to achieve these goals, a National Water Commission (NWC) was established to steer national water reform, with $2 billion committed over five years by the Federal Government to the Australian Government Water Fund. Three programs have been established: Water Smart Australia (with a focus on developing efficient water technologies and practices); Raising National Water Standards (aimed at developing consistent nation-wide standards for monitoring, measuring and managing Australia's water resources); and Community Water Grants (focused on supporting local communities with wise water use projects).

A National Water Summit was held at the end of 2006 to discuss how to deal with the 2005–06 drought. The summit ordered emergency work to protect urban supplies of water and established a working group to secure supplies by 2007–08. The leaders agreed to begin permanent water trading between Victoria, New South Wales and South Australia by 1 January 2007 to ensure that water goes to the highest value user. But as the State of the Environment (SOE) Report (2006) pointed out, 'Whether these reforms will be sufficient to restore the rivers to an acceptable level and redress the evident loss of biodiversity remains to be seen.'[59] Indeed, there is growing concern that initiatives such as interstate water trading will not be enough to restore the state of Australian rivers, because of the unseasonal nature of river flows. This is exacerbated by the fact that water is being harvested, stored and released (for irrigation) outside the natural flow regimes of rivers.

Despite a number of positive developments in water resource management over the years, the drought has been so severe that longstanding water allocation rules and water management systems are largely ineffective. As Professor Mike Young from the Wentworth Group of Concerned Scientists has noted:

> A lot of water management systems ... are in disarray. The models they were based on aren't calibrated to run under [the] severe and extended drought conditions that we're now experiencing ... regulations applying to dam releases, management of water storage and irrigation allocations were severely challenged, and in many cases, no longer relevant.[60]

A bold action plan to limit water wastage and secure the health of inland aquatic environments is needed. The over-allocation and over-extraction of water for agriculture is the most pressing issue. One solution is that the Federal Government enters the market to buy water from irrigators. This would force farmers to make some tough decisions about the viability of their farming practices. Dr Arlene Buchan, from the ACF, says that:

> Buying water gives farmers a choice about how to deal with the drought. They can decide to sell part or all of their water and use the money to get out of debt, invest in more efficient irrigation practices, change from irrigated to dryland farming or leave the land altogether if they want.[61]

Water resource management requires a sustainable balance between the competing needs of the environment, irrigation, industry and domestic use. Governmental intervention will be needed. While care and compassion are essential, they do not mean continuing to provide drought subsidies to support farming practices that cause massive environmental destruction. Three headline parameters identified by the NWC can help determine the balance of competing interests. These are: water quality, water availability and water use. Key questions include: How much water do we have? Who is using it? How much water do we need to store? What is the variability of water resources? In what areas do we have inefficient water use?[62]

First and foremost, Australia needs a coherent national water policy to deal with the ongoing water crisis. The management of water resources in Australia has traditionally been vested in state and territory governments. In January 2007, Prime Minister John Howard announced a $10 billion plan for the Commonwealth to take control of the Murray-Darling Basin, called the National Plan for Water Security. The plan would give the Commonwealth powers to: set a Basin-wide cap on surface and groundwater use; establish Basin-wide water quality objectives; set standards for catchment-level plans; impose seasonal allocations of water; direct rural bulk water supply systems; facilitate environmental water management; and set rules for water trading regimes. The plan includes paying irrigators $3 billion to sell their water rights in order to save the river system and spending $6 billion on overhauling outdated irrigation systems that waste water. At the time of writing, Victoria is the only state which has refused to sign up to the plan – on the basis that it lacks detail on how water will be managed at both state and Commonwealth levels. It also remains to be seen whether the plan will achieve the desired result of restoring the Murray-Darling River and securing water supplies to New South Wales, Victoria, South Australia and Queensland.

Second, more rigorous scientific assessment is needed to systematically identify the degree and extent of river health deterioration across Australia, as well as the relationship between drought and climate change. Third, more coordination and cooperation between federal, state and territory governments and communities would help any efforts to reduce water consumption, erosion, sedimentation, pollution and salinity, and to manage and monitor water allocation more effectively.

Professor Peter Cullen, also from the Wentworth Group of Concerned Scientists, has outlined some key actions for effective water management in Australia:

1. a moratorium on any further extractions of water from the [Murray-Darling] Basin until sustainable levels of extraction have been established;

2. the licensing and measurement of all extractions;

3. the establishment of a group of high-level scientific experts to advise a Murray-Darling authority body with an immediate task of determining the implementation of the Living Murray target (i.e. to return 1,500 gigalitres of water to the Murray);

4. a single register of all water entitlements to make registries compatible across state borders;

5. seasonal allocations of water;

6. the appointment of an independent environmental manager to help protect the general health of the river system;

7. infrastructure investment;

8.   greater integration of land and water management; and

9.   water markets that include cities and towns.[63]

HUMAN CONSUMPTION: THE CHALLENGE OF SUPPLY AND DEMAND

In addition to the problems of over-extraction and over-allocation of water for irrigation, there is another problem: an increasing population means a growing demand for water. Australia has more water per capita than many other countries in the world due to its small population relative to landmass. However, variability of supply and high levels of consumption have resulted in declining water reserves, especially in capital cities (with the exception of Darwin). The Water Services Association of Australia (WSAA) projects that a population increase to 17.3 million people in Australia's capital cities by 2030 (currently it is over 12 million), coupled with a close to 50 per cent decrease in available water, will mean that demand for water will far outweigh supply.[64]

In recent years, Australian households have reduced their per capita consumption of water from 120 kilolitres per head in 2000–01 to 103 kilolitres per head in 2004–05.[65] This reduction was due to water-pricing changes, education programs and greater water efficiency measures (dual-flush toilets, for example). Such measures are, however, not enough, and will not solve the problem of water scarcity in Australia. According to Quentin Grafton, an economist from the Australian National University (ANU), we need to make more changes to water pricing to reflect water's environmental and social costs.[66] Proposals have been made for a water trading system for metropolitan users which would allow those who reduce their water consumption to sell their water to big users. While such a scheme would help prevent the need for water restrictions, it would increase the price of water. There would therefore be equity issues to resolve.

A Morgan poll in February 2006 found that 68 per cent of Australians believed that governments are not doing enough about water conservation.[67] Furthermore, the 2006 SOE Report says that Australia is 'lagging behind the rest of the world on appropriate water reuse and storm water harvesting'.[68] It is essential that we make continued improvements not only in water efficiency (such as ensuring minimum efficiency standards for taps, toilets, appliances and showers), but also in harvesting rainwater and stormwater, and in recycling household water for non-consumption purposes, such as watering gardens and flushing toilets. Recycling water through treating sewage is currently being considered in places such as Toowoomba and Goulburn, and will possibly be considered for the rest of Australia as part of a long-term strategy. Education will play an important role in overcoming misconceptions and fears about recycled water.

Desalination, the removal of salt and other minerals from water in order to obtain fresh water suitable for consumption or irrigation, is another option. In 2006, the first desalination plant in Australia, the Perth Seawater Desalination Plant in Kwinana, was constructed, to supply Perth with 17 per cent of its water needs. The plant cost $387 million and has an annual running cost of just less than $20 million. It is the first plant in the world to use electricity generated from a wind farm. Perth is an Australian city that is using a 'security through diversity' approach to water. In addition to desalination, Perth has introduced water trading with irrigators, uses recycled water from the cities as irrigation water for agriculture, and is planting trees to offset its GHG emissions.

It is vital that in tackling Australia's ongoing water crisis, we appreciate the natural, cultural, spiritual and aesthetic value of water. This does not in any way change our responsibility to agricultural communities or our need to respond to the social impact of drought and water scarcity. It merely reminds us of the fundamental importance of water.

Disturbing the peace:
Biodiversity loss in Australia

Human activity is a key threat to Earth's rich and wondrous biodiversity. According to the ACF, today's extinction rate has not been matched since the dinosaurs disappeared 65 million years ago. Biodiversity loss is being further exacerbated by climate change – scientists predict this could drive more than one million species to extinction by 2050.[69] Tim Flannery argues that if we continue with 'business as usual' and do nothing to address GHG pollution, at least three out of five species 'will not be with us at the dawn of the new century'.[70] The IPCC's latest report echoes these concerns, stating that if global temperatures increase by even 1.5–2.5°C, extinction among 20–30 per cent of plant and animal species 'is likely'.[71]

THREATS TO BIODIVERSITY IN AUSTRALIA

Australia is recognised as one of the globe's 17 mega-diverse countries, containing exceptional variety – we have close to one million 'endemic' species not found anywhere else in the world. This can be linked to our geographical isolation, which has led to our having a vast range of unique habitats, and variable climatic conditions. Australia's biodiversity is currently under considerable threat from land clearing, climate change, the introduction of invasive species (both past and new) and other human-induced environmental pressures. The 2006 SOE Report announced that 'biodiversity continues to be in serious decline in many parts of Australia'.[72] The IPCC, in its 2001 report, concluded that Australia's biodiversity is particularly vulnerable to the projected change in temperature and rainfall over the next 100 years.[73] Many species and ecosystems are already vulnerable, endangered or critically endangered, with low resilience to external pressures. The Department of the Environment and Heritage (DEH) (now the Department of the Environment and Water Resources) has identified 383 fauna and 1300 flora species currently either under threat or extinct in Australia. In

2002, the NLWRA reported that 94 per cent of bioregions have one or more threatened ecosystems, and identified 2891 threatened ecosystems and ecological communities across Australia.

Protecting marine and estuarine biodiversity needs to be a national priority. Spanning the five ocean climate zones from the tropics to the polar regions, Australia's sea area is one of the largest in the world, containing over 4000 magnificent and diverse species. Australia has unique marine biodiversity, with a high number of endemic species. This is due to continental separation and the low nutrient status of its oceans – there is an absence of major upwellings (the wind-caused movement of nutrient-rich water to the ocean surface). Surrounding a dry continent, Australia's oceans are a bountiful source of recreation, tourism, sustenance and spirituality for many Australians. Indigenous communities, in particular, have strong cultural links with marine and coastal waters. Yet a range of human activities, including over-fishing, the introduction of invasive marine pests, chemical contamination, waste water pollution, coastal development, mining, oil drilling, tourism, global warming and ozone depletion, have led to the deterioration of Australia's marine habitats – coastal erosion, increased flood risk, habitat loss and major threats to biodiversity. From coral bleaching in the Great Barrier Reef to the decline in luxuriant meadows of sea-grasses, and the loss of mangroves, kelp and other marine habitats, human impact is taking its toll. A good start to the prevention of further losses would be a national policy, supported by state, territory and federal legislation. Such a policy should include clear recognition of Indigenous rights, and be based on ecologically sustainable practices, regional marine planning (including the extension of marine protection areas), and the long-term monitoring and research that are needed to protect our marine and coastal environments.

Wet tropics rainforests are another 'biological disaster on the horizon',[74] with amphibian decline documented in the mossy rainforests of eastern Australia and the rainforests of northern Queensland. Currently in Australia, 4 species of frogs are already extinct, 15 others endangered and 12 listed as vulnerable.[75] Rainforest and alpine-dwelling species such as the green ringtail possum, the broad-toothed rat and the mountain pygmy possum are also predicted to decline as a result of change in habitat due to higher temperatures. Global warming also threatens the eucalypt forests of Tasmania's world heritage area, the heathlands of Australia's southwest, the Alpine region of the Snowy Mountains and Victorian Alps, and the Kakadu National Park wetlands.

BIODIVERSITY POLICY IN AUSTRALIA

As a signatory to the United Nations Convention on Biological Diversity, Australia is committed to three main goals:

1. conservation of biodiversity;
2. development of national strategies for the sustainable use of biodiversity; and
3. fair and equitable sharing of benefits arising from resources.

Under the *Environment Protection and Biodiversity Conservation Act 1999* (Cth), various institutions and programs have brought biodiversity protection and management into the ambit of broader natural resource management. The Federal Government's $36 million 'Maintaining Australia's Biodiversity Hotspots Programme', for instance, concentrates on high conservation value areas that are still relatively intact. In 2003, the Threatened Species Scientific Committee announced 15 national biodiversity hotspots, and in 2006 the Committee announced a new approach to assessing ecological communities, one which will help regional bodies more as they develop appropriate responses to these problems.

Despite a wide range of national and state initiatives, there is still no integrated approach to biodiversity management and protection across all of Australia. Australian governments need to invest more resources in understanding the impact of change and how to restore biodiversity so that they can identify what they need to do to achieve ecological sustainability. In particular, a deeper understanding of the relationship between climate change, drought and biodiversity loss must be rigorously pursued in both policy and research.

A broad national framework was proposed by the Natural Resource Management Ministerial Council in 2004. It was titled a 'Biodiversity adaptation to climate change action plan for 2004–07', and was to be reviewed and revised in 2007. While this was a positive step, it is imperative that in addition to work done on habitat restoration, Australia immediately takes action to reduce its GHG emissions in order to help save our increasingly threatened biodiversity. It is crucial that in planning our actions relating to climate change, land and water, we take into account their impact on biodiversity – not merely for the benefit of humans, but for the intrinsic value of all other life forms inhabiting this planet.

Restoring the land: Protecting against land degradation in Australia

Since European settlement, agricultural production, urban development, transportation, industry and recreation have devastated Australia's landscapes. These practices have resulted in the degradation of soils and waterways, the reduction or destruction of habitats and the ensuing loss of biodiversity. Since 1973, around 17 million hectares of Australian forests have been cleared, with an estimated 1.5 million hectares of forests cleared between 2001 and 2004.[76] The major vegetation groups that have experienced at least 30 per cent clearing since 1750 include: rainforest and vine thickets; eucalyptus open forest; eucalyptus low open forest; eucalyptus woodlands; low closed forest; and tall closed scrublands.[77] In addition, unsustainable agricultural practices, weed infestation, rising water tables, salinity, inappropriate fire management and other unsustainable practices contribute to the degradation of native vegetation and to biodiversity loss.

A range of national and regional schemes for reducing deforestation and preventing land degradation have already been set up. The National Action Plan for Salinity and Water Quality and the Natural Heritage Trust are major programs aimed at protecting Australia's natural resources. A variety of programs and initiatives have also been established by the Department of the Environment and Water Resources to facilitate Indigenous partnerships in land conservation. Indigenous communities have, as a core part of their cultural and spiritual beliefs, special practices for managing the land and conserving biodiversity and these should be recognised and elevated at all levels of policy. The Regional Forest Agreements (RFAs) in Western Australia, Victoria, Tasmania and New South Wales are 20-year plans for the conservation and sustainable management of Australia's native forests.

The methods we set up to protect and manage land need to be based on an understanding of the interconnectedness of the landscape and the life it supports. The biggest gap in land management is the failure of governments to take this kind of holistic approach. Environmental legislation, for example, 'tends to focus on one issue, such as vegetation cover or water or chemical use, leaving land managers to decipher and apply apparently unconnected regulatory requirements across a range of highly connected activities'.[78] A holistic approach would see a major shift away from commodifying the land and towards recognising the interconnected economic, aesthetic and spiritual gains that result from land conservation and preservation.

An environmental crisis from within

The natural environment we depend on for food, water, shelter, aesthetic and spiritual sustenance is under serious threat. To tackle climate change, drought, biodiversity loss and land degradation, the Australian Government needs to develop comprehensive national policies that have ecological sustainability as their major goal. Governments at all levels need to offer their citizens vision, foresight and strong leadership. All areas of life will reap the benefits. Conversely, failing to care for our natural environment will not only destroy any hope for economic prosperity, but will entail an immeasurable deficit of spirit and soul. As Rachel Carson reminds us:

> To stand at the edge of the sea, to sense the ebb and flow of the tides, to feel the breath of a mist moving over a great salt marsh, to watch the flight of shore birds that have swept up and down the surf lines of the continents for untold thousands of years, to see the running of the old eels and the young shad to the sea, is to have knowledge of things that are as nearly eternal as any earthly life can be.[79]

We must strongly reject the fallacy that we have to choose between environmental preservation and economic prosperity. Greater collaboration among environmentalists, scientists, policy-makers and economists will help us do this. Global warming and its consequences should force a revolutionary shift in perceptions about human activity. It is time to view the environmental crisis not as 'out there' in the environment, but as a crisis within.[80]

chapter 4

human security: guaranteeing a decent life for all

Andrew Scott

People need security in childhood, through their schooling years, to underpin their search for jobs, and throughout their lives both at work and at home with their families, if they are to fulfil their hopes for optimal health and wellbeing. This chapter explores policies to strengthen security in all these phases and places.

The vital first years of life

Although we have come to expect our society to provide us with increasing economic prosperity and technical advancement, many key indicators show that the health, wellbeing and development of our children are not improving; indeed some things are worsening.[1] Inequalities between Australia's advantaged and disadvantaged children in terms of low birth weight, the incidence of diseases such as asthma, and educational opportunities and experiences, are increasing.[2]

The Brotherhood of St Laurence has proposed that Australia should now do what many other countries, including Britain and Canada, have done already, which is set a target and timeline to reduce child poverty. The Brotherhood's aim is for Australia to cut its rate of child poverty from the present level, which it estimates on the basis of OECD data to be about 12 per cent,[3] to 8 per cent or less by 2010, and to 3 per cent in 2020. This credible goal is supported by the Brotherhood's insight that:

> the more we invest in people at the start of their life – especially in the
> early years and during the key transitions from home to school, school
> to work and work to parenthood – the less we need to spend on them
> in remedial programs and health and welfare payments as they age.[4]

There has been some positive recognition of this principle by the Victorian Government following Jack Shonkoff's visit to Melbourne in March 2006. Shonkoff is the Chairperson of the US National Scientific Council on the Developing Child and co-author of *From Neurons to Neighborhoods: The science of early childhood development*.[5] He came to Melbourne as a keynote speaker at the Early Childhood Forum. As Australian journalist Jo Chandler pointed out:

> Jack Shonkoff was an idealistic young paediatrician in New York when
> he realised that if he wanted to make children better, he would have
> to give up medicine. He moved into academia, ultimately producing
> a landmark paper ... [that] put the scientific case that disadvantage
> had a toxic effect on the brain development of children ... [It] showed
> that for every dollar invested in their preschool program, there was
> an $18 return to the communities ... [including] savings ... on
> welfare benefits they never claimed ... [and from] crimes they never
> committed.[6]

The Nobel-prize winning economist James Heckman is a member of the
Council Jack Shonkoff chairs, and his research powerfully reinforces the
point that investing in disadvantaged young children is economically
efficient.[7]

The visit by Shonkoff, and his presentation to a Victorian Cabinet
social development committee, produced some policy action. The
Victorian Government announced in its subsequent 2006 Budget speech
a funding boost to protect vulnerable children. Its policy documents for
A Fairer Victoria have, as a major theme, 'giving every Victorian child
the best possible start in life', and have committed the state government
to establishing an Office for Children to undertake research into and
promote the development of more innovative approaches on early
childhood issues, including through programs which intervene early
to prevent problems, rather than treat symptoms after they appear,
and which make kindergarten and child care more accessible for
parents.[8] A series of Victorian Government funding announcements in
2006 committed resources to families in outer suburbs of Melbourne
that have high population growth and high concentrations of young
children. Their purpose is to strengthen child protection, foster care
systems, community-based childcare, kindergartens, and maternal and
child health services, with particular emphasis on vulnerable families,
including those who have children with a disability.

All the states have a very long way to go, however, before they
catch up to the countries which are most successful at investing in
children and preventing child poverty. Australia's preschooling capacity
is relatively poor, covering only 36 per cent of 3 and 4-year-olds in

2002, compared with the average of OECD countries of 68 per cent. Despite the research showing that preschool is the stage that has the greatest influence on educational outcomes, Australia is spending only 0.1 per cent of GDP on preschooling – the OECD average is 0.4 per cent.[9] Australia and the United States are among the lowest spenders in the developed world on early childhood education and care; Denmark, Finland, Norway and Sweden are the highest.[10] It is no coincidence that these four Nordic countries have a much lower rate of child poverty than Australia.[11]

United Nations research published in 2005 found that 14.7 per cent of children in Australia live in poverty; the proportions in the four main Nordic nations are 2.4 per cent in Denmark, 2.8 per cent in Finland, 3.4 per cent in Norway and 4.2 per cent in Sweden.[12] The same research shows that Norway managed to even further reduce its level of child poverty during the 1990s.[13] The Nordic nations appear to have driven child poverty down to these low levels by increasing government support to children in the most needy households.[14] Clearly, greater investment in early childhood programs is needed if child poverty in Australia is to be reduced.

Cutting child poverty to 8 per cent or less by 2010 and to 3 per cent in 2020 is achievable with appropriate investment in early childhood services and the direction of more funds to children in needy households.

Learning opportunities

Far too many government primary schools in Australia have long been suffering from dilapidated physical conditions. The teaching profession has for too long been undervalued. The gaps between the resources – and therefore the performance – of different schools are far too great. In the wake of the 2004 national election, Professor Richard Teese was moved to write with great passion about the secondary school funding gap between the haves and the have-nots widening further unless there is a fundamental change of policy direction:

The children of blue-collar workers have less than one chance in three
of reaching university – only half the rate of children from professional
and managerial homes. But they also finish school much less often.
If they do complete school, they are four times more likely to be
unemployed. Is it to reduce these gaps or to maintain them that the
Coalition Government will spend five times more on independent
school children than on government school children in the next four
years? ... The large independent schools, which have benefited most
from Coalition largesse since 1996, will continue to dominate the
academic scene ... This ... betrays the efforts of those whom we ask
to perform the hardest tasks in our school system, to deliver quality
where it is most required, to deliver equity where everything conspires
to abandon it.[15]

Two-thirds of Commonwealth funding for schools goes to the non-
government sector, notwithstanding the fact that only a third of
students attend these schools.[16] Analysis of Budget papers over the last
decade shows that funding for private schools has tripled, while the real
funding of universities has fallen.[17] Between 1995 and 2001, in spite of a
15 per cent increase in per capita GDP, Australia's total public spending
on tertiary education institutions fell by 11 per cent.[18] Further, in 1999
Australia allocated only 0.8 per cent of total GDP to public spending
on tertiary education, compared with an OECD average of 1.0 per cent.
Australians, however, put 0.7 per cent of GDP into *private* spending
on tertiary education, compared with the OECD average of 0.3 per
cent.[19] The Australian Labor Party (ALP) Opposition's unveiling of its
substantial and forward-looking 'Knowledge Nation' policy in the lead-
up to the 2001 election caused the Howard Government to increase
funding for university research somewhat. However, the latest OECD
data shows that the *proportion* of public spending on tertiary education
has continued to fall in Australia and now makes up less than half of
this nation's tertiary education funds. This puts Australia amongst the
bottom four countries in the OECD in terms of state support for tertiary
education institutions.[20] Considerably more support is needed.

The 2006 OECD *Employment Outlook* report shows Australia
spending only 0.04 per cent of its annual income to retrain the
unemployed, compared with the 0.54 per cent spent by Denmark; and

one clear finding from the OECD's 2006 reassessment of its 1994 Jobs Strategy was the importance of active labour market programs and skills training.[21] These are precisely the areas in which Australia has been least active over the last decade.

The World Economic Forum has continued to demote Australia in the global competitiveness rankings, down to 19th spot in its latest (2006) report. This is because of Australia's failure to try to move 'beyond simply using technologies developed elsewhere', to develop its own 'greater capacity for scientific innovation' through improvements in education – as is done in the much higher ranked Nordic and other northern European economies.[22] The decline in Australia's export performance in the last decade can be directly traced to the cuts in support for research, development and associated activities which were made in the Coalition Government's first Budget.

The first Howard Government Budget dramatically increased Higher Education Contribution Scheme (HECS) charges, by an average of 65 per cent.[23] Though HECS remained easier to bear than direct fees, after 1996 it hit students harder, and we soon had among the highest tuition charges in the world for public university education.[24] Australian universities are now among the least affordable in the world.[25] Between 1995 and 2000, the average OECD country increased the rate of enrolment in tertiary education by 27 per cent; Australia increased its tertiary enrolment by just 6 per cent.[26]

The funding of universities in Australia has shifted markedly: from the old basis of public provision to increasingly burdensome private personal debt and reliance on revenue from international students paying for 'full fee' places. This, together with the increased national government support of private rather than state schools, has had many negative effects. HECS charges have already doubled in the last decade – including a 25 per cent increase at nearly all Australian universities in 2003. The cost to individuals of post-school study in Australia has rocketed: total personal debt as a result of university fees has been rising by $2 billion each year since 2003–04. The national Department of Education has recently estimated that debt from HECS, and loans to cover 'full fee' degrees, will rise by at least 10 per cent a year until the end of the decade. If this occurs, the amount owed will double in six years, from $10 billion in 2003–04 to more than $20 billion by 2009–10.[27] It is also easier and easier for individuals who obtain university entry scores well below requirements to get into 'full fee' degrees ahead of those who have gained better academic results but are not as wealthy. In some cases, these 'full fee' places cost more than $200,000. Such practices compound the inequalities in the earlier stages of education, and so cannot be justified.

It is too daunting for many young people to accept the high long-term personal debts required when undertaking higher education. In May 2006 more than half a million young Australians (15 to 24-year-olds) were not in full-time learning or work.[28] Professor Simon Marginson predicts that, under present policies, for most Australian universities:

> The funding crisis will become perpetual. Students … will carry higher debts than any generation before them; but the best quality places will now be settled on the 'best quality' people, those with the means to pay.[29]

This is an unacceptable future. It is all the more unacceptable given that, as Marginson also points out:

> the government's [own] policy advisers are aware of the giant strides being made by … Finland [for example] through targeted investments in the knowledge economy, in which public outlays on universities are joined to private investment and export initiatives … [and how] Ireland has become one of the largest software exporters in the world, partly through the right investments in research and a high and universal level of training in an education system free of fees.[30]

Labor has pledged to cut the number of 'full fee' university places, compensate universities for the estimated $2 billion loss in revenue which will result, and increase funding to universities overall. In a major policy paper, Labor has declared that 'full fee' places are 'fundamentally unfair' because better-off students can gain places denied to those with higher marks. These create, in the ALP's eyes, 'the potential for higher education to become a mechanism for reproducing social stratification, in contrast to its longstanding role in Australia as a means of upward social mobility'. The ALP also proposes lowering the cost of degrees in skill shortage areas such as accounting, mathematics, engineering and agriculture by reducing their HECS charges. It is considering paying part or all of students' HECS debt if they work in areas of skills shortages and/or in country areas. These so-called HECS debt remissions would apply to graduate nurses and doctors in rural or remote areas, high school maths and science teachers and teachers in disadvantaged schools.[31] Further, the ALP is proposing initiatives to make teaching a more attractive profession, including more prospects of career advancement for long-serving teachers.[32]

Recently, arguments have been made for consolidating Australia's centres of tertiary research excellence and moving away from a uniform university sector. The Federal Government has signalled the possibility of such a change, with Education Minister Julie Bishop encouraging universities to merge or specialise, in a push to reduce the number of traditional public institutions by two-thirds. The Minister argues that Australia is too small to keep 37 generalist public universities and should contract to about 12 more viable institutions.[33] Consolidation of institutions could perhaps be part of reversing the drastic public underfunding of tertiary education in Australia.

However, the Minister has also sent out a contradictory signal, calling on state governments to take more responsibility for funding universities (which would reverse the transfer of funding responsibility to the national government which occurred in 1974), and calling on alumni and philanthropists to be a bigger part of the solution to the funding shortfalls of Australian universities.[34] This is an abrogation of the national government's responsibility to reverse the unique slide in funding to these vital institutions, and of its responsibility to restore adequate public expenditure to them so that they can fulfil their responsibilities in both teaching and research. Currently, many universities are spending too much of their time scrambling for private sources of funding for research projects which are not their real choices or priorities. They are also forced by present funding arrangements to compete against one another in areas such as the recruitment and teaching of postgraduate coursework students.

Australia needs to reinvest in and support a variety of post-secondary pathways. We need more nurses, for example; and a big part of improving the nation's skills base must be to restore and boost intakes to high-quality, traditional trade apprenticeships. While there has been a rise in the number of people in various shorter duration vocational training courses since 1996, the number of people commencing traditional trade apprenticeships barely grew from 1996 to 2003, and in none of those years did that number match the number who commenced in each of the preceding 15 years.[35]

The Technical and Further Education (TAFE) sector has not fared quite as badly as the university sector in terms of government funding in the last decade. Nevertheless, TAFE too is drastically underfunded.[36] Australia's investment in skills training needs to increase greatly – our current position is third lowest in the OECD. In a submission to the Council of Australian Governments (COAG) in September 2006, the directors of the TAFE institutes in Australia proposed sweeping reforms to attract more people into trades. The submission points out that federal and state governments have cut funding to the same sector which they expect to produce more skilled workers. The TAFE directors propose reforms including: reintroducing specialist technical schools, this time as colleges at Years 11 and 12, linking them to TAFEs to create a pathway to skills certificates; and creating new opportunities for adults and others unable to get apprenticeships as carpenters, or in the vehicle, engineering and manufacturing industries, through trade diplomas made up of initial full-time training at TAFE followed by on-the-job training. They also propose allowing more people to come from overseas to Australia as TAFE students, gain skills qualifications and ultimately residency, just as they can now do through universities, and increasing the financial incentives for students to become apprentices, and for firms to train them. 'Australia has relatively low levels of educational attainment,' the submission points out. 'Over 40 per cent of people in the workforce do not have post-school qualifications.'[37]

The streaming of students into 'academic' or 'technical' paths which used to take place in schools around Year 10 was ended in Australia during the 1980s. The intention was to prevent inequalities being entrenched at an early age. However, the resulting system may not have adequately recognised the variety of talents which young people have, nor the fact that many may be more suited to skilled hands-on work than to general academic study. There has thus been a move back towards encouraging Vocational Education and Training (VET) in schools and towards providing applied learning alternatives that are of equal status to the standard Year 12 qualification. Researchers are now examining how well different models of VET in schools work in terms of achieving the objectives of increased participation, more effective transitions (from school into suitable work or further learning) and the engagement of reluctant learners.[38] These findings will provide valuable data on the effectiveness of VET for different student groups, which will enable further policy efforts to tailor the later years of secondary schooling to bringing out the full range of our young people's abilities.

Federal and state governments, representing both the major political parties, are now, encouragingly, talking about the need for more vocational training. One option is to create new technical colleges. However, it is one thing to talk about such measures, and to use the term 'apprenticeships' at election time to send out positive reminders to voters of a time when there were more structured opportunities for young people to enter secure trades which were in lasting demand. It is another to follow through and fund quality programs which are able to play such roles now and in the future. This is the challenge to which Australia's governments must now rise.

The opening up of obvious, gaping trade skill shortages by 2006, and criticism of the misuse of temporary '457' visas to fill many of them with exploited guest workers, mostly from China and the Philippines, finally forced the Howard Government to announce more investment in improving the skills of Australia's current and future workers. The government has sought to stave off criticism of the chronic skills shortages which have developed during its tenure with an announcement in late 2006 of $837 million in new spending over five years.[39] The Australian Industry Group had earlier called for a larger public investment – $1 billion for a national Skills Fund over three years.[40] Meanwhile, trade unions are concerned that the skills funding must be for *broad-based* training which leads to portable qualifications. The emphasis will indeed need to be on large-scale, high-quality, lasting and properly accredited long-term programs, not cheap attempts at a 'quick fix', if a recurrence of the present problems is to be prevented. It is appalling that the Howard Government made such deep cuts to jobs and training programs and let these take their toll for ten years, and then was driven only by the political difficulties these inevitably produced to announce a partial reversal. Aside from the cynicism this displays, the damage done is so much harder to fix a decade on. Just as with climate change, the Federal Government has ignored something for a decade, until it has worsened into a crisis, and even then has responded quite inadequately.

In sum, there need to be substantial increases in funds for the most needy primary and secondary schools and for universities and TAFEs, with a priority to boost intakes to apprenticeships and other vocational education and training.

Finding suitable work

While the official unemployment rate in Australia fell below 5 per cent during 2006, actual *joblessness* is a far greater problem in Australia today than in the comparable stages of recovery from earlier economic recessions.[41] Joblessness is a broader concept than unemployment: it encompasses the *under*employed and those workers so discouraged by countless rejections that they have ceased to actively look for paid work. Their discouragement is understandable given that there are still 5.6 unemployed persons for every vacant job in Australia, according to official statistics.[42] The real extent of joblessness is approximately double the official unemployment rate, which means there are approximately one million Australians today whose labour is underutilised.[43] The proportion of men aged 15–64 in full-time jobs has fallen from

87 per cent to 67 per cent since 1970.[44] The proportion of working-age women in the labour force has risen, but is still very low compared with other OECD nations.[45] Approximately 700,000 people of working age are now on the Disability Support Pension.

A further dimension of underemployment is the high number of migrants from non-English speaking backgrounds who do not have their overseas trade and professional qualifications recognised in Australia. This is a longstanding problem which has recently been highlighted again. It continues to detract from this country's ability to realise the full, rich potential of its culturally diverse people.[46]

Policy-makers need to alter their definition of 'full employment' from the current official rate of about 5 per cent to a truer definition, such as 'an unemployment rate below 2 per cent, zero underemployment and no hidden unemployment'.[47]

There are now 357,000 families in Australia in which no one holds a job, and most of these are families headed by single mothers.[48] These women want to work.[49] However, there are enormous barriers to their finding jobs which allow them to meet all the demands placed upon them as single mothers. For a start, equal pay is still far from being a reality. Furthermore, women – who still make up the overwhelming majority of workers with caring responsibilities – want and need more secure jobs, and more appropriate and predictable working hours. The 'welfare-to-work' laws which took effect in July 2006 tend in the opposite direction, unfortunately, imposing further harsh compliance requirements on the unemployed, including 8 weeks' loss of income support for non-compliance, while providing no actual employment possibilities.[50] Highly respected community organisations including the Salvation Army and the St Vincent de Paul Society, which have worked for decades with the most disadvantaged Australians, have declined to participate in case management under this new regime, because of the severe and unfair penalties it imposes.

Ending joblessness means ensuring that enough work is available for all those who want it. This is possible if there is sufficient political will. Action is especially needed in geographic areas where there is entrenched joblessness. The fact that a few resource-rich 'sun belt' states are presently booming, while the number of jobs in parts of the more populous eastern states, including rural areas hard-hit by the long drought, stays stagnant, is a reminder of how ingrained and recurrent our regional inequalities are.

While too many people in Australia are unemployed or underemployed, too many others are working more hours than they want to or than are compatible with a balanced life. The changes to the labour market in recent decades have greatly intensified work for those who do have it. One in five employed Australians now works an average of 50 hours a week; and Australia is one of the few OECD countries to recently show a continuing rise in working hours.[51] Casual employment – or the proportion of employees without paid leave entitlements as a proportion of all employees – rose from one-fifth to one-quarter of all employees between 1992 and 2003.[52] Australia has the highest rate of casual employment, and therefore the greatest job insecurity – that constant worry about losing your job and powerlessness to affect whether or not that will happen – in the OECD.[53]

In 1996 the Coalition Government rushed into abolishing nearly all the active labour market programs that had been belatedly introduced by the former government ... and which were given little time to have effect. The 'work for the dole' program, their replacement, has proven a poor substitute in terms of job preparation and skills formation. It has benefited very few long-term unemployed people compared with the suite of programs which preceded it. Nearly ten years after they introduced it, the government is still talking about introducing a more substantial training component into 'work for the dole' activities, but even now, in the midst of the skills shortage crisis, this is only proposed as a token element, without independent accreditation to assure its quality.

From the outset, the present Federal Government's approach to employment services has been more about making short-term cost savings than supporting unemployed people in their search for suitable work. It has also been ineffective. A 2006 study by Melbourne City Mission found that more than half of the most vulnerable welfare recipients, such as early school leavers, the homeless, people with disabilities and single parents, have not had access to training or employment programs over the past two years. Despite all the government's rhetoric about reducing 'dependency' on pensions and other benefits, this study found that 'much more' effort is still needed to create pathways into paid work for marginalised job seekers. Like many earlier studies by independent community organisations, it found no evidence that the unemployed lack motivation. It did find that structural hurdles to finding work are still entrenched, despite a decade of 'reforms', including the contracting out of job placement services to private and not-for-profit providers under Job Network. The survey participants said they wanted to achieve financial security, and to start saving. When participants were asked about the benefits of working, other themes included: 'keeping busy', boosting self-esteem, and 'having a sense of structure and purpose'. The aim of one 18-year-old on a youth allowance was 'to support self, stand up tall instead of having to ask for money and afford a place to live. It all works together.'[54] The study found that the insistence on 'a continual cycle of ineffectual activities' – such as keeping a job-seeker diary – inevitably trips up people experiencing ill-health and other personal problems.[55] This report is powerful new evidence against the government's attempts to remodel Australia's welfare system on harsher, US-style lines.

The costs in the medium and long term of continuing unemployment are far greater than the costs of investing more now to form skills, and to rebuild public and community services to the extent necessary to reduce intractable concentrations of unemployment. Depending on the assumptions used for the calculations, Australia is poorer by between $20 billion and $40 billion a year as a consequence of our willingness to tolerate persistently high rates of unemployment and underemployment.[56] A major cause of entrenched unemployment in Australia is the long-term decline of local manufacturing industry. This has now reached a crisis point – the sector is falling below critical mass, which is particularly detrimental to South Australia, New South Wales and Victoria, where the manufacturing sector was once substantial. The proportion of the labour force employed in manufacturing has fallen particularly rapidly in Australia, to the lowest level in the developed world.[57]

Australia cannot indefinitely borrow 5–6 per cent of national income without a strategy for strengthening local production of both goods and services. The ratio of imports of goods and services has been rising, from 18 per cent of GDP in 1984–85 to 21 per cent in 2004–05.[58] Manufacturing still matters, and not only because of its importance in providing employment for many who have been hit by economic restructuring since the 1970s. It also matters because Australia simply cannot improve and diversify its export performance in the world unless it restores, adapts and builds on some of its remaining manufacturing industries. Dr Peter Brain's National Institute of Economic and Industry Research (NIEIR) argues that the poor Australian 'manufacturing experience since 2000 can be directly attributed to the large reductions in manufacturing assistance made by the Coalition Government in 1997'.[59] The Irish, Finnish, Danish and Swedish experiences, among others, show the importance of manufacturing in small economies. Manufacturing succeeded in these countries because they gave it the assistance needed to innovate, expand and export. The NIEIR report proposes an annual:

> sustained $1 billion (in 2005 prices) policy package (that is additional to all current funding) focused on increasing, either directly or indirectly, the demand for Australian manufactured products ... designed around six segments. Each segment is designed to alleviate obstacles that prevent Australian manufacturers from reaching their full potential. The components ... are: $300 million investment allowance; $300 million research and development assistance scheme; $225 million increase in the export market development grant scheme; $75 million technology diffusion program; $50 million incentive program to attract foreign equity into small and medium sized manufacturing businesses; and $50 million strategy to attract and train highly skilled labour for the application of advanced manufacturing technologies.[60]

NIEIR calculates that if this $1 billion program were maintained from 2007 to 2020 it would make a significant contribution to expanding the demand for Australian-manufactured products, including: creating at a minimum almost 300,000 direct and indirect jobs; and increasing GDP by at least $54 billion in 2005 prices. The Business Council of Australia, in conjunction with the Society for Knowledge Economics, has released a national innovation blueprint which highlights the superior research and development investments made by other nations (including Ireland, Finland and Denmark). This peak employer organisation argues the need to: recognise innovation as a critical national priority; align efforts by governments and business to boost innovation; strengthen linkages and collaboration between all elements of Australia's innovation system; implement specific policy and investment measures to strengthen Australia's research networks and institutions; enhance policy focus and strategic investment in education and training to improve the innovation capabilities and culture of our people; and improve and sustain a business environment suitable for innovation.[61]

Kevin Rudd, on his election as national Leader of the Opposition in December 2006, immediately spoke of the need to take steps to ensure that Australia has a future as a manufacturing nation. This marks a rare and welcome return of industry policy to the centre of Australian political debate; it now needs to be followed by specific policy commitments. One area for much greater potential growth in output and employment in Australia is in the manufacture, operation and maintenance of wind power turbines, solar hot water systems, photo-voltaic panels and other renewable energy technologies. National government policy needs to more explicitly support the uptake of these.

Employment in environmental work is one of the fastest growing areas of employment worldwide. Repairing soil, reducing pollution and waste, improving energy efficiency and developing renewable energy are generating millions of jobs in many parts of the world. Researchers have shown how, by pursuing a 25 per cent renewable electricity target by 2020, at least 16,600 new clean energy jobs can be created in Australia.[62] One promising opportunity for support from a combined environmental and industry policy is the manufacture in Australia of hybrid cars.

In order to combat unemployment, it is necessary to spend a very substantial further amount, probably more than $1 billion over three years, specifically on training and on public sector jobs for unemployed people in regions of high joblessness. These jobs would offer rewarding work in areas of unmet community need, including environmental projects, community services and the infrastructure needs of local voluntary bodies such as the fire and state emergency services.

Jobs which will provide useful work for the unemployed, and which will also improve the environment, include: weed and pest control, particularly in drought-hit rural areas; general community maintenance; cleaning and restoration of urban creeks and other waterways; construction of bicycle paths; soil conservation and revegetation work; and recycling of waste products. There is also potential for more jobs in eco-tourism.

The jobs program could also extend into human services needed in local communities, including caring for the aged, for children and for people with disabilities. The health and welfare sectors of the workforce are among those now facing skill shortages and an ageing workforce. These sectors need to be supported through better planning, both in the interests of meeting the community's need for their services and as part of a policy to reduce unemployment.

Bringing fairness back into work

The radical new reductions of Australians' rights at work are exacerbating inequality and insecurity. Following the passing of the *Workplace Relations Act 1996* (Cth), individual contracts became much more widespread in Australia and reduced employees' rights and power.[63] After gaining control of the Senate in 2005, the Coalition Government quickly moved to introduce even more, and more draconian, laws. The Act which makes these changes is titled 'WorkChoices', yet it actually limits the real choices available to employees by giving much more power to employers. The body which it creates is titled the Australian Fair Pay Commission, yet the term 'fair' is not even included in that body's wage-setting parameters. The Act reduced the role of the former independent industrial relations umpire, the Australian Industrial Relations Commission, which had helped to promote fairness in the Australian workforce for more than a century. Although the first decision of the Fair Pay Commission, in late 2006, surprisingly awarded a substantial rise to low-paid workers in Australia, there can be no confidence – given its composition and charter – that it will act similarly in the future in comparison with the body which it has in effect superseded.

Following the restriction of award conditions to just 20 'allowable matters' in its 1996 Act, the government restricted them even further in the 'WorkChoices' Act. The Act curtails the right to strike to an extent normally associated with dictatorial regimes. It strictly controls and limits the right of trade union officials to enter workplaces. One of its most distressing provisions is the outlawing of any occupational health and safety training provided by unions. The Act also removes workers' rights to collectively bargain with employers about long service leave, about notice of termination, and about skill-based career paths. It removes protections against unfair dismissal. The 'WorkChoices' Act immediately generated many alarming cases of exploitation – a mere foretaste of the effect it will have if it is allowed to continue to operate in the coming years. For example, Charmaine, a hairdressing teacher, was on her way to work when another driver's car collided into hers and she was injured. Doctors fitted a head and neck brace and told her to take a month off to recuperate. When she rang work to explain, her boss said that she would never recover from a neck injury and would have to be let go. Charmaine said, 'You can't sack me because I was in a car accident that wasn't my fault', but her employer said that the changed laws allow a small company to sack on the spot. Charmaine has asked the Human Rights and Equal Opportunity Commission (HREOC) for help, but in the meantime is unemployed. HREOC reports that complaints soared by 70 per cent after 'WorkChoices' was introduced.[64] Information uncovered by the *Sydney Morning Herald* shows that in the first six months of 'WorkChoices', 45 per cent of Australian Workplace Agreements (AWAs) removed all the award conditions the government had promised would be protected by law, and a clear majority removed some of these conditions, such as shift work and annual leave loadings.[65]

The International Labor Organization (ILO) has expressed serious concerns that, through these new laws, Australia is in violation of international conventions concerning workers' rights: in particular, Convention Number 98 on 'The Right to Organise and Collective Bargaining'. Under the new laws, union officials and employees can be fined tens of thousands of dollars just for asking an employer to include, in a collective agreement: protection from unfair dismissal, or union involvement in dispute resolution; or protections against employees being replaced by labour hire or contractors.[66]

'WorkChoices' individualises the employment relationship, discourages teamwork, and treats an individual employee as if she or he is absolutely equal to a corporation, where in reality she or he is nowhere near equal in power. The new law promotes 'flexibility', but only on employers' terms. This will mean even poorer prospects for skills formation – employers' short-term and narrow skill requirements will determine training, not employees' needs for a full, lasting and portable qualification. It will place those who sign individual agreements at risk of losing long-term established conditions including public holidays, annual leave loadings, and overtime entitlements. A submission to an Inquiry into the Bill made by no less than 151 distinguished Australian academics, of diverse opinions, put a powerful case against these laws, concluding that they 'contravene long established international labour standards, strengthen employer prerogative, create new hazards for many working Australians, [and] widen inequality and disadvantage the most vulnerable'.[67] Unfortunately, the advice of these experts has not been heeded.

The 'WorkChoices' Act should be abolished, along with the system of individual contracts known as AWAs which preceded it and which has been instrumental in reducing employee entitlements. Abolishing the Act is a necessary condition for Australia moving to a new and fairer system with better pay and conditions.[68] A new independent industrial relations umpire needs to be installed.

The new arrangements will need to honour Australia's ILO obligations. The arrangements will also need to enshrine workers' rights to collective bargaining, recognise the legitimate role of trade unions, and include procedures which maximise health and safety at work, including guaranteeing training opportunities for elected health and safety delegates. The new arrangements should also seek to realise the positive new possibilities which are opened up by the 'WorkChoices' Act. For instance, it is considered possible to enact a new law to protect the right to collective bargaining through a number of constitutional avenues, including the corporations power (which the High Court has now upheld as a valid basis for 'WorkChoices'), the external affairs power, and the states agreeing to refer power over industrial relations to the next national government.[69]

Reducing the clash between work and life

The latest industrial relations changes are also adding to the increasingly intolerable time pressures on family life. Many employers are freer under the new legislation to assert their managerial prerogative to deny workers what they need. This will be bad for families, including for children who already have too little time with their parents. In the English-speaking countries we tend to set up a dichotomy between paid and unpaid work; these are conceptualised in different terms in many European nations. We should start with the same assumption as Sweden does and which its experience has proven correct: that both men and women want to work and play a role in raising children.[70] We should then proceed to make our industrial relations arrangements more family-friendly, to both enable and reflect this. The approach in the Nordic nations includes allowing parents to spend time with their newborn and young children, including explicit provision for substantial periods of paternity leave, as well as maternity leave.

Australia and the United States are now the only OECD nations without statutory provision for paid maternity leave. The Federal

Government has failed to act on a well-considered proposal for paid maternity leave from HREOC following the inquiry HREOC completed in 2002. Australia's workplaces need to change to better enable work to be combined with caring. The ALP is now in an ideal position to promote this as part of its alternative to 'WorkChoices'. To date, however, it has only committed to legislation which will allow workers to *ask* for two years of unpaid maternity leave, plus the right to return to work part-time or with flexible hours. Employers would still be able to refuse this request on so-called reasonable grounds. Paid parental leave should be made available as a right. There need to be government policies to encourage more high-quality, well-paid part-time jobs. Currently some more enlightened elements in the private sector are well ahead of the government: they are responding intelligently to employees who want more control over working hours and recognising the benefits which these will bring to their companies' productivity. For employees to gain more control of their working hours, there must first of all be fewer casual jobs. Without this it is not possible for families to predict their finances adequately. Family-friendly working practices need to be a high priority in the arrangements which replace the falsely named WorkChoices Act.

Australia's current child care arrangements have been widely criticised, including by backbench Liberal MP and former Minister Jackie Kelly, who has called them a 'shambles'.[71] The ALP is proposing some measures to expand child care and improve its quality and affordability, in order to help families balance their work and family commitments better.[72] Even more changes than it has suggested are urgently required as part of a major expansion of preschool education arrangements.

A secure roof over everyone's head

There are high levels, yet declining proportions, of home ownership in Australia, with younger people being priced out, and especially vulnerable to lifelong debt because of the acute problems of housing affordability. In the December quarter of 2006, according to the Housing Industry Association and the Commonwealth Bank, affordability plummeted to its lowest level ever since measurements were first taken, which was more than two decades ago.[73] An average Australian first home buyer now needs in excess of 30 per cent of their disposable income to service minimum monthly payments on a new mortgage. On census night in 2001, the ABS estimated that 100,000 people were homeless. In November 2006, following the fourth interest rate rise in two years, it was reported that suburban growth corridors in the major capital cities were being hard hit, with increasing numbers of home-buyers turning to welfare agencies for emergency food and financial relief. Homeless services provider Hanover said that between 10 and 20 per cent of its homelessness prevention was for mortgagees. Community financial counsellor Garry Rothman said that irresponsible lending was causing people to lose their homes, and that the explosion of mortgage brokers in a deregulated industry had resulted in increased issues of warrants of possession:

> It's a time bomb and it's already started going off … There are a lot of mortgages out there that are not sustainable … People are being sold mortgages that give them no leeway and things like an interest-rate rise or petrol increases can tip them over.[74]

Eminent researcher Hugh Stretton has advocated governments in Australia cooperating to finance and build 40,000 new houses each year. He makes the particularly useful suggestion that one of the conditions of this work should be that the builders are required to attract and accept set numbers of apprentices into the various trades involved in the houses' construction.[75]

A detailed policy response to Australia's housing affordability crisis, which is broadly consistent with Stretton's approach, has been proposed by Julian Disney, Professor and Director of the Social Justice Project at the University of New South Wales.[76] Its central feature is national government expansion of rental housing for low-income people. Disney argues that:

> The Commonwealth should take the lead in negotiating with the
> States a National Affordable Housing Agreement, renewable every five
> years, to integrate, rationalise and strengthen government assistance
> for affordable housing. The Agreement should include major tax
> reform and stronger public investment as well as increasing the role of
> local governments in helping to meet affordable housing needs.[77]

Disney points out that most government housing assistance is currently provided in tax concessions for home-owners who are relatively wealthy, not to those who are building their careers and raising families. He points out that less than a fifth of current government assistance for housing in Australia goes to low-income renters, yet it is they who suffer the problems of affordability most. The priority must be to change the balance of government assistance, by providing more help for low-income renters. As Disney highlights:

> Very few but the most deeply disadvantaged people can now obtain
> public housing. Moreover, a very high proportion of new public
> tenants are housed in outer areas which have difficult social problems,
> few work opportunities and unfavourable reputations.[78]

He proposes that a substantial portion of the expanded public housing stock should be available on limited-term tenancies to people in the workforce whose income is presently too high to obtain public housing. This would help reduce counterproductive concentrations of severe disadvantage in public housing and meet the broader need for job mobility in metropolitan areas. He also argues that developers should have to commit a modest proportion of new housing for management by accredited non-profit organisations as affordable housing for low-income people.[79]

Disney further argues for more adequate and timely provision of basic community infrastructure such as schools, hospitals and recreational facilities, to attract more businesses and workers to the outer suburbs of the capital cities where housing costs tend to be lower. In his view:

> General tax and rate revenue should continue to be the main funders
> of infrastructure for these community purposes … [although] The
> Commonwealth Government's new Future Fund could be used
> as a vehicle for developing a substantial and sustained program of
> community infrastructure development, especially in provincial cities
> and regional centres.
>
> Governments could establish 'affordable housing bonds' which provide
> private investors with a guaranteed rate of return and are used to
> provide low-cost housing and related infrastructure development.
> Government funding of, say, $250 million (less than 3% of next
> year's Budget surplus and less than 2% of the Future Fund's opening
> balance) could trigger private funding at least equivalent to the current
> government investment in low-cost housing.[80]

A more modest but still valuable option he proposes is to provide
Commonwealth grants through a program such as Building Better
Cities. At very little cost, this program helped to start a number of
important regional developments in the early 1990s. It also often
attracted substantial private investment to complement the initial
public seed money.

Improving our health

In terms of health, Australia stands out as comparatively well off
overall. We live longer and are healthier than ever before. Both the
life expectancy and the 'healthy' life expectancy rates in Australia are
among the highest in the world. We have universal health insurance,
under which we are all covered for public hospital treatment and for
most of the costs of our visits to general practitioners. In the United
States, by contrast, 45 million people have no health insurance at all.
We compare well with other wealthy countries in other respects too:
for example, we do not have hospital waiting lists as long as those in
Britain.[81]

However, Medicare universalism has been eroded under the
Howard Government. The government was elected on a promise to

maintain Medicare. This followed the Coalition parties' reluctant acceptance of substantial public financing of health care – due to the sheer popularity of the system. Since 1996, however, the government has introduced a series of privatisation measures. Bulk-billing rates have fallen, with more people having to pay for going to the doctor. The gap between the Medicare rebate and the amount actually charged by general practitioners has grown. The Liberal and National parties claim to support Medicare, but, as analyst Gwendolyn Gray writes, their real preference remains for a predominantly private system.[82]

The private health insurance tax rebate introduced by the Howard Government takes away resources which are urgently needed to repair the public health system. In principle, it should be abolished. If a pragmatic electoral approach deems this too difficult, it should at least be means-tested. This will release more resources to repair the public system rather than putting them at the disposal of the richest and least needy Australians. Priorities in the repair of the public health system are to ensure an adequate number of hospital beds and the future training and supply of an adequate medical workforce, including doctors, nurses, and technicians.

The diseases arising from wealth, such as obesity, are likely to lower Australia's high life expectancy. The financial cost of obesity in Australia has been estimated as $3.8 billion in 2005. Of this, productivity costs are estimated as $1.7 billion (45 per cent), health system costs at $900 million (23 per cent) and carer costs at $800 million (21 per cent). Then there are further costs – taxation revenue foregone, and welfare and other government payments – which amount to an estimated $360 million (10 per cent), and other indirect costs, estimated to be $40 million (1 per cent). The net cost of lost wellbeing (the dollar value of the burden of disease, netting out financial costs borne by individuals) is valued at a further $17.2 billion, bringing the total estimated cost of obesity in 2005 to a staggering $21 billion![83] The prevalence of obesity is lower in Australia than in the United States, but it is higher here than in Britain and much higher than in France and Japan.[84] Obesity and the factors which contribute to it, such as lack of physical activity, and insufficient fruit and vegetable intake, are more frequent in disadvantaged people than among the well off.[85] Strategies to reduce obesity must be sensitive to the different opportunities available to different socio-economic groups. We also need to be mindful that we simultaneously have a serious problem of anorexia and associated eating disorders among young women who feel under pressure to look like the fashion models who are paraded in so many advertisements.

The determinants of health include: biomedical factors; individual health behaviours; socio-economic influences, including people's different levels of income, education, and geographic access to services; and broader social determinants, including the degree of social cohesion and the state of the environment.

The national government is currently focusing on individual behaviour, tackling it 'disease by disease'. There is proven value in this approach. The 2003 Abelson report, for instance, has shown that there are quantifiable savings to government and returns to the community from public health programs aimed at altering individual behaviour, such as those targeted at reducing tobacco consumption and at risky behaviours which make coronary heart disease, HIV/AIDS and road trauma more likely.[86]

However, there is currently little national government policy interest in tackling health inequalities. Some state governments, though, are placing more emphasis on family and 'place' in their health policies. These approaches need to be strengthened and extended. A renewed policy emphasis in Australia on tackling the social determinants of poor health would be cost-effective and would shift resources back towards the most needy. The government should set targets to reduce health inequalities.[87]

In Britain, more attention is being focused on reducing health inequalities. Sweden is playing a leading role in tackling the socio-economic determinants of bad health, continuing that country's longstanding tradition of focusing on societal wellbeing. Sweden's comprehensive national public health strategy has 11 objectives concerning the determinants of health, of which 6 refer to structural factors (participation and influence in society, economic and social security, for example) and only 5 to lifestyle choices by individuals (such as good eating and increased physical activity). The strategy aims to reduce housing segregation and social isolation, to channel resources to needy schools, to reduce unemployment, and to increase participation in healthy activities. Australia could benefit greatly from a similarly integrated approach.

It is particularly important to tackle the inequalities which are increasing through the shift in funding from governments to individuals, from public to private, from the unhealthy poor to the comparatively healthy well off. The countries with higher *public* expenditure on health end up having lower overall expenditure on health as a proportion of GDP. Only 45 per cent of health expenditure in the United States is public expenditure, yet the United States ends up having to spend 14 per cent of its GDP on health. In Britain, by contrast, 85 per cent of health expenditure is public; and that nation ends up spending less than 8 per cent of its GDP on health.[88]

Most people's experience of modern medicine consists of short, rushed appointments with GPs who are clearly under pressure to move patients through quickly and who tend to react to the immediate symptoms of the particular complaint in isolation, often by prescribing pharmaceutical products (for which there are always many advertisements in the surgery). People's desire for better quality, more holistic treatment is one of the reasons for the rising popularity of naturopaths and other alternative and complementary therapies.[89] However, many of these practitioners are not recognised for Medicare coverage. This makes the services of naturopaths and other alternative and complementary therapies more expensive, and thus more difficult for the less well off to afford.

There is, nevertheless, increased policy interest in preventive medicine, due to concern about the financial sustainability of Medicare and the Pharmaceutical Benefits Scheme, and the importance of reducing future economic costs. This interest originates especially in the Treasury, for example in its Intergenerational Report,[90] which very curiously, however, omits environmental questions. Environmental influences are being more widely recognised in the health literature, partly through the work of the Australian Research Alliance for Children and Youth. These influences now need to be taken into account more fully by government policy-makers.

Labor has indicated that it will not put forward another 'Medicare Gold' type policy: that is, a policy whereby the Commonwealth would have assumed responsibility for all hospital costs of people over the age of 75. Some Opposition health policy pronouncements have signalled increasing national responsibility for health to help reduce the federal/ state blame-shifting which particularly bedevils this policy area. This is positive as far as it goes – but more than this is needed.

Two areas of health which particularly need attention are mental health and dental health. Mental health difficulties are widespread. One in five Australians, at some stage in their life, encounters these difficulties, varying from mild or temporary to severe or prolonged. Mental illness is particularly common among young adults (aged 18–24), affecting one in four in this age group. In a 2004–05 ABS survey, 13 per cent of all adults surveyed reported experiencing high or very high levels of psychological distress in the preceding four weeks.[91]

Mental illness covers a wide range of disorders that affect the way people think, feel and act. These include anxiety, depression, bipolar disorder, schizophrenia, and personality disorders. Depression accounts for six million full work days lost each year in Australia.[92] There is increased recognition now that mental illness affects the brain, just as other illnesses affect other parts of the body. This recognition has helped to reduce the stigma and shame formerly associated with mental illness.

The ABS reports that 'mental health problems and mental illness are among the greatest causes of disability, diminished quality of life, and reduced productivity'.[93] The UK *Depression Report* of 2006 argues that cognitive behaviour therapy provided by well-trained clinical psychologists and psychological therapists can cure over half of agoraphobia, obsessive-compulsive and other severe anxiety disorders over 16 weekly sessions of rigorous, systematic treatment.[94] The report says that such treatment would be highly cost effective, costing less than $2000 per person and enabling many of the people who have been disabled by depression and anxiety for years and supported by disability pension to return to fully effective employment. Yet little public funding is currently allocated to treatment of depression and anxiety.

In 2006, COAG announced substantial new funding for mental health. However, there remains concern that because this package is focused on Medicare rebating for psychologists and psychiatrists, it will not benefit the many Australians who live in parts of the country where psychologists or psychiatrists are not available. Also, many Australians who need mental health care will still not be able to afford the gap between the Medicare rebate and the full cost of those practitioners' fees. More mental health workers of various types are needed, and they need to be more evenly distributed around Australia. Greater integration is required between service providers to bring the private sector psychologists and psychiatrists into greater contact and interaction with the public sector hospital emergency wards, nurses, mental health crisis teams and social workers. Gaining access to suitable housing is also particularly crucial for people suffering from mental health difficulties.

Public resources also need to be reinvested to reduce inequality in public dental services, which are not covered by Medicare. In an important new study, the Australian Council of Social Service (ACOSS) highlights how 40 per cent of adult Australians cannot get dental care when they need it. The ACOSS study emphasises that:

> Oral health is fundamental to overall health, well-being and quality
> of life. A healthy mouth enables people to eat, speak and socialise
> without pain, discomfort or embarrassment. The impact of oral disease
> on people's everyday lives is subtle and pervasive, influencing eating,
> sleeping, work and social roles. The prevalence and recurrences of these
> impacts constitute a silent epidemic.[95]

The study goes on to point out that 'over a quarter of Australian adults experience ... painful aching because of problems with their teeth, mouth or dentures'. It finds that those with particularly poor oral health and who are most unlikely to be able to access dental care are low-income adults, people living in rural and remote areas, Indigenous people, nursing home residents, people with disabilities, young adults on income support payments, and single-parent households. Of the adults not eligible for public dental care (2.3 million people), 23 per cent report that they delay or avoid dental treatment because of its cost.[96]

In response, ACOSS proposes a number of precisely costed recommendations, including the following:

⇨ A course of free basic dental treatment to concession card holders. The Australian Government to fund the cost of basic dental care for adult health card holders consisting of the cost of either an oral health exam, scale, clean and x-ray or basic treatment such as fillings or treatment for acute gum disease. The cost to the Commonwealth will be $480 million in the financial years 2007–08 and 2008–09.

⇨ More people to qualify for health cards. The income limit to qualify for Commonwealth Low Income Health Care Cards to be increased from $21,840 to $26,208 for individuals and from $39,936 to $47,923 for a family with two children. (This would only be for the purpose of access to publicly funded dental care.) The cost of this is included in funding for the first Recommendation (see above).

⇨ Better supply of oral health professionals. A proportion of the Commonwealth's funding (10 per cent in the first year) to be reserved for measures to ensure appropriate supply and distribution of oral health professionals, including dentists, to meet future needs. The Commonwealth's specific responsibilities to be the development of a national dental labour force plan and funding for the training of oral health professionals in universities. The cost of this is also included in the funding for the first Recommendation (above).[97]

It is crucial to remember that action and resources to tackle the causes of ill-health will help prevent many health costs from arising at all. Investing in preventive activities is the best way of avoiding having to spend money on illness. We need to ask more questions about the causes of increased anxiety and depression in our society. Unemployment, worries about money, punitive welfare provisions, and time stresses on individuals and families – all affected by government policy – clearly contribute. This means that many future improvements in health will require policy action in areas outside health. Policies to prevent poverty and joblessness, to relieve financial pressure on individuals and families, to create greater security (confidence that employment at a decent standard will continue and that family relationships can be kept intact) and to increase the range of educational opportunities are the best way of ensuring a healthier society.

Case study

THE NORDIC NATIONS: COMBINING EFFICIENCY, EQUALITY AND SUSTAINABILITY

The nations of Nordic Europe provide living proof that economically successful, socially fair and environmentally responsible policies can succeed. The four principal Nordic nations (Sweden, Norway, Denmark and Finland) are consistently assessed as among the most economically efficient or 'competitive' nations in the world by the World Economic Forum. They also always rate as the most equitable nations in terms of income distribution. Sweden, which has the largest population of the Nordic nations, is much more equal than Australia and Britain and twice as equal as the United States, according to the Luxembourg Income Study (assessed via the ratio of the disposable money income of people in the top 10 per cent to the disposable money income of people in the bottom 10 per cent).

This mix of strong economic performance and relatively equal income distribution makes a big and positive difference in many facets of life. While there is a strong work ethos and commitment to 'productivism', working hours remain within reasonable limits for work/life balance. (In 2005, workers in Australia worked on average 1811 hours a year, compared with 1360 hours in Norway, 1551 in Denmark, and 1587 in Sweden, according to OECD data.) These countries also pay attention to the working environment: positive environments (those in which workers have reasonable variety and the chance to work in teams) maximise employees' morale, commitment and output.

Particularly successful Nordic corporations such as Volvo and Scania are associated with innovative workplace design and a high quality of management (which involves proper consultation with workers).

The Nordic nations are notable for:

⇨ driving child poverty down to unparalleled lows and enshrining the rights of children;

⇨ comprehensively tackling housing and health inequalities;

⇨ improving gender equality and providing family-friendly workplace arrangements, including 12 months' paid parental leave, a minimum of two months of which must be taken by fathers;

⇨ fostering knowledge through high levels of private and public investment in research and development;

⇨ being generous aid donors to the world's poorer nations and taking in asylum seekers at relatively high rates;

⇨ adopting a thorough and serious approach to democratically tackling long-term policy issues in a way which involves the different sections of society;

⇨ leading the push within the EU for action to cut GHG emissions by 20 per cent by 2020; and

⇨ developing renewable sources of energy (Denmark in particular is a world leader in the use of wind power).

There is much that Australia can learn from these countries' successes in these fields.

While there were setbacks to the Nordic nations in the international economic recession of the early 1990s, they have continued to hold on to values such as universalism, full employment and equality. These values have helped – rather than hindered – these countries resume their strong overall economic, social and environmental performance since that time.

As Swedish scholar Dr Jenny Andersson writes (specifically in relation to Sweden), most people there continue to emphasise the interdependence of growth and security. The Swedish word for security, 'trygghet', has a broad meaning that goes beyond issues of material concern and refers to notions of comfort, wellbeing and belonging.[98] In Sweden, security is still regarded as a precondition of change, whereas in the United States, Britain and Australia, the greater dominance of economic liberalism requires individuals to be induced and coerced to accept the process of change as a precondition of security.[99] This is a very important difference. The international evidence is that the Nordic approach is more beneficial socially than ours.

The four main Nordic nations have the world's highest labour force participation rates for women.[100] In all four nations, the labour force as a proportion of the population is higher than it is in Australia.[101] Unemployment, including hidden unemployment, is still a problem in the Nordic nations, as in Australia. However, mainstream political and policy debate in these countries goes beyond the narrow official measurements of unemployment to confront the broader problem of joblessness, which confirms the quality of the democratic discourse and the breadth of policy ambition there. Those who are not employed in Nordic countries benefit from far more comprehensive and higher quality skills training than do Australian unemployed people at present. These countries, moreover, do not suffer the serious vocational skills shortages which have lately emerged in Australia as a result of inadequate public and employer investment in training.

The universal approach to welfare provision in Nordic Europe also guarantees a decent minimum income for all and prevents the spiralling hostility towards some categories of welfare recipients which occurs in countries with more selective and minimal welfare arrangements. There continues to be widespread public support in the Nordic nations for equality, for a strong welfare state and for continuing to take the 'high road' to prosperity. The resilience of these distinctive nations rebuts claims that 'globalisation' is eliminating all policy options for nation states.

In three of the four main Nordic nations – Sweden, Finland and Denmark – manufacturing for export continues to be economically important and supported. The Norwegian economy, by contrast, is like Australia's in that it relies much more on resources. However, unlike Australia, Norway uses its present resource riches wisely, building up reserves to ensure that it will be able to benefit from those resources in the much longer term. Norway aims to sustain its national inheritance, in line with the legacy of its former long-serving Prime Minister, Gro Harlem Brundtland, who led the preparation of the landmark 1987 international environmental report titled *Our common future*.

Nordic Europe is providing policy leadership to the world. Australia can benefit greatly from closer study of its achievements.

chapter 5

investing in the future: an economy which serves society

The Australian economy grew more quickly as it became more integrated into the global economy in the 1990s and early 2000s, productivity rose and efficiency increased. Yet in the twenty years since Australia embarked on its journey to globalisation, many Australians have experienced precisely what such a major reorientation might be expected to produce: greater job insecurity, increased surveillance by employers in the workplace, a new dependence on part-time employment, and a growing sense that democratic elections make no difference to the prospects of ordinary people. Many Australians have benefited but some have been pitchforked into an underclass that is permanently excluded from full-time employment.

Professor Stewart Firth[1]

Joan Kirner, former Premier of Victoria, used to tell of a talkback radio program in the early 1990s in which a caller was criticising the planned closure of a bush nursing hospital in her town. Not only would this greatly reduce the quality of medical services available to people in the district, she said, but it would also remove a lively focus of community activity. The talk-show host asked whether Australia could any longer afford public facilities such as this hospital, to which the woman replied: 'We live in a society not an economy.' The woman's comment highlights the issue of the priority which should be given to economic policy. The economy should be the servant of society rather than the reverse, and economic activity is a means to the end of human wellbeing rather than an end in itself.

After a quarter century of liberal economic dominance it is timely to examine its benefits and costs, identify lessons, and consider whether or not re-evaluation of national goals and public policy would be beneficial. If we accept the goals discussed in Chapter 2 of improving wellbeing, increasing happiness and contributing to the common good, what are the implications for contemporary economic strategy?

Evaluating the economic liberal era

As background, it is relevant to briefly review the evolution of economic policy during the last quarter century. Under Prime Ministers Gough Whitlam (ALP) and Malcolm Fraser (Lib), tariffs were the first target of Australian liberal economists. At the beginning of the 1980s a committee of inquiry was established into financial regulation, but the Fraser Government did not have time to implement the committee's recommendations before they lost the 1983 election. The social democratic strategy with which Bob Hawke led Labor to government in 1983 was immediately attacked by liberal economists in the Treasury, within business and in New Right think-tanks. The initial concern of the Hawke Government for employment growth was affirmed by the national economic summit. The Prices and Incomes Accord with the union movement enabled both wage restraint and more stimulatory monetary and fiscal policy for the first half-dozen years. Unemployment and inflation fell simultaneously and substantially as a result of the Accord. However, the opposition of international financial market operatives to public expenditure caused the Labor Government to be cautious about major improvements to services such as education and health.[2] Hawke and his Treasurer, Paul Keating, gradually adopted a liberal economic version of the market fundamentalist policies inaugurated by UK Prime Minister Margaret Thatcher (Conservative) and US President Ronald Reagan (Republican). Keating decided to do exactly what his department advised, so floating of the exchange rate and banking deregulation followed. As former Treasury official, now CEO of Westpac, David Morgan, commented later, 'Treasury always had its own agenda. It got more of its agenda up in the decade of the Hawke/Keating Government than for the rest of the postwar period combined.'[3]

Towards the end of the 1980s the Treasury used the size of the current account deficit and growing overseas debt to justify macroeconomic contraction, persuading Keating to adopt policies which caused what he memorably called the 'recession we had to have'. Government outlays were constrained and interest rates shot up. The major benefits that the Accord had produced between 1983 and 1989 were squandered, and unemployment rose from under 6 per cent to 11 per cent within a couple of years. The Labor leadership accepted the economic liberal view that privatisation and deregulation were the symbols of economic responsibility and would increase efficiency. The government focused on reducing inflation rather than on economic growth, let alone improvements in wellbeing or social equity. Privatisations of the Commonwealth Bank, Qantas and the Commonwealth Serum Laboratories were divisive and of dubious economic benefit.

There was, however, considerable variation in the goals and policies of particular ministers. Some ministers treated social justice as a subsidiary goal, while others achieved many significant social democratic advances. There were major initiatives in health insurance, education, income support, the environment, multiculturalism, and Indigenous and foreign affairs. As Prime Minister in the first half of the 1990s, Keating introduced valuable active labour market measures in the *Working Nation* White Paper and negotiated an important National Competition Policy Agreement with the states. However, during the Hawke–Keating years taken as a whole – that is, between 1983 and 1996 – the tendency to uncritically accept the advice of the Commonwealth Treasury, sometimes in ways contrary to the Labor Party platform, meant that unemployment fell only marginally and inequality in the distribution of income, wealth and power increased.[4]

The liberal economic ascendancy reached its zenith under Prime Minister Howard, through further reductions in the extent and quality of public services, further privatisations, further deregulation for large corporations and further reductions in public investment. The relatively steady economic growth which had begun under Labor in 1991 continued. Howard's good fortune was to be in government when American consumer demand made the United States the engine of global growth. When American growth faltered, the US Federal Reserve relaxed monetary policy, driving down interest rates everywhere, including Australia. Rapid growth in Japanese, Chinese, European, Korean and Taiwanese commodity imports and steady growth in imports by Southeast and South Asian countries at the start of the new century kept Australia's terms of trade strongly positive, restricting the deterioration in the current account and diverting attention from the country's growing international debt. Australian consumers kept domestic demand high by spending most or all their household income, and in recent years by net borrowing.

Many of the benefits and costs of economic liberalism have been mentioned in earlier chapters. For the last 15 years the momentum of national economic growth has been maintained, enabling substantial growth of average incomes. At the beginning of the 1980s and again at the end, Treasury recommended contractionary policies; these recommendations were accepted by the Fraser and Hawke governments, and both times led to recessions. Treasury has not repeated that misguided advice since, despite the continuing growth of the current account deficit, which was said then to justify such tight fiscal and monetary policies. In other words, lessons were learnt from those episodes of contraction, and for the last 15 years Australian economic policy has generally contributed to economic growth. Most corporations have prospered and their profits have risen. Employment has grown strongly and unemployment has fallen. Increased funding for the states from the GST has financed improved access to health, education and some other community services. The Coalition has responded to increased demand for improvements in human services from corporations, families and the ageing. Significant improvements have been made, often for the relatively well off, such as support for private schools, the private health care rebate, and tax cuts for superannuants. For those who feel threatened, expenditure on the intelligence services has been massively increased, there have been major overseas military deployments and sophisticated weapons have been ordered.

Ironically, though, some of those outcomes have only been achieved by abandoning liberal economic goals. Revenue from taxation in Australia, which provides 31.6 per cent of GDP, is slightly higher now than ever before, though it remains well below the OECD average of 36.3 per cent.[5] The growth in demand for human services which follows naturally from rising incomes and the ageing of the population has offset the effects of privatisation, contracting out and cuts in many services. The role of the state has grown rather than declined and there has been a pronounced tendency to centralise policy-making in the national government, despite the traditional Coalition preference for decentralisation. The High Court's 2006 decision to confirm the validity of the national government's industrial relations policies, based on the constitutional corporations power, strengthens this centralising tendency even further. Welfare policies have become harsher, imposing more stringent conditions for access to income support on the unemployed, single parents, the disabled and new migrants. Despite the unpopularity of policies such as privatising Telstra, some attention has been given to electoral opinion. Public affection for the iconic Snowy Mountain Scheme led Howard to abandon its sale and there was strong reaction against the proposed sale of Qantas to overseas buyers. Opinion polls showing strong community opposition to the sale of Medicare Private led to deferral of its privatisation.

There have also been direct costs, and neglect of other vital goals. The most obvious macroeconomic cost has been the growth of the current account deficit, which was 5.6 per cent of GDP in 2005–06.[6] Such a high deficit with the rest of the world will eventually have to be substantially reduced. In 1980 Australia owed 6 per cent of GDP to the rest of the world, but by September 2006 this had risen to 53 per cent. This matters because debt becomes a circular problem: the larger it is, the more costly it is to service and reduce. Also, it would be prudent to reduce risks of damage from any future potential crisis caused by international financial market volatility. From 1996 to 2004 the growth of Australian exports was among the lowest in the OECD: Australia failed to become a clever country. Commodity exports did all the work and the composition of exports changed little. Our top ten merchandise exports in 2003 were coal, petroleum, gold, iron ore, aluminium, beef, aluminium ores, wool, wheat, and passenger motor vehicles. Only one, motor vehicles, was an elaborately transformed manufactured good (an ETM). Except for those motor vehicles, the list was much the same as it had been eight years before, and so was the proportion of Australia's merchandise trade accounted for by ETMs (21 per cent compared with 23 per cent). Services accounted for 21 per cent of Australia's total exports in 2003, much the same as five years before. The big changes occurred earlier, between the mid-1980s and the mid-1990s, when the first effects of freer trade were being felt. Reduction of the external deficit will be necessary. As eminent economist Professor John Quiggin concludes, 'The success or failure of economic liberalism may be judged, in large measure, by observing whether this adjustment takes the form of increased exports, driven by higher productivity, or of reduced imports driven by a contraction in economic activity' – as happened in 1989.[7]

Many of the opportunities which favourable domestic and international circumstances have created have been neglected. As a result, skilled labour is in short supply; 11.4 per cent of the workforce are unemployed or want additional work, as noted earlier; infrastructure is defective and deficient; and household debt has reached over 150 per cent of household income, with resulting increased vulnerability to rising interest rates. The relentless, obsessive drive for productivity gains in the public sector has reduced not only employment but also the quality and accessibility of many Commonwealth services. Training and employment opportunities in the public sector have been reduced – for apprentices, for other young people, for people with disabilities and for Indigenous people. The government has also refused to consider funding the expansion of employment essential to providing early childhood education, care for the aged and care for those with debilitating disabilities.

As in Bush's America, the government's policies concerning tax, spending and regulatory decisions have entrenched corporate priorities rather than those of the whole nation. The economic liberal policies have always been unpopular with voters, especially privatisation and cuts to human services. This has not prevented the Howard Government from shifting power towards the already powerful: employers, corporations, media moguls and itself. The wealth and power of high income-earners has been enhanced by large tax cuts, concessions and deregulation, while the insecurity of the vulnerable has been increased as income support has been cut, eligibility reduced, intrusive, pedantic regulation elaborated, and services restricted.

Fundamental conditions and rights at work have been abandoned by severely restricting union activities and establishing structures and procedures hostile to collective bargaining, despite these being contrary to international labour conventions agreed to by all member countries of the ILO, including Australia. The economic security of the majority has been undermined by this revolution in workplace relations. This is damaging working conditions, especially for those at the highest risk of being made redundant: young people entering the workforce, women and older workers. Australia's century-long tradition of fair play in employment has been destroyed. Intrusive micro-regulation of individuals has also been multiplied – by the party which purported to aim for small government, deregulation and freedom. Many Australians feel they are being told what to do more than ever before, especially in the workplace and in dealings with government agencies.

The evidence that economic liberalism sometimes entrenches market failure is accumulating. The growth of GHG emissions is the clearest example, but concentration of ownership, and so capacity to control prices or collude in controlling prices, is growing in numbers of industries, including media, manufacturing, recycling and retailing. The wave of corporate deregulation and privatisation was necessarily followed by re-regulation of the private monopolies which had been created, but questions remain about whether or not these arrangements will in fact ensure genuinely competitive outcomes. The degree of regulation of much individual activity has actually been intensified: we all experience the delays and frustrations of complex and detailed administrative arrangements of both private enterprises and public authorities. It is simply wasteful to retire or retrench public servants and then to re-engage them for higher fees from their home-based consultancies.

Political scientist and historian Stewart Firth vividly summarises the benefits and costs:

> The proponents of a globalised, free trade might well be right about
> the stimulus this fundamental change of direction has given to the
> economy – higher growth rates appear to suggest that – but the
> fear is that a globalised Australia where only efficiency matters will
> be less identifiably Australian, less democratic, less equal and more
> ravaged by environmental degradation. Australians will no longer be
> citizens but merely employees and consumers in the global economy.
> Efficiency is only one criterion against which the success of a society
> can be measured. Some say other criteria matter more, such as national
> identity, democratic responsiveness, social equality and environmental
> preservation, all of which should be balanced against efficiency rather
> than subordinated to it.[8]

A reaction against the extremes of market fundamentalism is underway in most of the rest of the developed world. In the United States, the Democratic victory in the 2006 congressional elections was a clear indication that the electorate was not only sceptical about the invasion of Iraq, but also critical of Bush's domestic mismanagement and the corruption of his administration.[9] Local opposition from both Democrats and many Republicans defeated proposals for the privatisation of schooling by issuing vouchers. The decline of the stock market in the early 2000s repelled potential supporters of privatisation of social security, forcing Bush to abandon it. Despite opposition, many Republican as well as Democratic Congress members supported an increase in the minimum wage in 2007. The economic liberal push to cut the public sector has been superseded by the 'war on terror', which has been used to justify massive increases in military spending and in the domestic security industry. Bush's enormous fiscal deficits are being condemned in many political forums, and the tax cuts for the wealthy which were their other cause – as well as wasteful spending on irrelevant weapons – will have to be curtailed to reduce budget deficits. The American economic liberals have failed to obliterate many aspects of Roosevelt's New Deal, just as Australian economic liberals have failed to erase much of Chifley's social democracy. The political spectrum in the United States and Australia is moving back to a choice between big-government conservatives and moderate social liberals or social democrats. Executives have learnt that there is more to be gained from cooperative governments with plenty to spend, particularly on corporate welfare, than from a relentless struggle to cut public outlays:

This unrecognised defeat for economic liberalism fits with the experience of relative stability of public expenditure in the non-English-speaking developed countries. It is surprising that John Howard did not recognise this structural shift in the US, but perhaps he judged that since his term as Prime Minister would end sooner than the presidency of George Bush, there would be little personal benefit in beginning the inevitable distancing that would be required of Australian policy when the American electorate rejects neo-conservative and libertarian Republicanism in November 2008, as the disillusionment and exasperation with Bush shows they are likely to do. Most developed countries have given somewhat more attention to employment growth and poverty reduction amongst legitimate economic goals than they did in the 1980s and early 1990s as already described in relation to the EU.[10]

The adoption by the Commonwealth Treasury of a mission 'to improve the well-being of the Australian people' could be an attempt to broaden the department's purposes. It remains to be seen whether that will change their orientation in practice. The description of policy outcomes being sought is not reassuring. Treasury expresses its first goal, of a 'sound macroeconomic environment', as 'characterised by stable prices, low interest rates, healthy economic and employment growth and a sustainable external position'. The goal of full employment of earlier decades has been discarded. 'Horizontal and vertical equity' are included amongst the principles of tax policy but not amongst the characteristics of a 'sound macroeconomic environment'. There is no mention of wider concerns or constraints, such as environmental sustainability or the social purposes of policy.

In addition to the goals of public policy, several other major considerations must frame economic policy. The necessity of containing climate change by reducing GHG emissions has already been discussed. The size and rate of growth of the population is vigorously debated and must be explicitly addressed. The goal of reducing inequity in the distribution of income, wealth and power must be affirmed and embedded in economic strategy.

Population and immigration

Global population size has a major effect on GHG emissions and water use, so slowing global population growth would contribute to sustainability. In that context it is argued by some that Australia's population is too high for continental environmental sustainability, and by others that it is too low for optimal economic sustainability. But is fertility a major challenge for Australia, as Peter Costello has argued? It is difficult for one of the two most sparsely populated countries in the world (the other is Mongolia) to convince itself or others that it is overpopulated, not least because of the complexities of the calculations involved in such a conclusion. Though 80 per cent of the continent is semi-arid, 57 per cent of land is used for agricultural activity, mostly grazing. Average Australian agricultural exports are able to feed about 55 million people at Australian levels of consumption. About 84 per cent of the population live in the fertile, temperate, most densely populated 1 per cent of the continent. Nevertheless, in a country and age in which there is high productivity in agriculture (mostly for export), in which 75 per cent of the workforce is employed in providing services to others, and in which most of the population prefer to congregate in cities, Australia could support a considerably larger population if this were desired. Environmental sustainability depends not only on the ratio of population to fertile land but also on the rigour of conservation measures, including the extent of use of renewable energy, water recycling and pollution-minimising technologies, and the commitment to maintaining biodiversity through adequate protected areas and complementary policies.

These points are not, however, reasons for seeking to motivate increased fertility. There does need to be better support for those who want to have children, through more family-friendly workplace and parental leave provisions, but Australia should avoid contributing to global overpopulation. As Australia's birth rate fell below replacement in 1976 and has remained so throughout the last 30 years, the country's population will start to decline naturally in 2033 unless it is increased by continuing immigration. Sustained immigration can mean adding to the supply of skilled people, reducing the growth of the 'dependency ratio', increasing family reunion, and taking a share of refugees. The net migration gain is likely to continue at around 110,000 a year.[11] This would increase Australia's population to 28 million people in 2050.

Asylum seekers are a special category of immigrants about whom there has been intense controversy. As suggested in the first chapter, there is a strong humanitarian and legal case for Australia to be more welcoming. Basic decency requires that asylum seekers be allowed to sustain themselves and contribute to society through paid work, rather than being isolated and imprisoned behind razor wire – at enormous cost to society, and to the aid program. Australia should return to applying the UN Convention on Refugees, which it ratified in 1954, and should, like Canada, incorporate the Convention and its Protocol into the Migration Act to guarantee that application.[12] Most types of bridging visas, which cruelly withhold access to employment and social services, should be abolished. All the detention centres should be closed. Not only would this end much inhumanity and save over $130 million a year – which is taken from the aid budget and which should be used for poverty reduction in developing countries; it would also signal to the world that Australia is seeking to deal with refugees responsibly, justly and legally.[13] That would mean that all refugees who arrive without a visa would be treated in the same way as those who arrive by air without a visa and then apply for refugee status. That is, they would be issued with a visa which would allow them to work and receive services until their case is processed – which should be expected to happen quickly and with courtesy. It is crucial that anyone concerned with justice and humanity in Australia actively oppose the current immoral, unjust and illegal system. It would also be appropriate for Australia, as one of the contributors to the terrible slaughter and social chaos in Iraq, to sharply increase its intake of Iraqi refugees, as we did for refugees from Vietnam in the late 1970s and early 1980s.

It is vital that public policy include strengthening social harmony and combating racism. The reduction of English-language teaching and advisory services for migrants is an entirely false economy. If Australia is to become an equitable, humane society it is essential that accommodations be sought which recognise diversity while affirming agreed national moral and legal standards. This is a necessary condition for Australia to continue to accept not only 110,000 permanent settlers each year, but also 200,000 short-stay business visitors, 100,000 students, 60,000 people on working holidays and 4 million tourists – today's numbers.

An effective means of contributing to restraining global population growth would be to increase our contribution to the UN Fund for Population Activities (UNFPA) from a derisory $4 million a year, as it is now, to at least the level of the Netherlands – over $70 million. Australia's tokenism is a hangover from the time when independent Senator Brian Harradine (whose vote the Coalition needed in the Senate) was bullying AusAID to withdraw support for family planning. Though he left the Senate several years ago, his legacy lingers, and should now be discarded. The populations of most developing countries are still growing at annual rates of 2–3 per cent; the rate is higher still in others, such as Papua New Guinea. UNFPA estimates that the cost of providing family planning services for all countries would be around $14 billion a year, and that the vital complementary services for maternal health and prevention of sexually transmitted diseases would add a further $10 billion a year. Developing countries themselves are providing about three-quarters of the $5 billion which is currently being spent, but they clearly need significant external support to ensure the availability of adequate services for all women. It is difficult to imagine a more cost-effective means of reducing the rate of global population growth and so reducing growth of GHG emissions than for Australia to sharply increase its annual contribution to UNFPA. Much more assistance for the education of girls and women is an essential complementary policy – there is still discrimination against girls attending school in many countries.

Addressing poverty, disability and exclusion

The Australian Council of Social Service (ACOSS) wrote in a 2003 submission to the Senate inquiry into poverty that 'people in poverty ... live under conditions that would be widely regarded by the community as hardship, experience a lack of socially defined necessities, or have substantially less command over resources than the community finds acceptable'.[14] Poverty needs to be understood as deprivation of several kinds, even if it is measured using income.[15] The ABS expenditure survey indicators of financial stress include going without meals or home heating sometimes, inability to have a special meal once a week, to go out once a fortnight, or to pay gas, electricity or telephone bills on time. The Senate Community Affairs Committee inquiry into poverty concluded in 2004 that estimates of the poverty rate varied between 13 and 19 per cent, which implied that between 2 million and

3.5 million people are living in poverty. Groups at high risk of poverty include Indigenous and unemployed households, sole-parent families, young people in low-income households and households of working age whose main source of income is welfare payments (such as those with people with a disability, and carers). About 20 per cent of Australians have a disability which significantly impedes their life at some time, though some recover. People with a disability are disproportionately represented amongst the poor. A case study illustrates their problems and those of many others:

> Amy is a single mum with adult children and had a full-time job and a relatively modest mortgage which was under control. Then she became seriously ill, and after an operation spent months in hospital and was left with a permanent disability. Her absence from work was so lengthy and her mobility and pain problems so intense that Amy lost her job and her disability meant that she was unable to find another. Thus she joined the ranks of those on the Disability Pension. Through the next five years Amy found herself falling through the cracks in the government's support system, and needed to fund, out of her meagre resources, her own wheelchair, and mobility devices – her shoes, orthotics, callipers, walking frames and ramp. She knew that the cost of some of these could be covered by the government's assistance scheme for aids but there is a five-year waiting list, and putting her life on hold for this length of time was impossible.

> Amy managed – by increasing the mortgage on her home. Her equity had been previously built up slowly over time, as she worked in low-paying jobs that allowed her the hours she needed to care for her children. Now the bank is sending threatening letters and the situation is scary. She has a qualification in accounting, and knew that she could have accessed her needs through credit, but she also knew of the risks. Either way, her situation was very frightening.

> It is not only Amy's access to shelter that is under threat. So is her access to social connection. Her car is old and she cannot afford to replace it, and even covering the registration, which used to be more significantly reduced for pensioners, is a challenge. Her house was cheaper because it was distant from the shops, but with the State Government putting a cap on half-price taxis, using these to cover the basics of shopping is not an option. The Commonwealth Government's answer to people living with a disability who are

socially isolated is to do voluntary work, and they will pay a mobility allowance of $30 a week – the equivalent of 1.5 trips between North Dandenong, where Amy lives, and Dandenong. Even funding the trip home is a challenge.

If the rate of the Disability Pension was increased to realistically cover subsistence, the taxi cap adjusted more generously, access to aids such as wheelchairs improved, and pensioner car discounts increased for both those with a disability like Amy and for the unemployed, Amy could meet her mortgage repayments, would have better mobility and be in an improved position to return to the workforce and to live independently and productively.[16]

The UN World Summit on Social Development in Copenhagen in 1995, attended by Prime Minister Paul Keating on behalf of Australia, agreed that countries should prepare national plans to define, measure and eradicate absolute poverty and reduce overall poverty by declared target dates – a commitment which was successfully proposed and advocated by the Australian delegation. By the time of the Special Session of the General Assembly held in June 2000 to review progress, 39 countries had set targets for poverty reduction, 78 countries had prepared plans and a further 40 were in process.[17]

The European Union considers social exclusion and poverty inter-related issues, and has adopted European goals and encouraged preparation of national action plans. The British Government responded by making a commitment to eliminate child poverty within a generation, and preparing indicators to monitor progress and specific strategies for different groups. Ireland commissioned a report, established a Combat Poverty Agency and prepared and implemented a national anti-poverty strategy.

International experience shows that setting targets and preparing a strategy focuses attention and strengthens consistent action. ACOSS urges adopting the targets of reducing the overall level of poverty by a quarter and halving child poverty over a 10-year period and preparing a national strategy in cooperation with the states and territories through the Council of Australian Governments (COAG). Establishing an Anti-Poverty Commission could contribute to overseeing effective implementation of the strategy. Many of the essential elements of such a strategy are mentioned in Chapter 4 and later in this chapter. They include: strengthening the macroeconomic policy focus on employment growth; investing more in education and skills training, transitional employment schemes, early childhood education, preventive and primary health and dental care; improving income support; and removing poverty traps in welfare payments. Introducing a national housing strategy with a component for tackling homelessness is also vital.

After four years of negotiation, a new UN Convention on the Rights of People with Disabilities was adopted by the UN General Assembly in December 2006. The Howard Government initially opposed negotiation of the treaty, arguing that the rights of people with disabilities were adequately covered by the Universal Declaration of Human Rights and other conventions, but there was agreement from most other countries to the preparation of the treaty and it is now completed. The convention has a preamble and 25 articles, beginning with general principles and definitions. It moves through commitments to equality and non-discrimination, liberty and security of the person, freedom of expression and privacy, to living independently, equal access to education, health and employment, participation in public life, physical accessibility, an adequate standard of living and monitoring. The convention will set a framework for effective policy for people with a disability in all countries. It is essential, therefore, to urge the Australian Government to swiftly sign and ratify the treaty. The Senate Community Affairs Committee completed an inquiry into services for people with disabilities early in 2007 which makes valuable recommendations.[18]

Everyone engaged in public policy recognises that one of the major challenges in coming decades is population ageing. Both Labor and Liberal governments have given much attention to older people's income security, so that is not likely to be a high priority during the next half dozen years – unless the tax cuts relating to superannuation in the 2006 Budget become an excessively large drain on revenue. One reform which certainly deserves consideration is to raise the age of retirement for women and men wherever it is still compulsory or conventional, because with the rapid growth of healthy life expectancy, working life can naturally be gradually extended too.[19] Issues requiring immediate attention include increasing the flexibility of retirement arrangements so as to enable those who want to continue in paid employment past the conventional retirement ages to do so. When official economists are so concerned about the rising 'dependency ratio', it is absurd to force people who want to work to retire. Fuller recognition and support for the enormous range of voluntary contributions to innumerable community services which can be made by older people are also vital.

The contingencies social security payments have to deal with are so much more varied now than they were 60 years ago that some policy thinkers have suggested replacing all payments and tax allowances to people in particular categories of need with a basic income payment to all. Such a revolution would not only be enormously costly, but its introduction would be likely to cause great uncertainty and perhaps insecurity. Oxford Professor Sir Tony Atkinson proposes instead a 'participation income' which would be complementary to existing provisions: 'The state would guarantee a level of income, fixed as a percentage of median income although varying with personal circumstances such as age and health, and would fill any shortfall not covered by existing state provisions.'[20] Atkinson recommends that such an income guarantee should recognise sickness, disability or other inability to work, but for all others be conditional on community participation, indicated not only by seeking work but also by undertaking training, caring for others, and doing approved forms of voluntary work. If such a program began by guaranteeing a basic income to parents of every child, child poverty could be dramatically reduced. Careful study of these possibilities would be warranted for Australia, where there are considerable gaps, inequities and poverty traps in the provision of income support. The half a million family carers are another major group whose contribution is inadequately supported. The cost of replacing their work with that of paid carers is estimated to be equivalent to about 3.5 per cent of national income, so improved long-term income support for carers would be both fair and cost-effective.[21]

Economic policy for wellbeing, sustainability and the common good

Refocusing national economic policy to give a central place to improvements in the quality of life would have many implications for economic development strategy and macroeconomic policy. Income growth would continue to be important, but it would be measured by increasing median income rather than by growth of GDP. This would immediately build an indicator of equity into mainstream economic policy. Atkinson goes beyond this and argues attractively for a Strategy for Incomes within which attention would be explicitly given to how the fruits of growth should be distributed.[22] This would provide a firmer basis for consideration of how wellbeing, the quality of life and the common good could be addressed in each area of macroeconomics – fiscal, monetary, international and incomes policies.

This framework requires a more sophisticated balance between economic goals, including reduction of unemployment and containment of inflation. Growth of employment contributes more to increasing personal and national economic security – strengthening personal sense of purpose, reducing the terrible waste of unemployment (of people who want productive work not being able to get it), increasing efficiency in the use of people's time and energy, improving equity by reducing poverty and strengthening social integration – than any other economic or social achievement. A simultaneous focus on employment and inflation is more feasible early in the 21st century than it was in previous quarter century because inflationary forces are less strong. What economists describe with the ugly term the 'non-accelerating inflation rate of unemployment' (the NAIRU) has fallen. Globalisation intensifies international competition, reducing the capacity for enterprises to determine prices. Wage pressures have declined, partly because of demographic changes, partly because of increased worker insecurity, partly because of trade union weakness – though greed for exorbitant executive salaries has intensified.

Australian fiscal policy is caught in a doctrinaire and partisan trap. Budget surpluses have become the symbol of fiscal responsibility. This is absurdly restrictive. Budget surpluses are desirable when the economy is growing strongly, as a way of dampening demand, but so are deficits when the economy is beset with contractionary influences. Taxation and outlays should be used pragmatically as a counter-cyclical influence. Even the OECD recommends that if commodity prices fall and the terms of trade turn down 'it will be important to allow the automatic stabilisers to work, including ... at least temporary modest fiscal deficits if that downturn were severe'.[23] During the recent long upswing it has been appropriate for Treasurer Peter Costello to budget for a surplus, but it would be irresponsible of him or of Labor to promise surpluses throughout a forthcoming term of government, because the economy's needs cannot be known so far in advance. And it would be irresponsible for spokespeople from either party to criticise the other party for suggesting that they might run deficits if the economy needed a stimulus.

Liberalisation of financial markets has been the most influential change in the macroeconomic environment during the last 30 years. Following financial deregulation, the Reserve Bank's ability to influence financial markets was limited to influencing the money supply, resulting in more volatile money supplies and interest rates. Financial volatility increases risk and the cost of investment, and sometimes leads to financial crises. Around the world there were over 100 episodes of systemic financial sector crisis during the last two decades of the 20th century.[24] The human, social and economic cost of these crises has been enormous, with the loss of employment and the increase in poverty lasting long after the financial effects have eased. In a liberalised financial market, the power of short-term capital flows to destabilise economies ensures that preferences of financiers are constantly in the minds of national economic policy-makers, skewing economic and social priorities towards reduced expenditure.

Nobel Laureate Professor Joe Stiglitz argues that the emphasis on the independence of central banks, on the ground that monetary policy is a technical issue, misrepresents the nature of their decisions, because

monetary policy necessarily has political dimensions.[25] Independent
central banks have tended to be preoccupied with reducing inflation
and to give less weight to the impact of their policies on employment.
Changes in monetary policy inevitably have distributional consequences.
Two improvements would be: first, for the Reserve Bank to take more
seriously the goals of economic and employment growth which are
included amongst their statutory purposes; and second, to ensure that
the Board is representative of all major sectors of the community and
therefore more likely to be attentive to the interests of all, not just of
financial markets.

The emphasis on stable prices without a complementary
employment goal tends to lead to Australian monetary policy being too
tightly constrained. The size of the current account deficit contributes to
this stance because of the need to attract capital. That is why Australian
interest rates are amongst the highest in the developed world. Yet it is
scarcely possible to overestimate the importance of the availability of
credit at manageable interest rates to entrepreneurs in small and medium
enterprises. Every increase in interest rates discourages investment and
so constrains employment growth. The former Governor of Australia's
Reserve Bank, Ian Macfarlane, said when delivering the ABC Boyer
Lectures in 2006 that households will bear the brunt of the next
economic recession because their rapid build-up of debt has made them
particularly vulnerable to a bust in the price of property assets. These
factors deserve greater weight in the Reserve Bank's decisions.

An additional arm of macroeconomic policy that is commonly
neglected is social dialogue leading to the negotiation of a national
economic and social strategy by business, unions, government and
civil society together. This approach has been a valuable instrument
in many countries – in Australia during the Accord in the 1980s, and
in many European countries, including Austria, Denmark, Ireland
and the Netherlands.[26] It can also be a significant means of increasing
participation in political processes, so contributing to the accountability
and transparency of governments. While it is unlikely that the Accord
could be repeated in Australia in the form in which it was negotiated
in the 1980s, the value of forming economic strategy in consultation

with all social partners has been largely neglected since then; it could be re-emphasised with benefit.

Raising the revenue

Tax expert Professor Neil Warren concludes: 'The tax system, both Commonwealth and State, continues to fail the three key principles of a good tax system – to be equitable, efficient and simple.'[27] The extent of poverty, and of the inequality of income and wealth in Australia – and their continuing growth during the last decade – described in the first chapter, indicate the importance of strengthening progressive measures in the tax system that constrain inequality. Our tax system is not contributing sufficiently to reducing inequity. One reason is the disproportionately high tax burden on low and middle income families; the very rich seem to be able to avoid paying their fair share. Professor Patricia Apps of the Sydney University Law School shows that:

> the effective rate scale that now applies is no longer progressive but tends to exhibit an inverted U-shape, with very high rates on below average incomes … The focus has been on switching towards a less progressive income tax schedule and a highly targeted benefit system.[28]

Tax rates for lower income earners can be high because of the interplay of tax and targeted family payments systems. When family incomes rise, the combination of increasing income tax with loss of means-tested government payments causes many families to have effective marginal tax rates of over 50 per cent, when the top marginal tax rate for high income earners is 45 per cent. In 2006–07, about 910,000 Australians, 7.1 per cent of the working age population, kept less than half their additional private income.[29] The proportion of adults caught in this anomalous trap was only 4.8 per cent in 1996–97. Of families paying high effective marginal tax rates in 2006–07, about half lose over 60 per cent of every additional dollar earned and smaller numbers lose over 70 per cent, though fortunately the proportions of deprived people are slowly declining. Although one in five sole parents loses more

than 50 per cent of additional income and so is at the greatest risk,
surprisingly, almost two-thirds of people experiencing this deprivation
are parents with partners and dependent children on middle incomes.
This has been compounded by the introduction of the GST and of user
charges for many public services. The Committee for the Economic
Development of Australia (CEDA) argues that 'the Australians facing
the strongest [tax] disincentives to work are mostly lower and middle
income earners'.[30] Low income earners and those paying high effective
marginal tax rates must be the focus of any changes to rates of income
tax and to allowances.

Maintenance of an effective, equitable redistributive tax system is
a necessary means of constraining the growth of inequity, for income
taxes are the only mechanism available which increases the contribution
to public revenue as income rises. The Howard Government's tax cuts
for high income earners have reduced the already modest extent of
that redistribution. It is essential that there be no further tax cuts for
high income earners during the next few years. One means of curbing
the explosion of CEOs' incomes would be to remove their employers'
ability to describe their pay above a threshold as a corporate claim, as a
cost of production for the company. If a generous annual threshold of,
say, $500,000 were set for executives' incomes, and any payment above
that could not be claimed by companies as a cost of production, that
would be an incentive to limit their pay.

Tax systems don't just have to be equitable, efficient and simple;
they also have to raise sufficient revenue to fund desired services.
There has been a common claim that voters want tax cuts so much
that they would accept poorer services, but this is simply inaccurate.
The 2005 Australian Survey of Social Attitudes suggests that attitudes
have changed only slightly since the 2003 survey, with 47 per cent of
respondents in the later survey preferring increased social spending and
34 per cent reduced taxes. Shaun Wilson concludes that:

> Although it is clear that Australians are worried about the state of
> public services and infrastructure, and are willing to forgo tax cuts
> to pay for improvements ... both politics and policy remain highly
> sensitive to the fiscal discontent of mortgage-holders, higher income

earners and the politically disaffected – a potentially powerful coalition of interests in favour of tax cuts. The dynamics of support for a low tax model suggest its critics must find a rationale for tax rises that best accords with these interests and sensibilities. One possibility would be to extend the taxation of wealth, which is popular with most anti-tax voters because it addresses their interest in tax equity, but this carries political risk.[31]

Certainly the Australian tax system is deficient in excluding any taxation of wealth. There is an especially strong case for reintroduction of an inheritance tax to limit the extent of inequity in the distribution of wealth passed on from one generation to the next. However, the electoral difficulties with such a proposal are substantial. The most politically acceptable way of raising tax is to undertake to use the revenue generated for a highly desirable service: the Medicare levy is the most obvious example. The most urgently required taxing of a specified object is carbon emissions, to more closely reflect their true environmental cost. The proceeds could be used to subsidise research into and introduction of renewable energy. Huge advances in use of renewable forms of energy production are already being made in other countries. Germany is adding 2000 wind turbines each year and is now nearing a total of 20,000. Japan heavily subsidised the purchase of rooftop solar panels by home-owners. The resulting increase in the volume of installations was so strong that manufacture and installation costs have fallen, driving down the price to the point where the subsidy is barely necessary because home-owners are able to produce power for the same price as charged by the big utilities. Electricity in Japan is expensive because of the scarcity of energy sources, but this illustrates the principle required to remove the massive market failure of unpriced GHG emissions. Australia has far more sunshine than Japan, so Commonwealth funding to kickstart nationwide installation of solar panels makes complete sense. Funds for solar energy research should also be swiftly and substantially increased because 'huge technological breakthroughs' are now reported to be tantalisingly near.[32]

Professor Julian Disney argues that the exemption of owner-occupied homes from capital gains tax and tax deductibility of the costs of investment in property for rent (negative gearing), especially in combination with concessions on capital gains, are excessively generous.[33] They do distort incentives by increasing returns on 'unproductive' housing and so diverting potential investment from manufacturing and tradeable services. Yet those concessions also contribute to reducing the cost of buying a home and increasing the supply of housing, and so perhaps to limiting increases in house prices. These suggestions would generate too much political opposition for any major party to adopt as policy during the next parliamentary term or two. Disney makes a stronger and more feasible case when drawing attention to Australia's lack of the kind of inheritance or gift tax that exists in most other developed countries.

Some revenue increases would be possible through improving the efficiency and comprehensiveness of tax administration. A potentially effective means of reducing tax avoidance is to increase international tax cooperation. Governments are limited by international competition in both the forms of tax and the tax rates they can apply. There is also an urgent need to reduce opportunities for evasion and avoidance and to minimise the danger that countries will strive to increase their revenue in ways that deplete the global commons. There is a growing imperative to improve arrangements for cooperation between national tax authorities and to strengthen their capacity for efficient and equitable tax administration.[34] Establishment of an international tax agency would facilitate such cooperation and fill a serious gap in the framework of global public goods.[35]

These brief comments mention only a few of many tax issues which deserve attention. There has not been a full-scale review of the tax system since 1975, yet there is widespread discontent with the system's complexity and inefficiency as well as with its inequity. Establishment of an independent, expert, comprehensive inquiry into tax reform is now justified and appropriate.

Investing in wellbeing

Fiscal policy does influence society and the economy. Personal wellbeing and employment growth can be encouraged cost-effectively by well-chosen expenditure increases aimed directly at equitable improvements in services for all, especially education, training, health, housing and employment programs, and at income maintenance for the impoverished and excluded. There is a striking correlation between national average incomes and government revenue as a proportion of GDP. Countries with high income levels resulting from past economic growth tend to have higher levels of government expenditure, reflecting greater demand for the services that are commonly provided by governments, such as health, education and income security.[36] The 1991–96 tax revenue of low-income countries averaged 13 per cent of GDP; in lower middle-income countries it was 18 per cent; in upper middle-income countries, 20 per cent; and in high-income countries, 30 per cent.[37] This empirical relationship completely contradicts the normal justifications for the economic liberal goal of cutting public expenditure. Social spending is essential to achieve universal access to education, health and infrastructure, and for other programs that improve many aspects of everyone's wellbeing and that reduce inequity.

Increased public investment in these services, as well as in infrastructure, generally improves productivity and so raises private profitability. Peter Costello's policy of frugality in both Commonwealth and state expenditure is misguided. His claim to be preparing for a future economic downturn by preventing infrastructure investment is short-sighted – such prevention merely retards improvement in economic efficiency. His view is especially misjudged since the Commonwealth has no net public debt. While the decline in public investment from one half of private investment in the 1960s to barely a fifth today does not prove neglect, it does suggest the possibility of inadequacy.[38] Professor Peter Sheehan, Director of the Centre for Strategic Economic Studies at Victoria University, argues persuasively that:

Australia has, for the last decade or so, been living off its existing stock of human knowledge and social capital, and not doing nearly enough to replenish those stocks to be economically viable or socially coherent over the long term … Thus investment in physical, human and social capital should be at the centre of our fiscal strategy.[39]

Borrowing for investment in activities which generate income is entirely economically responsible. Just as households responsibly take out a mortgage to purchase a house – provided the amount of the mortgage is realistically related to expected income – so governments should borrow for investment which generates future returns for the community. Facilities constructed this year are of benefit both immediately and for future decades. Why shouldn't future as well as current beneficiaries contribute to the cost? Few companies fund all their investment out of current profits. The pride of the NSW Government in being the only host to finance an Olympic Games without borrowing was misplaced: though the Games left Sydney with major improvements in sporting facilities for use in future decades, recurrent services such as education were further starved of funds. As financial analyst and commentator Alan Kohler writes compellingly, 'Governments in Australia don't build infrastructure any more, no matter how sensible it might be, and no matter how much demand there might be from super funds for the government bonds needed to finance it. Politicians prefer to enrich investment bankers and not issue government bonds.'[40] Rejection of public borrowing for investment has been one of the absurdities of market fundamentalism.

Fortunately, some of the states are cautiously starting to borrow again in order to invest, but they are still without the support of the Federal Treasurer, who remains committed to balancing the whole cash budget, rather than just the recurrent budget, over the course of the business cycle. This leaves no room for net borrowing over the medium term for investment. A step towards greater realism would be to distinguish between the recurrent or operational budget and the capital budget and to recognise the good sense of borrowing to fund capital expenditure. In a situation where there is no Commonwealth debt, and innumerable high-priority needs for physical and social investment, there could be no legitimate complaint about such a change. As Fred Argy writes:

> [O]ur discussion leads to one clear conclusion: governments need to abandon once and for all their opposition to public debt *per se* and determine their appropriate infrastructure financing options on a case-by-case basis, with no presumption against borrowing ... For serious progress to occur, Canberra needs to make additional capital grants to the states, earmarked for specifically agreed projects.[41]

It would be entirely appropriate to make such grants out of borrowing, rather than requiring that they be funded from recurrent revenue, as happens at present.

Labor plans to establish a national infrastructure authority, Infrastructure Australia, to drive planning and investment and report to COAG. Its first task would be to conduct a national infrastructure audit to assess future needs and set priorities. Financing would be conducted through a Building Australia Fund which would put to work the assets of the Future Fund, other public investment and also possibly public–private partnerships. However, public–private partnerships are normally inefficient because private investors seek high returns to take risks which would be more appropriately borne by governments and involve payment of wastefully high fees to financial intermediaries (such as Macquarie Bank and Babcock and Brown); they also lack transparency and accountability. Calling tenders for construction generates competition and is the proven way of using public funds efficiently.

The Australian federal system is more unbalanced than that of other federations because the states have responsibility for 41 per cent of all government outlays while raising only 15 per cent of total tax revenue.[42] This fiscal imbalance gives the Commonwealth all-too-tempting opportunities to both cut taxes and deny the states sufficient funding to finance comprehensive, high-quality services. The states are forced to be mendicants, and to tax jobs, land, transactions and gambling. As the population ages, health costs multiply, forcing erosion of state expenditure in other areas unless those state resources are increased or their other responsibilities are reduced, such as by transferring responsibility for health to the Commonwealth. The High Court's landmark November 2006 decision in the industrial relations case increased Commonwealth power even further, 'obliterating' powers that state governments previously considered unquestioned – those covering such areas as health, education and transport, as Justice Callinan said in his minority judgment. Justice Kirby said that the imperative to ensure a 'fair go all round', which was at the heart of federal industrial law, was being destroyed in a single stroke, and that the decision ran the risk of 'destabilising the federal character of the Australian Constitution' (*New South Wales v Commonwealth of Australia*; *Western Australia v Commonwealth of Australia* [2006] HCA 52 (14 November 2006) at 562) and further reducing the states to service agencies of the Commonwealth. This undermines the principle of subsidiarity: that services be managed by the level of government where they are most efficiently handled and which is as close as possible to users.

Another possible way of reducing fiscal imbalance would be to extend the states' taxing powers, by empowering them either to tax spending (given that they already receive revenue from the GST), or to introduce a levy on income negotiated through COAG. This could be collected by the Commonwealth and transferred to the states and territories for service provision, and no doubt offset by a reduction in income tax. John Quiggin estimates that a progressive levy averaging 5 per cent would be sufficient to eliminate vertical fiscal imbalance.[43] This would provide a sounder basis for responsible government, allowing the states to raise the revenue they need and requiring that they take responsibility for its efficient use. The Commonwealth would still have the power to collect most personal and company income tax. Both the Labor and Liberal parties are advocating continuing debate and innovation about the roles and financing of the Commonwealth and the states.

Economic vitality

One of the principal rationales used by economic liberals for cutting public expenditure was that this would prevent public sector activity squeezing out the private sector. Underneath that assertion is the assumption that the business world has more vigour and entrepreneurship than the public sector. Unpacking that assertion suggests a more complex reality: it seems that particular activities are most effectively undertaken in particular sectors. Most economic activities are most efficiently undertaken in a competitive private sector. Yet relying only on private initiative tends to result in insufficient investment in research, education, training and health, and insufficient spending on infrastructure. Countries seeking economic vitality do well to recognise the value of active encouragement of both public and private sectors and of cooperation between them.

Research, development and demonstration are essential to enhancing economic vitality. 'Innovation is critical to Australia's growth and preparedness for emerging economic, social and environmental challenges', writes the Productivity Commission.[44] Yet during the last decade Australian expenditure on research and development (R&D) has stagnated at around 1.6 per cent of national income. The ratio of higher education expenditure to GDP fell from 1.7 per cent in 1995 to 1.5 per cent in 2000. Another more positive indicator of the nation's knowledge base is investment in software, which grew from 1.1 per cent of GDP in 1995 to 1.7 per cent in 2003. Putting those three indicators together for the year 2000 shows that investment in knowledge was 4 per cent in Australia. This compares with the average for OECD countries of 4.8 per cent. Sweden spent more than any other OECD country, at 7.2 per cent of GDP, and the United States spent 6.8 per cent. It is clear that, as a Parliamentary Library paper cautiously concludes, 'the amount Australia invests in its knowledge base is on the low side'.[45]

The government's *Innovation report 2005–06* recognised that Australian gross domestic expenditure on R&D is well below the averages for the OECD and the European Union – we are placed 18th among OECD countries. In Sweden and Finland, business spends two and half times as much on R&D as we do; in the United States it spends twice as much as it does in Australia.[46] Australian universities are also funded to undertake less research than their Nordic equivalents, though the differences are not as great and Australian universities do more research than those in the United States.[47] In 2006 only 18 per cent of applications to the Australian Research Council were successful, which means that the amount of money available through the principal source of university research funding is quite inadequate to respond to scholars' initiatives. Even recognising that some of the proposals are likely to have been recondite or poorly conceived, this rejection rate suggests considerable waste of intellectual energy, and that there is such unsatisfied demand for funds that major increases, towards the levels in Nordic countries, would be justified.

The neglected 2001 *Agenda for the Knowledge Nation* prepared by a taskforce chaired by Barry Jones contains many recommendations deserving of swift implementation, including: doubling overall R&D as a percentage of GDP; removing impediments to commercialisation of research; building on Australia's strengths in medical research; dramatically improving support for technologies for environmental sustainability; expanding online education; recognising the high cost-effectiveness of investing in early childhood learning; increasing Commonwealth support for public education; and much, much more. Adoption and dissemination of innovation as well as discovery are essential, and the former will not be possible without greater attention to the latter. ACTU Secretary Greg Combet suggested that a Leading Technology Development Allowance of 20 per cent of eligible investment costs (that is, being taxed 20 per cent less) could be offered in addition to existing depreciation schedules for investments at the technological frontier.[48]

The current boom in global demand for Australian mineral resources is saving us from an even greater deterioration in the current account deficit, but there is no evidence that mineral exports alone will be sufficient to pay for expected imports, whether or not prices for minerals fall. The answer does not lie in attempts to curtail Australian demand for imports, but in seeking growth in exports through investment in manufacturing, infrastructure and services (see Chapter 4). In the 1960s and 1970s, when Australia's current account deficit was small, investment averaged 29 per cent of GDP; it is now 26.4 per cent.

There has been a tendency to give too little attention to the service sector in all discussion of economic policy. Production and employment are conventionally perceived as about physical goods rather than face-to-face services. Yet the service sector is the area of most economic and employment growth. Services employ three-quarters of the labour force, the principal industries being retailing, health and community services, education, government administration and defence, communications, wholesaling, finance and property, culture and recreation, and personal services. The ILO reported early in 2007 that for the first time the services sector has become the biggest source of employment worldwide – it covers some 40 per cent of the world's workers.[49] As well, trade in services amounted to 20 per cent of the total value of global cross-border trade. That proportion is rising, and not just in the naturally international service industries of finance, telecommunications and transport. These trends need to be recognised in Australian economic strategy, because they are essential to employment growth and to the services essential for improvements in wellbeing.

Countering market failure is another vital means of stimulating economic vitality. Advocates of market fundamentalism are often distinctly selective about areas for which they advocate increasing competition. They are noticeably silent on regulation of privatised monopolies, media concentration, the restrictive practices of surgeons and lawyers, ownership of local monopolies such as toll roads, airports and shopping centres, and regulatory protection for pharmacies, or for Qantas on the Pacific route. The consequences of failure to ensure adequate scrutiny of a privatised monopoly are vividly demonstrated by AWB's contravention of UN sanctions against Iraq by payment of $290 million in bribes to the Saddam Hussein regime. The 'small, close knit and powerful monopoly trading powers [of AWB] should never have been left unchecked: bad business practice and scandal were sure to follow' concludes Professor Stephen Bartos of Canberra University.[50] Federal MP Lindsay Tanner (ALP) argues correctly and toughly that business lobby groups expect the Labor Party to accept labour market deregulation – 'to put our low-income heartland to the sword, but it hasn't got the guts to challenge well-heeled vested interests in its own backyard'.[51] Strong action by the Australian Competition and Consumer Commission (ACCC) is essential.

This chapter has outlined means to advance the wellbeing of Australians and the common good through strengthening economic security, social justice and vitality. Following a compelling case study of Ireland, the next chapter discusses the same goals in relation to the global search for security, peace and justice.

Ireland's economic transformation: Strategy and pragmatism

Roy Green

How did Ireland transform itself from the economic basket case of Europe to a post-modern success story in two decades? Just think back to the 1980s, when unemployment was 17 per cent and inflation 20 per cent. It seemed then that there was no way out. Ireland's strategy of investing in its human capital had produced the highest proportion of computer science and engineering graduates of any country in the world after Japan, but they were all going abroad to get jobs. The outlook could not have been bleaker.

Fast forward to 2007 and the picture is so different that many Irish can scarcely believe they are living in the same country. They have experienced the fastest growth of employment, output and productivity of any country in the OECD, and their country has become a hub for global corporations producing personal computers, software, medical devices and pharmaceuticals. There has been considerable analysis and debate about the lessons of Ireland's turnaround, as might be expected.

Some claim it is a triumph for economic orthodoxy, as growth was associated with a fiscal squeeze, low corporate tax and pro-market policies. Others argue the contrary, that carefully designed intervention by an array of public agencies, combined with policy pragmatism, made the difference. Who is right?

Inevitably, there is some truth in both interpretations, but one thing is certain – Ireland's transformation was not a spontaneous outcome of market forces. Left to itself, the economy would have limped along a low-skill, low-productivity path, jobbing for routine work that could be performed more cheaply there than elsewhere. The circuit breaker was a 'social partnership', somewhat like Australia's Accord, involving business, trade unions, community organisations and a less than reputable government of the day. However, while the politicians were discredited by scandal and corruption, the country's leading civil servants were hard at work preparing plans that would be implemented through a far-sighted partnership with civil society. These were summed up in the *National Development Plan 2000–2006* as follows:

> There is a strong link between investment in the research and
> innovation base of the economy and sustained economic growth …
> The accumulation of 'knowledge capital' will facilitate the evolution of
> the knowledge-based economy.

The first task, however, was to achieve macroeconomic stabilisation, giving up the idea of a public spending-led revival in a small marginal economy and opting instead for wage restraint, at least in the short term. This was combined with fiscal consolidation, in return for substantial European funding for infrastructure renewal, entrepreneurship and skill development. Together with the already high-performing graduate labour market, the elements were put in place for investment attraction. However, further elements were required. A separate investment attraction agency, the Industrial Development Agency (IDA), was established, with the strategic as well as very practical goal of targeting future global growth sectors based on new technologies and skills. The framework for this activity would be developed by Ireland's innovation agency, Forfás, which drew on international thinking but also did some of its own. In parallel, a new agency, Enterprise Ireland, was given the task of linking foreign direct investment (FDI) companies to supply chains and clusters, with the intention of embedding companies in the local economy.

In this context, Ireland's low corporate tax was a significant factor, but it was not the only one in FDI attraction policy and the associated rapid growth of the small to medium enterprise (SME) sector. The major catalytic role in the 1990s was played by the key public agencies, which identified where Ireland would be able to position itself in European and global markets and then designed and deployed the policy instruments to achieve the desired outcomes. Nothing was preordained, and to some degree it might be said that Ireland's targeting of new growth industries was fortuitous, but the fact is that they did it – and prospered.

By the end of the 1990s, new challenges had emerged. Ireland had become the largest exporter of software in the world, and the fifth largest exporter of computers, but these exports embodied research and technology that was imported, not home-grown. The same applied to other sectors, such as medical devices and pharmaceuticals. The problem was examined by a high-level group of business and union leaders, senior civil servants and outside experts, who concluded:

> Whereas in the past, products manufactured in Ireland were designed elsewhere, in the future, more of the ideas, the designs and the technology must originate here. Companies in Ireland will have to innovate and gain leadership positions in their target markets.[52]

Already Ireland had begun a huge program of investment in research in universities and institutes of technology, through both competitively funded projects and 'innovation partnerships' with industry. Now it was essential not only to generate the ideas that might lead to new products and processes, but also to encourage effective knowledge transfer and commercialisation. New Centres for Science, Engineering and Technology (CSETs) were established at Irish universities in collaboration with some of the largest FDI companies in Ireland, with a view to devolving R&D capability from head offices and building local capability. Is this the market at work, or making the market work better? The Irish are not particularly interested in the answer to this question at a philosophical level. They are the ultimate pragmatists.

Consider this example. One of Ireland's new CSETs is at the forefront of stem cell research. It hired back world-renowned Irish researchers at the Mayo Clinic who had emigrated in the dark days of the 1980s. In 2006, the European Union required a vote on whether embryonic stem cell research could be pursued legally in the member states. The Irish Catholic bishops counselled the government to vote against the measure ... and it might have done so only a few years ago. But there is a new religion abroad, one aiming to make Ireland a leading knowledge-based economy as part of an ambitious European strategy. The government supported the majority vote to pursue embryonic stem cell research, along with its new friends Finland, Sweden and Denmark, among others.

Now Ireland is a successful high-wage, high-productivity economy – it is this combination that persuades FDI companies to stay rather than shift to lower cost locations. These companies pay high nominal wages, but they enjoy high productivity and thus low unit labour costs, largely as a result of sustained investment in human capital over a 40-year period, supplemented by an increasing commitment to research and innovation. As the Enterprise Strategy Group pointed out, 'Knowledge creation and diffusion are at the core of economic activity. Knowledge is embodied in people, and it is the quality of the human resources that will determine the success or otherwise of firms and economies in the years ahead.'[53] If there is any single key to Ireland's transformation, this investment must rate highly, but it does so in the context of an imaginative and flexible approach to policy-making which, to paraphrase Keynes, avoids being the 'slave of any defunct economist'.

chapter 6

advancing global security and justice

[The argument for pre-emption] represents a fundamental challenge to
the principles on which, however imperfectly, world peace and stability
have rested for the last fifty-eight years. This [argument] … could set
precedents that resulted in a proliferation of the unilateral and lawless
use of force, with or without justification. We have come to a fork in
the road … We must decide whether it is possible to continue on the
basis agreed [in 1945], or whether radical changes are needed.

Kofi Annan, September 2003

Though military conflict is in decline globally, terrible violence persists in many countries and regions, including Iraq, Lebanon, Palestine and Israel, the Darfur province of the Sudan and Sri Lanka, and there is serious instability in several of Australia's neighbouring countries. In many countries, governments repress their people or have abandoned standards set in the UN Universal Declaration of Human Rights. There is debilitating poverty in parts of the developing world, often associated with inadequate supplies of food, water and housing, let alone of educational and health services. HIV/AIDS and other pandemics continue to be globally threatening. The failure of the United States to bring peace and order to Iraq illuminates the enormity of the Australian misjudgment of uncritical compliance with American preferences. It is therefore imperative to rethink Australian foreign policy. This chapter suggests that Australia's national interest requires that we adopt a more independent stance towards the United States and re-engage with the rest of the world through the United Nations in order to contribute to rebuilding a rule-based and more peaceful and just international system.

The United States and Iraq

The Iraq war has created a momentous dilemma for the world. What principles can the international community now use to limit the use of force? The central controversy before the invasion of Iraq was about the legality of the proposed action. The question was would the United States (and the United Kingdom and Australia) comply with the UN Charter and maintain the international rule of law? In Chapter VII of the Charter, the use of force is prohibited unless authorised by the Security Council or in self-defence when armed attack occurs or is imminent. Opening the General Assembly in September 2002, the UN Secretary-General at the time, Kofi Annan, said:

> [A]ny State, if attacked, retains the inherent right of self-defense under
> Article 51 of the Charter. But beyond that, when States decide to use
> force to deal with broader threats to international peace and security,

there is no substitute for the unique legitimacy provided by the United Nations.

President Bush also spoke at that General Assembly opening, arguing that the United States wanted to help the United Nations enforce the resolutions passed by the Security Council on Iraq. If the Security Council did not agree, he said, the United States and a 'coalition of the willing' would act alone.

Some Americans, labelling themselves realists, argued that states no longer act according to the international structure of law founded on the UN Charter. Charter rules governing the use of force in international affairs had been ignored so often since World War II, they said, that they had effectively ceased to form part of international law, and accordingly it was no longer contrary to international law for states to act in breach of them. Sir Brian Barder, former British High Commissioner to Australia, commented:

> The idea that a law ceases to be a law if it is sufficiently often disobeyed seems oddly defeatist, not to say perilous, even if applied to international as distinct from domestic law. It is no doubt true that the US is now so uniquely powerful that it can do what it likes, however illegally, with impunity. But that's a far cry from saying that international law actually licences the United States ... to use force against another state whenever it feels so inclined and in complete disregard of its treaty obligations ... And to tell the rest of the world that we have got to 'recognise' this new American hegemony and 'the failure' of the whole UN experiment is surely outrageous.[1]

The United Nations was formed in a wave of postwar idealism. Its goals, set in the Preamble of the Charter, include 'to save succeeding generations from the scourge of war', to affirm 'fundamental human rights', to establish the basic conditions for justice and the rule of law, and 'to promote social progress and better standards of life in larger freedom'. With such goals, it is not surprising that opinion polls show that large majorities of people in all countries continue to support the United Nations. The American-led invasion of Iraq was the most direct challenge to the UN violence-minimising system in 60 years. If America can pre-emptively attack whichever country it considers threatening, why can't others also? If the conditions established in the UN Charter for containing use of force can be disregarded, what system is left? The illegal American invasion of Iraq supported by the Blair and Howard governments was not only wanton aggression; it also caused a crisis in the international system.

To propose new approaches to force minimisation, Kofi Annan appointed a High Level Panel on threats, challenges and change, of which former Australian Foreign Minister Gareth Evans was a member. The panel reported in December 2004 under the title *A more secure world.* Their extensive recommendations included restarting disarmament, reaffirmation by nuclear states of their previous commitments not to use nuclear weapons against non-nuclear states, and the adoption of five criteria (by the Security Council) which would have to be satisfied before use of force is authorised. The five criteria are: whether the threatened aggression is sufficiently serious; whether the primary purpose of the proposed military action is to avert a threat; whether the proposed action is the last resort; whether it is the minimum necessary; and whether the proposed action is likely to have less destructive consequences than inaction. The Secretary-General called for adoption of these criteria by the Security Council in his preparatory recommendations to the Global Summit which was held in New York in September 2005. It surprised no one that the Bush Administration was stubbornly opposed to this. However, many other countries did support this clarification of the conditions under which use of force could be authorised by the Security Council, and as late as three weeks before the Summit a compromise was included in the draft outcome document, saying, 'we recognize the need to continue discussing principles for the use of force, including those identified by the Secretary-General'.

Then, in a recess appointment – that is, an appointment made when Congress was not in session and thus without Congress's agreement – President Bush appointed John Bolton as US Ambassador to the United Nations, and within ten days he was advocating 750 amendments which would have emasculated the Global Summit outcome. Intense day-and-night negotiations followed, and anything which had not been agreed to a day before the summit began was simply deleted. As a result, the whole section on disarmament and non-proliferation lapsed. However, the outcome document includes a clear statement of principle: 'We reiterate the obligation of all Member States to refrain in their international relations from the threat or use of force in any manner inconsistent with the Charter of the United Nations.' The question is whether US administrations and other governments will accept and abide by that principle. So the outcome document of the largest Global Summit meeting ever held says nothing about constraining use of force, disarmament or nuclear non-proliferation. Fortunately, however, sufficient concessions were made by all countries, including the United States, to allow several other significant agreements to be finalised, including establishment of a Peacebuilding Commission, a Democracy Fund, a small police force suitable for rapid deployment and a Human Rights Council. There was recognition that the global community has a responsibility to protect vulnerable populations when their governments are not acting to prevent genocide. That UN Summit in September 2005 illuminated much about the state of global politics, by demonstrating the difficulty of achieving international agreement while the United States tries to dominate global affairs. It has also shown, though, that despite that impediment, multilateral agreement about some significant issues can still be achieved. UN forums continue to contribute to international peace and justice.

The consequences of the invasion of Iraq have been so terrible that they destroy the legitimacy of the Bush doctrine of pre-emptive attack in the minds of any but the most doctrinaire neo-conservative advocates of US hegemony. The cost to Iraq is incalculable when we take into account the 650,000 Iraqis estimated by the John Hopkins School of Public Health to have been killed between January 2002 and July 2006 in conflict-related deaths, and the even greater number of injured.[2] Millions of Iraqis have been displaced or have left the country as refugees and several Iraqi cities have been ruined, together with large parts of the country's infrastructure. The population has been traumatised in ways that it will take generations to heal. The US coalition and the Iraqi Government have violated human rights standards and international law by imprisoning large numbers of Iraqis and others, including David Hicks, without charge or trial, and torturing many of them.

There has been massive corruption and inefficiency in the privatised military and reconstruction activity – which has so far failed to deliver improvements in basic services. The national heritage has been looted. In addition to the fortress in central Baghdad, US military bases are being constructed. Most US and allied personnel have legal immunity from Iraqi law and so impunity from prosecution. Total US budgetary costs of the Iraq War, including foreshadowed military expenditure, future medical costs, and interest on national debt, are estimated by Nobel Laureate Joe Stiglitz to be US$1300 billion, and that does not include non-budgetary costs such as the value of life lost or impaired.[3] This is getting close to twice Australia's annual national income. Leading European philosopher Jürgen Habermas writes, 'Make no mistake, the normative authority of the United States of America lies in ruins.'[4]

Opinion polls taken in Iraq show that the occupation is highly unpopular. A large majority of Iraqis say that the occupation heightens insecurity and sectarian violence. Yet reconciliation between Baathist Sunnis, Kurdish nationalists, the Shiite majority and other political groups is extremely difficult. The Iraqi Government proposed a 'National Reconciliation Plan' in June 2006 but the US opposed key elements of it, causing a stalemate. Vice-President Dick Cheney told *Time* at the end of October 2006 that 'we're not looking for an exit strategy. We're looking for victory.' The bipartisan US Iraq Study Group which reported in December 2006 opened its summary by saying 'the situation in Iraq is grave and deteriorating', recognising that the American invasion has become an unmitigated catastrophe. The report concludes that 'no one can guarantee that any course of action in Iraq at this point will stop sectarian warfare, growing violence, or a slide toward chaos'. Many experts are talking of America's defeat in Iraq.

Cheney speaks with absolute certainty that the United States is trustworthy because it is on the side of goodness; its intentions are innocent. Yet the United States is currently the world's most aggressive nation. There are only two countries which have launched attacks on others in recent years, the United States and Israel, and they are close allies in their aggression. Cheney is clear that the Bush Administration would, if necessary, use force against Iran. 'The US is keeping all options on the table in addressing the irresponsible conduct of the regime ...

We will not allow Iran to have a nuclear weapon,' he said to *Time*. Max Rodenbeck, *The Economist*'s Middle East correspondent, writes, 'obviously America poses a far greater threat to Iran than Iran does to the United States. And perversely, it is this threat more than anything else ... that bolsters Iran's oppressive and unpopular government.'[5]

The global primacy of the United States suggests that it is important to pay close attention to the forces driving its policies. The Bush revolution in foreign policy has involved 'an unprecedented assault on international law', writes UN elder statesman Sir Brian Urquhart, not only by invading Iraq but also by abandoning commitments made by the United States during the previous 50 years in one treaty after another, covering such things as arms control, conflict resolution, human rights, climate change and treatment of prisoners.[6] By eschewing the international rule of law and multilateral negotiation in favour of unilateral pre-emptive military action, the Bush Administration has deliberately undermined international cooperation and diplomacy, and therefore the United Nations also.

The American delusion of national exceptionalism – that it should not be expected to comply with the rules which apply to other countries – has its origins in more than the megalomania of the neo-conservatives around Bush. Many Americans maintain their country's historic sense of being God's own country with a manifest destiny to lead the world to liberty and democracy. The strong tendency to use military methods to resolve issues, combined with budgeted military expenditure next year of $620 billion – about half global defence spending – amounts to a bad case of militarism. The *New York Times* editorialised that 'the budget barrels along with unrealistic long-term projects that the services and the nation will ultimately be unable to afford, piling on stealth destroyers and air combat fighters designed for the cold war'.[7] Historian Arthur Schlesinger Jr asked, 'who can doubt that there is an American empire? – an informal empire, not colonial in polity, but still richly equipped with imperial paraphernalia: troops, ships, planes, bases, proconsuls, local collaborators, all spread around the luckless planet'.[8]

The rationale for aggressiveness since 9/11 has been the so-called war on terrorism, but this too has been riddled with misjudgments. The threat of terrorism has been grossly and endlessly exaggerated: for an American, the probability of being killed by terrorists is about the same as the probability of being killed by an allergic reaction to peanuts. Six times more Americans are killed every year by drunk drivers than died in the World Trade Center.[9] The danger from terrorist use of so-called weapons of mass destruction is much less than is often asserted. Chemical and biological weapons are extremely difficult to make and use and there is no evidence that any terrorist has come close to acquiring nuclear weapons. Military action is rarely the most effective way to counter terrorists. Armies exacerbate the problems rather than solving them, as in Iraq. 'The point of terrorism is not to defeat the enemy but to send a message', writes Harvard expert Louise Richardson.[10] She says that since terrorists seek revenge, renown and reaction, Bush has given al-Qaeda a far greater reward than it ever dreamed of winning.

There is growing recognition in the United States that the invasion of Iraq has been America's most disastrous folly since Vietnam. The Democrats' victory in the US congressional elections of 2006 was the most hopeful political event relating to foreign policy in a developed country so far this century. A major strength of American civic culture is the vigour of public debate. The critique of the Bush doctrine is generally far more comprehensive and incisive in the United States than in Australia. Whoever is elected US president in 2008, the extremist unilateral stance will pass and multilateral engagement will increase. This does not mean that American militarism will automatically fade, but it is probable that fiscal pressures will receive more attention and that military expenditure will take a share of the cuts essential to restoring budgetary balance. Yet the Australian Government apparently does little to prepare for such an evolution of the American political climate.

Rethinking the American alliance

When Australia was the only country to join the United States and United Kingdom in the invasion of Iraq, many Europeans and people from developing countries were surprised and asked why. The reason starts with the trauma of near-invasion by the Japanese in 1942 and gratitude to America for protecting Australia. Australians often forget, though, that this action was a by-product of America's need for a base from which to organise their response to the Japanese. President Roosevelt told Richard Casey, later Australian Minister for External Affairs, in 1941, that while the United States would go to the defence of Canada if it were attacked, Australia and New Zealand were so far away that they should not count on American help. The treaties signed at the start of the Cold War are strong bonds. The ANZUS Treaty of 1951 was a formal expression of Australia's dependence on the United States for protection and has been a central element of Australian defence and foreign policy ever since.[11]

The view that shared values have provided, and continue to provide, a strong basis for the alliance is misleading. There are similarities – of language, ethnicity and political institutions – but also substantial differences. Perhaps the Howard Government's claim of 'shared values' is simply a muted way of noting the extent to which it has complied with the market-fundamentalist economic ideology and the neo-conservative foreign policies of the Bush Administration. The national purposes of Australian and US foreign policy diverge in crucial ways. Australia has no global ambitions, and those related to the region are for stability and economic advancement rather than dominance. Shared values should not, and need not, be the determining force for an alliance in any case. The claim that they are is close to saying that WASPS should stick together, a xenophobic paradigm which more and more Americans and Australians would reject. The viability of a strategic partnership needs to be determined principally in terms of strategic issues.

The central fact about the Australian–American alliance is that it does not mean much to the Americans. Australia's support has been of value to US administrations seeking to legitimise their actions – in Korea, Vietnam and the Iraq wars – but Australia's military contribution to those wars was marginal. No doubt the communications stations have been useful to the United States. But has Australian compliance added to our security? The explicit mention of Australia in the US *National*

Security Strategy is reassuring to some. Bush has been personally grateful for Howard's support. Australia has supported the United States in five major wars, but what difference does that make? The United States did not contribute the troops which the Australian Government asked for to assist with peacekeeping in Indonesia, for instance. Professors Stuart Harris and Amin Saikal of the ANU write that:

> The US has long made clear that the US national interest comes first in its actions. For Australia this was made very evident over its involvement in East Timor, where the US, while helpful, extended only limited assistance, emphasising the priority of its own national interests, including its relations with Indonesia.[12]

An issue of potentially greater importance is the possibility of conflict in the Taiwan Strait, an area in which Australian and American national interests could well be sharply different.

The American alliance probably has practical benefits. By increasing the community's sense of security, the alliance has in the past enabled Australia to keep military expenditure lower than it would otherwise have been. Kim Beazley (ALP) said, when he was Defence Minister, that the US defence association saved Australia 1 per cent of national income. A second benefit claimed by supporters of the alliance – readier access to American weaponry – currently means little. The US administration is seeking to waive licensing rules for Australia to buy certain classified types of military equipment but Congress opposed the proposal. Australian policies did not give Republican congressional leaders sufficient confidence to relax controls on exports of weapons to Australia – this might, apparently, have played into the hands of terrorists! Another benefit claimed for the alliance is the sharing of intelligence. This is looking more like an impediment to well-judged policy. Australia incurred substantial costs from uncritically accepting the 'intelligence' provided by the United States about Iraq.

The Howard Government's closeness to the Bush Administration has had political, financial, military and human costs. This uncritically pro-American stance restricts Australia's capacity to express its own international priorities, and has weakened Australia's independence and standing with regional neighbours, as well as undermining its reputation at the United Nations. By refusing to require that David Hicks be returned to Australia or at least charged and swiftly tried, the Howard Government weakly acquiesced in American injustice. To the extent that it has any significance, Howard's obedience is reinforcing aggressive and illegal American policies. The likelihood of pressure to participate in further military expeditions is increased. Opportunities to act as a catalyst and supporter for conflict resolution, peacekeeping, and development are lost. Integration of our defence force with theirs through interoperability of force structure and procurement adds to defence costs, as do additional military expeditions. The relatively low risk of becoming a terrorist target increases.

The Lowy Institute poll published in October 2006 showed that two-thirds of Australians think too much notice is taken of the United States in foreign policy. Australia would be more secure in an orderly multilateral system than in a world where the only superpower reserves the right to unilateral pre-emptive use of military force. The issue is not whether to retain or renounce the US alliance. To abandon the American alliance would erode what little scope for influence is available to Australia, might lead to increasing defence expenditure and would probably be electorally unacceptable. Rather, the immediate issue is about the policies adopted and advocated by Australia within the alliance. Australia should affirm the value of the United Nations' multilateral framework and urge US multilateral engagement and adherence to international norms, treaties, and law. Australians can also support the majority of Americans who want their country to be an honourable participant in the multilateral system. We can cooperate with those within the United States who seek peaceful and just solutions to conflict. We would do well to seek greater independence and autonomy, based on firm clarity about national goals. The alliance can be maintained while our foreign policy becomes more realistic about the nature of the United States and clearer about our national interests. We can then seek to be cooperative when we can, yet firm in urging US engagement with the United Nations and respect for international law.

The American alliance is sometimes discussed as if Australia faced a threat of invasion, yet there is no interest anywhere in attacking this country. Australian governments have been spending large amounts on sophisticated weapons for 20 years to prepare to repel an invasion when no such threat exists or is likely. As Paul Monk writes, 'in Australia's case, both now and for decades past, there has been no serious possibility of such an invasion'. And later: 'in the eyes of a number of observers … the most realistic threats to the country's future security and prosperity do not consist of an invasion of the kind against which so much has been invested in capital equipment since the 1980s'.[13] Much more serious threats are those relating to vertical and horizontal nuclear proliferation (that is, increasing sophistication of nuclear weapons by nuclear states as well as acquisition of nuclear weapons by additional countries), climate change or disease pandemics, all of which can only be effectively addressed through multilateral action.

Undermining the United Nations

International goals such as peace, prosperity, justice and sustainability can only be effectively pursued through a cooperative, rule-based global order, applied and enforced through multilateral institutions. Yet the Howard Government has cooperated with the Bush Administration's relentless campaign to weaken the United Nations. As well as being ideologically opposed to multilateralism, the Bush Administration and its neo-conservative operatives have been attacking a constraint on the United States' pre-eminence and retaliating for the refusal of most countries to support the invasion of Iraq. Some criticism of the United Nations was justified: a proportion of UN peacekeeping troops in the Congo were seriously undisciplined, and some people associated with the Oil-for-Food program were corrupt. The scale of these transactions was small compared with the bribery paid by over 2000 corporations to Saddam Hussein's government – including the $290 million paid illegally by Australia's AWB. But they have been rigorously investigated, several people have been charged and procedures to prevent such abuse have been tightened. It is essential that the constant struggle to improve the United Nations' efficiency and effectiveness be rigorously maintained – as indeed such a struggle needs to be for every complex organisation.

A more general criticism of the United Nations is that it is ineffective in resolving conflicts, but those claims are often attempts to use the organisation as a scapegoat for the unwillingness of governments to negotiate seriously and to compromise. The UN Secretariat was not responsible for delaying peace enforcement in Darfur, the region of western Sudan that has been racked by conflict and displacement of population: in fact Kofi Annan campaigned for years for effective action against genocide in Darfur. The causes of the delay lay instead in the reluctance of African states to intervene in opposition to the Sudanese Government, the possibility of a Chinese veto and insufficient political investment by the other permanent members of the Security Council. One of the principal functions of the United Nations is to provide forums at which issues can be discussed and conflicts negotiated. Failure to reach agreement is due principally to differences in national positions.

The inability of the United States and the United Kingdom to persuade, bully or bribe the majority of Security Council members into supporting a resolution sanctioning the proposed invasion of Iraq is considered by some scholars to be the biggest US diplomatic failure since World War II. By that refusal the Security Council demonstrated as never before its value as a forum for negotiation about the use of force, because it denied legitimacy to the invasion. It also demonstrated the power of public opposition in most countries to American aggression, as some governments, including those of Mexico and Chile, were unable to act in ways contrary to the wishes of most of their people. Yet the United Nations could not prevent the illegal invasion, and this demonstrates its limits when challenged by a determined superpower. As Yale historian Professor Paul Kennedy writes about the drafting of the UN Charter:

> Despite all the language of the UN Charter requiring compliance with Security Council resolutions, if a powerful state should decide to defy the world body and go it alone, there was little that could be done to

prevent that happening, unless, of course, the other powerful states were willing to move to military enforcement and thus run the strong risk of starting World War III. If lesser states broke the rules they might well get spanked.[14]

Such failures draw attention not only to the limits of the present sanctions available to the international community through the United Nations but also to outdated aspects of its structure. The most publicised part of the report of Kofi Annan's High Level Panel on threats, challenges and change was about reform of the Security Council. There is much justified criticism that the Security Council's membership reflects the structure of global power in 1945, which has meant that the countries defeated in World War II have been excluded from permanent membership, as have all but one developing country (China). The High Level Panel proposed increasing 'the involvement in decision-making of those who contribute most to the United Nations financially, militarily and diplomatically'. Of their proposals, the one attracting most support involved creating a new category of semi-permanent seats for a longer term than the present two years for elected members, for which countries would be eligible to seek re-election after their term expired. Although several countries have obvious claims for long-term membership – India, for example, because of its population, and Japan, because it is the second largest economy, and both because of their contributions to the United Nations – there is opposition from other countries to every candidate. Yet surely global realities must be recognised in the Security Council's composition if its credibility is to be sustained.

The engagement of the Howard Government with the United Nations has been particularly uneven. The government, which came to office determined to reduce Australia's participation in UN peacekeeping, became the largest force contributor to one of the largest UN peacekeeping operations in the world, not just for a few months, but over a period of years. Australia's commitment of troops to East Timor was easily its largest since the Vietnam War – 5500 of INTERFET's peak strength of 11,500 – and it enjoyed widespread support from the Australian public. Some Australian troops stayed until the end of the UN mission in 2004, and returned again after the breakdown of order in 2006. The Bougainville peacekeeping mission (over 5000 regional peacekeepers over five years, most of them Australian) and the Regional Assistance Mission to the Solomon Islands were examples of regional, not UN, peacekeeping, but were nevertheless entirely welcome. Yet during the decade from 1996 Australia has often been either a passive observer or an impediment to some of the effective work of the United Nations. Australian support for American unilateralism, opposition to control of GHG emissions, denigration of the Human Rights Commission, and neglect of the United Nations' work on economic, social and environmental policy has disappointed developed and developing countries alike.

Two of many possible examples illustrate the problem. In March 2002 the Australian Government sent a parliamentary secretary to head its delegation to the International Conference on Finance for Development held in Mexico. Australia was the only developed country other than Portugal not represented by a minister, and deceitfully described its representative as the Minister for Development Cooperation. The meeting was attended by more than 50 presidents and prime ministers, and the US delegation included President Bush, Secretary of State Colin Powell, and Secretary of the Treasury Paul O'Neill. A meeting on 'Action against Hunger and Poverty' called by Presidents Lula and Chirac at the United Nations on 20 September 2004 was also attended by over 50 heads of state or government and by cabinet ministers from many other countries, including the United States. But there was no name plate for Australia. It was reasonable that Alexander Downer not attend, because the meeting was during the election campaign, but the Australian Ambassador to the United Nations should have participated.

There have been some positive policies as well as Australian advocacy of international support for independence for East Timor, including support for the International Criminal Court, despite intense US opposition. But these activities are not what Australia is now best known for internationally. The appointment of Robert Hill as Ambassador to the United Nations is welcome, because he is genuinely supportive of the United Nations and of Australian multilateral engagement, but he is constrained by government policies.

Renewing multilateral engagement

Many constructive ways in which Australia could express renewed multilateral commitment are possible and feasible. Eight high-priority practical possibilities follow. First, Australia could adopt a more mature strategy for contributing to global security, through reaffirmation of a rules-based international order. Among the principal requirements for ending the scourge of war is for international society to reaffirm preferences for peaceful conflict resolution rather than violence, to negotiate rather than confront, and to adhere to the rule of law rather than acquiesce in domination by the United States. Australia could become a sophisticated advocate of that approach. Clarifying the enormity of the costs of war would strengthen motivation for diplomatic negotiation to address conflicts, as would strengthening international exchange, communications networks and transactions including trade, and advocating stronger treaties and adherence to treaty commitments.

Second, Australia could undertake active study, research and consultation about feasible means for improving the United Nations' effectiveness. During the last two or three years, Britain, Canada, France, Germany, and three Nordic countries have all sponsored public discourse on multilateral issues through commissions of inquiry, research projects, international consultation and public information campaigns (including support for national UN Associations) leading to articulation of reform proposals and innovative policies for the multilateral system. They have then led international discussion about their proposals. If the Australian Government is serious about contributing to UN reform it could undertake such valuable preparatory work also.

Third, terrorism needs to be put in perspective, if only because it can generate exaggerated fears. For example, there have been no deaths from terrorism within Australia. A sophisticated, multifaceted strategy is required for tackling terrorism, including, simultaneously: homeland defence; pursuit and punishment of terrorists; action within countries of origin, supported, whenever sought, from outside; addressing the political repression and exclusion that causes grievances; and tackling injustice, poverty and despair through major upgrading of programs for social, political and economic development. The best way to protect ourselves against terrorism is simply to act justly.

Fourth, increases in military spending contribute little to a campaign against terrorism. In fact, they add to the dangers. The military dominance of the United States adds to the risk that it will take improper military action. America cannot 'at once be as powerful as it boasts and as vulnerable as it fears'.[15] Reconsideration of recent and planned increases in Australian military expenditure is warranted. There are many far more cost-effective ways of reducing risks and assisting development. Restraint of military expenditure could release funds for desperately needed Australian economic and social programs as well as for assistance to other countries.

Does Australia really need far higher military spending per person than Japan, Germany, Italy or Spain, and two-thirds more than Canada? Since 1995–96, real Australian military spending has been increased by 37 per cent. What change in the strategic environment justifies that? The *increase* in the 2006–07 Budget alone was $2 billion (to about $20 billion) compared with the *total* aid budget that year of less than $3 billion. Are those respective outlays well judged? What external threat justifies spending over $50 billion on expensive purchases of sophisticated weapons? Invasion from the north with conventional weapons is among the least likely military contingencies Australia might face, and therefore should not be the conceptual foundation of our defence policy. Announcing the spending of $6 billion for 24 Super Hornet fighters in March 2007 seemed to have more to do with boosting the government's national security credentials than with addressing an alleged air combat gap.[16] Will spending a minimum of $16 billion on 100 joint strike fighters and $6 billion on three air warfare destroyers make us safer than spending on ways of reducing the motivation of terrorists? The Howard Government's defence doctrine focuses on interoperability with US forces anywhere in the world rather than on 'air and naval domination of the sea-air gap between the Australian and Asian land masses'.[17] Is this a change that the majority of Australians really want, especially when the choice is between spending

$20 billion a year on the military and improving the quality of health and education?

The current defence strategy should be rigorously reviewed, starting with a thorough assessment of external threats. This might lead to identification of ways of cutting military outlays, making way for more cost-effective means of reducing international conflict. A 2005 Research Note from the Parliamentary Library suggested that:

> the global rise of non-state threats, such as Islamic terrorism ... at the same time that conventional military threats to Australia fade away, brings with it questions about how the nation should think about its security requirements.[18]

For some years, the Australian Defence Force (ADF) has focused on the kinds of internal conflict being encountered in Australia's neighbouring states. This is a valuable use of the ADF, who have indeed brought order to the Solomons and East Timor. Increased contributions to UN peacekeeping would also be valuable.

Fifth, nuclear weapons, not terrorism, continue to be the major threat to global survival. Yet the Bush Administration has both abrogated the treaty limiting anti-ballistic missile systems – to facilitate research on missile defence – and revived the idea of developing nuclear weapons for first use rather than for defence. The research violates the Nuclear Non-Proliferation Treaty (NPT) and undermines the commitment of other signatory countries to stop developing nuclear weapons capability. It also risks breaching the firewall between conventional and nuclear weapons. The NPT is essentially a bargain: nuclear weapons states agreed to progressively disarm in return for renunciation of acquisition by the rest. The revival of American nuclear weapons research and the refusal of France, Russia, the United Kingdom and the United States to undertake no first use threatens the survival of the treaty. At the 2000 NPT review conference, the five nuclear states (the fifth is China) party to the treaty gave an 'unequivocal undertaking ... to accomplish the total elimination of their nuclear arsenals leading to nuclear disarmament'. The Bush Administration's backing away from this commitment was a major cause of the deadlock at the 2005 NPT review conference.

The Blix Commission on Weapons of Mass Destruction which reported in June 2006 argues, correctly, that:

> so long as any state has such weapons – especially nuclear arms
> – others will want them. So long as any such weapons remain in any
> arsenal, there is a high risk that they will one day be used, by design or
> accident. Any such use would be catastrophic.[19]

The commission proposes incremental steps towards outlawing nuclear weapons: taking all nuclear weapons off high-alert status; making deep reductions in numbers of nuclear weapons; prohibiting the production of fissile material; urging all nuclear states to make no-first-use pledges; bringing the Comprehensive Nuclear-Test-Ban Treaty into force; and reviving the commitments of all parties to the NPT, especially steps towards nuclear disarmament by the nuclear weapons states. Australia's role in this global survival strategy must include joining with the strongest advocates of the Blix Commission's strategies, continuing to sustain obligations of the South Pacific Nuclear Free Zone Treaty and rigorous scrutiny of the uses of uranium exports.

Sixth, most countries have adopted the Millennium Development Goals (MDGs) for universal primary education, gender equality, reduction in child and maternal mortality, combating disease, ensuring environmental sustainability and support for developing countries, but the Howard Government has not committed to them. The MDGs must be adopted for Australia, where they are not met in many Indigenous communities and other impoverished locations; they should also be the focus of Australia's aid program.

Many impoverished developing countries are caught in a poverty trap: they do not have the capacity to generate sufficient domestic savings and investment, or an economy that is attractive to foreign investors, or even the resources or industry to trade their way out of poverty. So they require increased aid to fund infrastructure and services essential to their economic and social development. Australia could readily increase aid to them because our national income has been growing rapidly, there is no Commonwealth Government debt, and the Budget is in surplus. Australia occupies a unique global position because of the intersection of our history, geography, economy, society and culture with those of developing countries, yet we are not being responsive to their needs. The swift public contributions to disaster relief after the 2004 tsunami demonstrated clearly that voters would support increased government aid for poverty reduction.

In 2005, Australian aid was still only 0.25 per cent of national income compared with the *average* for all donor countries of 0.47 per cent. Government plans would only increase aid to around 0.35 per cent by 2010, at the most. This would be half the UN target of 0.7 per cent and not even two-thirds of the EU countries' commitment of 0.56 per cent by 2010. We need to prepare a new strategy of Australian aid, one that includes our impoverished neighbours across the Indian Ocean in Africa, and set targets so that we accept a fair share of developed countries' responsibility for achieving the MDGs. When Nelson Mandela visited Australia in 1990 he appealed for assistance to non-racial sports bodies and to education, technology, management, health and culture: 'We depend on your assistance to help us to attain equality, not only in our country but in the community of nations universally.' The words of Jeffrey Sachs, Director of the Earth Institute at Columbia University, to his American compatriots in 2006 apply equally to Australia:

> We stand by as millions die each year because they are too poor to stay alive. The inattention and neglect of our policy leaders lull us to believe casually that nothing more can be done. Meanwhile we spend hundreds of billions of dollars per year on military interventions doomed to fail, overlooking the fact that a small proportion of that money, if it were directed at development approaches, could save millions of lives and set entire regions on a path of economic growth.[20]

An effective strategy for international development would benefit from new sources of finance to fund economic development. Early in 2006 many countries supported a proposal by France for introduction of a levy on air travel to raise funds for development, the first such internationally agreed national tax to generate additional finance for development. It is an extraordinary anomaly that airline fuel has been exempt from tax since just after the end of World War II. Many other innovative sources of financing, for these and other goals, are being discussed, including a carbon tax and a currency transaction tax (Tobin tax); research into and debate about them continue to grow.[21]

Seventh, there is a major democratic deficit in the structure of international economic and financial institutions because of the disproportionate dominance of developed countries. The existing institutions are either exclusive, such as the G8 and the OECD, have unbalanced membership, such as the World Bank and the IMF, or are insufficiently timely and decisive, such as the current working arrangements of the UN Economic and Social Council (ECOSOC).[22] In 2001 the UN Secretary-General appointed a high-level panel chaired by Ernesto Zedillo, former president of Mexico, to examine global economic governance and provision of finance for development. In its report the Zedillo panel argued that:

> despite recent worthy efforts, the world has no fully satisfactory
> mechanism to anticipate and counter global economic shocks ... Global
> economic decision-making has become increasingly concentrated in
> a few countries. Tensions have worsened as a result. For a range of
> common problems, the world has no formal institutional mechanism to
> ensure that voices representing all relevant parts are heard.[23]

The Zedillo panel proposed the creation of:

> a global council at the highest political level to provide leadership on
> issues of global governance ... it would provide a long-term strategic
> policy framework to promote development, secure consistency in the
> policy goals of the major international organisations and promote
> consensus building among governments on possible solutions for
> issues of global economic and social governance.[24]

In addition, the panel suggested that ECOSOC should be upgraded.

Reform of the structures of governance of the international financial institutions is also essential, and is widely supported. Governance of both the IMF and the World Bank is asymmetrical and unequal: the lenders are the principal shareholders and the borrowers provide the income. Since 1945, voting strength has shifted towards the developed countries, which now have about 61 per cent of the votes of both the IMF and the World Bank. This ensures that they have a controlling influence over the policies of both institutions. Increasing the representation of developing countries even further would involve changing quotas and voting rights. If this were achieved, it could be expected to lead to more rigorous evaluation of the conditions which the World Bank and the IMF impose on developing countries, some of which have contributed to decline rather than growth.[25]

Surely Australia has sufficient interest in discussions about development and international economic governance to warrant participation in them? All Australian governments since World War II have been actively involved with all aspects of the multilateral system – until the last decade. A couple of decades ago Australia led the way in the establishment of the regional Asia Pacific Economic Cooperation (APEC) forum. There is a tendency amongst some Australians to be fearful of the rest of the world and to withdraw behind the Bush Administration. Yet the Australian economy is the 14th largest in the world. In the past we have been influential, and we could be again. Our influence would increase if we once again exhibited autonomy and participated in global discussions as an independent agent.

Finally, the eighth suggestion is for governments to demonstrate renewal of Australia's traditional commitment to multilateralism through improved accountability. Australia has always paid its dues to the United Nations on time, which is something for which we can be grateful. But in addition, the Minister for Foreign Affairs could make regular statements to Parliament on Australian action at the United Nations, and other ministers could report on action at the World Bank and the IMF, the ILO, the WHO, UNESCO and so on. Such statements should include a record of how Australia voted. They could provide much of the material for campaigns to inform the public about the purposes, work, achievements and difficulties of the UN system.

Australian governments and NGOs could do much to educate the public about the value of the incremental improvements in global policy that are agreed to at UN meetings. Most people have heard of some achievements of the UN system, such as peacekeeping, eliminating smallpox, controlling SARS, providing relief in emergencies and setting environmental, human rights and labour standards. Fewer are aware of the good news in the *Human security report*, published in late 2005, which found that there has been a dramatic decrease in the number of conflicts and mass killings, an even more striking decrease in the number of battle deaths and a complete turnaround in the number of conflicts peacefully resolved.[26] Since the early 1990s, there has been an 80 per cent decrease in the number of conflicts causing 1000 or more battle deaths in a year. More civil wars have been ended by negotiation in the past 15 years than in the previous two centuries. There are many reasons for this striking improvement, including the end of colonialism and of the Cold War, and the decline in the number of authoritarian governments. But the main reason is just that there has been a huge increase in the international effort to prevent, manage and resolve conflicts. For example, between 1990 and 2002 the number of UN diplomatic missions aimed at preventing wars increased sixfold.

International discussion of issues such as these eight has been relegated to the margin or paralysed by American unilateralism, but the election of Democratic majorities to Congress in November 2006 created many new possibilities. For example, the United States may start to pay its dues to the United Nations on time, and so be up to date with a central part of its legal obligations to the rest of the world for only the second time for a decade and a half. When Ban Ki-Moon took office as the UN Secretary-General on 1 January 2007 he offered a fresh symbol of leadership, adding to the possibility of improved collaboration between the United States and the rest of the world (including Australia) through the United Nations. Innumerable issues are waiting to be addressed. Australia's circumstances lead naturally to rethinking our foreign policy and to advocating strengthening of the international rule of law, upgrading our contribution to nuclear disarmament, reducing GHG emissions and fostering equitable development, and in all these ways contributing to international peace and justice.

chapter 7

revitalising australian democracy

The citizen is at the heart of a properly functioning democracy. Indeed the core principles of democracy are popular control over public decision making and political equality ... It is crucial that decision making is not left to a small minority with privileged access to influence and power ... Free speech, transparency of government operations and diverse media sources are all essential to achieving these ends. So are fair dealing between government and citizens and high standards of ethical behaviour by officials.

Carmen Lawrence, 2005[1]

What would a revitalised democracy look like? Political scientist Anthony Arblaster reminds us that through most of history the idea of democracy actually meant what we now call 'direct' democracy – namely people governing themselves through participation in the processes of decision-taking and policy-making. The representative type of democracy we are now familiar with was a relatively late arrival on the scene.[2] In Australia, as in many other parts of the world, the passions and high hopes which were associated with first winning the right to vote have been disappointed as voting has become an act of limited influence in a process dominated by professional politicians. Direct, or participatory, democracy implies far greater involvement by citizens in debate, through influential membership of a wide variety of organisations, movements, community action groups and parties. Politics can have a civilising influence. It is 'a way of ruling divided societies without undue violence'.[3]

Arblaster emphasises how wide the gap is between the ideal of a fully democratic society and the realities of the Western democracies of today. Democracy, he argues, remains a relevant ideal and a challenge to conventional political thinking, because 'representative or indirect democracy is at best an inadequate substitute for personal participation'.[4] There are obvious practical obstacles to applying the ideal of participatory democracy to large, modern societies faced with complex problems. However, while it is true that we can't all fit into one room as a mass assembly, technology makes it possible to link citizens in new ways. Television and the internet have led to new forms of participation which do not depend on physically meeting together. Instead we can form virtual assemblies. As Arblaster points out, 'modern technology has made the direct participation of the people in political debate and decision-making a perfectly practicable possibility'.[5] This is a possibility we could aim to explore and realise.

Australia's democracy is not healthy at present; nor is the quality of public life high. The principal characteristic of contemporary Australian politics is voters' disengagement. Most Australians aren't following national politics. Pollsters Saulwick and Muller report that 'Generation Y', the 16 to 24-year-olds, is living 'as though politics did not exist'.[6]

This may be overstating the situation, because there are numbers of vigorous issue-focused organisations run by young people with a passion for social justice, housing, environmental sustainability, international development, human rights, the United Nations and so on. Nevertheless, disenchantment is widespread – and not only in that age group. Reasons probably include accumulated loss of confidence in the parties; personal dislikes; distrust of one or other or all the parties; the apparently invincible dominance of one party for more than a decade; and the length of the economic upswing. Sixty per cent of Australians believe that the Federal Government is entirely or mostly run for a few big interests.[7] Globalisation is widely perceived as reducing Australian sovereignty and our capacity to control our destiny. James Walter, Professor of Political Science at Monash University, has written about the widespread view that 'liberal internationalism … comes to constitute a veto on local politics, crowding out alternatives and destroying political imagination'.[8] The sense of powerlessness about national and international affairs, and the horror of the violence and destruction in Iraq (and many other places), are so disturbing that many simply turn off the news. However, political discussion has been somewhat resuscitated by the election of Kevin Rudd as leader of the Parliamentary Labor Party and the approach of the 2007 national election.

It could be argued that lack of concern about politics simply reflects general satisfaction with the times. 'The economy is growing steadily, so leave it to the government', seems to be a common attitude. Others find the professionalism of politics alienating. Some analysts believe that disengagement is due not only to loss of confidence in political processes, but also to declining trust more generally within society – though the evidence is ambiguous. Confidence in institutions such as companies, police forces, churches and universities fell during the last decade, but that does not mean that interpersonal trust has declined.[9] For whatever combination of these reasons, the normal tendency to parochialism has been intensified: we all tend to be preoccupied with personal survival and growth, with family, friendships, work, sport and other leisure activities. The times are so anguishing for some, alienating for others, frightening for a few and disempowering for many that a high proportion just withdraw. 'Consumers prefer home renovations to politics; material indulgence to the exercise of social conscience,' concludes Hugh Mackay.[10]

Australia is not alone in experiencing voter disengagement. There were substantial falls in voter turnout between the 1960s and around 2000 in such countries as the Netherlands (where voter turnout fell 19 per cent), Switzerland (33 per cent), the United Kingdom (16 per cent) and the United States (26 per cent).[11] Despite being political system innovators a century ago, Australians have not been noted for the extent of our political engagement, though voter turnout is naturally high because of compulsory voting. In the federal elections in 2004, 94 per cent of those eligible voted, the second highest level of voter turnout in OECD countries.[12] This does not, however, contradict the opinion poll evidence of extensive political disengagement.

Threats to Australian democracy

Increasing disengagement is not an accident, for during the last decade there has been a sustained attempt by the Commonwealth Government to suppress public discussion and manipulate political processes. A royal court has run government. The king, John Howard, and the courtiers in his office have dominated Commonwealth public policy. Regal authoritarianism has eroded the openness, vitality and maturity of Australian political processes. The executive has been dominant and Parliament has had little independence. As will be shown, Senate Committees have been decimated; incumbent members of Parliament have been entrenched; fears have been exaggerated; civil liberties, including freedom of expression, have been curtailed; the use of political propaganda has exploded; the public service has been disempowered; and many community organisations have been bullied into silence. Even the High Court has cooperated in strengthening Commonwealth powers. Justice Kirby noted in his minority comment in the industrial relations case that the majority decision did not baulk at giving the executive an exceptional range of power to act without approval from the Parliament.

After 1 July 2005, when the Howard Government's majority in the Senate became operative, the Senate's capacity for rigorous scrutiny and review of government activity was decimated, further reducing the transparency and accountability of the Federal Government. The passage of legislation became a sausage machine.[13] The number of Senate Committees was reduced from 16 to 8. The number and length of inquiries was cut: a notable example was the derisory two days of hearings on media policy in September 2006. The government now chooses which issues will be reviewed, how reviews will be conducted, for how long they will last and who will be allowed to give evidence. Public servants have been forbidden to answer questions during the Senate Estimates Committee hearings and the length of those hearings has been reduced. Access by Australians to committee hearings has also been strangled. During 2005 the Law Council of Australia, the Vice-Chancellors of Australian universities and the major churches and peak charitable organisations were all prevented from presenting evidence in particular inquiries. The Law Council wanted to argue that sedition laws are dangerous, the churches that the industrial relations laws are anti-family and the peak welfare groups that the welfare to work changes hurt the already poor.

Incumbent members of Parliament are being entrenched. Parliamentary entitlements have been sharply increased, giving sitting members – the majority of whom are from the governing parties, of course – major advantages over other candidates. MPs now receive annual printing allowances of $150,000. The annual postage allowance was increased in 2005 from $27,500 to $45,000. Unused portions of these allowances can be rolled over to election years, when rules explicitly allow them to be used for printing of how-to-vote cards. 'Unfortunately, such increases blur the boundary between the legitimate needs of an effective member of parliament, and the illegitimate use of incumbency to further partisan interests,' comments ANU academic Norm Kelly.[14]

Recent legislative changes have reduced electoral impartiality. The *Electoral and Referendum Amendment (Electoral Integrity and Other Measures) Act 2006* (Cth) – another example of new-speak – could only be passed after the Coalition won control of the Senate. It involved steps towards the Americanisation of the Australian electoral system. Colin Hughes (Australia's first electoral commissioner) and Brian Costar (a professor of parliamentary democracy) write that:

> it is regrettable that some members of ... the Liberal Party ... now seem to regard their party as the south-west Pacific version of the Republican Party – or at least its Texan branch – and want to import some of the least democratic elements of the United States' electoral procedures.[15]

The Act closes the electoral rolls on the day on which the Prime Minister decides to advise the Governor-General to call an election – which is, of course, entirely unpredictable – and reduces to three days the time available to existing voters to update their enrolment. Before the last election over 400,000 people enrolled or updated their enrolment during the seven days they had after the election was called. Those who leave enrolment until after an election is announced are now not able to vote in that election. Extra proof of identity is required when applying to enrol. All convicted prisoners have been deprived of the right to vote, a move which flies in the face of modern thinking, which acknowledges the benefits of preparing prisoners for their move back into society by restoring their responsibilities as members of the community. It disproportionately impacts on young males (men make up 93 per cent of the prison population), and particularly Indigenous male Australians, who are imprisoned at 12 times the non-Indigenous rate.[16]

The legislation also addresses what Associate Professor Graeme Orr, of the Griffith University Law School, calls 'the single greatest issue confronting elections in the developed world ... the influence of private money' by in fact reducing transparency.[17] The threshold at which political donations have to be declared was raised from $1500 to $10,000, and this upper level is indexed to the rate of inflation, allowing donors greater and increasing secrecy. This means that donations from corporations and the wealthy are less rigorously scrutinised, even though those from trade unions face a more stringent disclosure regime. This legislation was not only opposed by Labor, the Greens and the Democrats; it was also criticised by the non-partisan Australian Electoral Commission. Hughes and Costar contend that 'the Coalition's 2006 legislation aims to solve problems that do not exist, and ... its effect is anti-democratic'.[18] As soon as electoral circumstances allow, Labor, Greens and Democrats must collaborate in repealing this regressive legislation. They might also consider banning foreign donations and setting upper limits on donations from all entities.

One of John Howard's commonest campaign tactics is to exaggerate threats. Carmen Lawrence writes accurately that 'this is amongst the most secretive of governments, more interested in manipulating people's fears than [in] taking them on as partners in public policy'.[19] Fear has always been a powerful element of Australian politics: of the French in the earliest years of British settlement, of Asians until the 1960s, of Communists during the Cold War, and, during the last decade, of asylum seekers and terrorists. Authoritarian leaders have often fanned the fears of their citizens so as to control them more easily. Security is a major growth industry. Fear of terrorism has provided the rationale for sharply reducing civil liberties. The Law Council of Australia, which speaks on behalf of the Law Societies and Bar Associations of every state and territory, objected to the government's 2005 anti-terrorism legislation, particularly to the introduction of control and preventive detention orders. 'The legislation offends our traditional rights and freedoms. The laws have properly been described as draconian. The justification advanced for their introduction has been meagre,' the Law Society wrote in a letter to the Prime Minister. The annual Press Freedom Index for 2006 moved Australia from 31st to 35th place 'because of anti-terrorist laws potentially dangerous for journalists'.[20] The Australian Society of Authors continues to oppose the sedition provisions because they threaten freedom of expression. 'We appear to be moving from liberal democracy towards the national security state,' writes *Australian Financial Review* journalist Geoffrey Barker.[21] Passage of this legislation demonstrates why introducing a charter of basic rights and freedoms in a Human Rights Act is essential to protect Australians' liberties.[22]

Unprecedented amounts of public money have been spent by the Federal Government on nakedly partisan advertising. Between 1996 and 2005 the Howard Government spent $1062 million on advertising, including $95 million on the advertising blitz before the 2004 election.[23] During 2005–06, $40 million of public funds was spent on advocacy for the controversial 'WorkChoices' legislation alone. The Auditor-General and parliamentary committees have made recommendations for guidelines to prevent misuse of public funds for partisan advertising, but so far no Australian government has introduced laws requiring (or even allowing) scrutiny of government advertising prior to publication. This improper, manipulative expenditure is another of the cascade of American practices designed to manipulate the electorate that has been imported. Others have included negative advertising and push-polling (in which respondents are asked questions of the 'what-do-you-think-about-x-beating-his-wife?' type to spread rumours which have no factual basis), which were introduced by Liberal Party officials after visits by their staff to the United States in the early 1990s. Another irritating example is the closing of all Commonwealth government bookshops, which increases the difficulty and cost of obtaining information and analysis about the basis for policies.

Long before these regressive changes, the Australian national Parliament was already less influential than legislatures in other democratic countries. A clear example of this is that neither the House nor the Senate can make a dollar of difference to the Budget. Once the Prime Minister and Cabinet are elected by the party which wins government, they have autocratic control of the money until the next election – unless they don't control the Senate. In that situation, the Senate can delay passage of the Budget but senators still cannot amend the Budget without the government's agreement because any amendments also have to be passed by the House.

In other areas Prime Minister Howard often makes decisions that have been planned and reviewed only by ministerial staff, thus excluding even the public service. Ministers often do not consult adequately with their senior departmental staff. This disenfranchises public servants, and makes them tentative, hesitant and reluctant to speak their mind.

This is all far more pronounced under Howard than under Keating. Impartial advice is no longer sought; ideas about ways of implementing the government's ideology are all that is asked for. Other views from within the public service and from experts or interested groups in the community are commonly not sought or are neglected. This tends to cause public service advice to become partisan. Appointments to boards, commissions and other advisory bodies go only to those who share the government's ideological positions. Members of advisory bodies who are not sufficiently 'blue' (conservative) are replaced or neglected when making new appointments.

Public comment by civil society has been repressed.[24] The government is hostile to NGOs, an attitude fanned by the Institute for Public Affairs (IPA), which received $50,000 from the Howard Government to study NGOs. This was like letting a cat carry out a study of the habits of mice. NGOs are being threatened with loss of tax deductibility for contributors or having their public funding cut or abolished if they criticise government policy. The Australian Pensioners' and Superannuants' Federation, National Shelter, the Association of Civilian Widows and the Australian Youth Policy and Action Coalition lost their funding. The UN Association of Australia was receiving $100,000 a year in the mid-1990s; that was cut to $8000 a year shortly after the Howard Government was elected and even that was withdrawn at the end of the decade. Organisations undertaking work for the Federal Government sometimes have confidentiality clauses in their contracts which prevent them commenting publicly on any aspect of public policy. Critical comment by churches, welfare and environmental organisations is commonly met with ministerial abuse rather than openness to dialogue.

Journalist Margo Kingston did not exaggerate when describing the government's 'five-phase plan' to shut NGOs up or shut them down as: first, stop funding NGOs that speak out, thus intimidating others into silence; second, strip activist NGOs of charitable tax status; third, set up a government 'non-government organisation'; fourth, use public service and 'intelligence' organisations to spy on awkward NGOs; and fifth, require NGOs to qualify for a 'licence' to talk to government.[25]

This contrasts starkly with Howard's remark after the 1996 election that more people would now 'feel able to speak a little more freely and a little more openly'. Coalition tactics may be silencing some groups, but resentment is growing. NGOs working for economic and social development in developing countries, for example, describe their relationship with the government as having changed from partnership to subcontracting – 'like having a gardening contract'.

The deterioration in the quality and vigour of analysis and public discourse in Australia is a direct consequence of these destructive policies. Many Australians think the American people have conformed to President Bush's policies, but there is greater intensity and vigour in the critique of Bush in the United States than there is of Howard in Australia. It is a national tragedy that passionate, sustained critiques of political ideology and its consequences are so rarely heard now in Australia.

Concern about political disengagement is justified because uninformed voters are less able to make well-judged choices about their representatives and leaders. Many argue that this is what has happened in Australia during the last couple of elections. Such a weak democracy is more likely to be manipulated by particular interests and to be unresponsive to marginalised groups. There is clearly a link between being uninformed and being more easily manipulated. When information is readily available and there is a commitment to truth-telling, spin is easier to detect and dismiss. Since disengagement is particularly pronounced among the young, there is a great risk that alienation might become cumulative and increasingly difficult to change.[26]

Consequences of growing media concentration

The media are the most powerful influence in a democratic society. Some aspects of the Australian media exacerbate political disengagement. The most notable feature of Australian media is the concentration of ownership: Rupert Murdoch, Kerry Stokes, the foreign owners of the former Packer company Publishing and Broadcasting Ltd, and Fairfax control most of it. 'Murdoch is arguably the world's most powerful media executive,' writes John Cassidy in *The New Yorker*:

> His company, News Corporation, owns Fox Broadcasting network, the Twentieth Century Fox film studio, the book publisher HarperCollins, the *Post*, *The Weekly Standard*, MySpace, and part of DirecTV, the biggest satellite-television provider in the country. News Corp. also owns five British newspapers and more than a hundred and ten Australian newspapers, and controls satellite-television providers in Britain, Italy, and Asia.[27]

Ownership of media is more concentrated in Australia than it is in any other developed country, with the possible exception of Italy. News Corp. alone owns about 70 per cent of Australia's newspapers. Over 80 per cent of Australians believe that media ownership in Australia is too concentrated among a few rich families. Media conglomerates have become propaganda arms of government in return for regulatory advantages such as relaxation of ownership limits. Robert Manne comments, 'Without the backing of News Corporation before, during and after the invasion of Iraq, it is hard to see how a blunder as comprehensive as Howard's could have had so little impact on his reputation and that of his government.'[28] Such support explains the Howard Government's wish to change the media laws in order to allow further increases in concentration of media ownership. Clear Channel, the radio network that owns 1200 stations in the United States and which has an interest in eight stations in Australia (these currently have an audience reach of half the population), also has a strongly conservative ideological position. Most major metropolitan Australian newspapers habitually advise readers to vote for the Coalition parties at election time – none regularly commends Labor – and only the ABC, SBS, some Fairfax staff and a few journalists in other companies attempt to cover all significant points of view. Since every corporation has its own subculture, diversity of ownership is a necessary – though not sufficient – condition for achieving diversity of content.

The government's *Broadcasting Services Amendment (Media Ownership) Act 2006* (Cth) facilitates further concentration of ownership. Reduction of restrictions on cross-media ownership allowed media proprietors to expand from one of the main forms of commercial media – television, radio and daily newspapers – to consolidation of any two of them, provided there continued to be five media owners in metropolitan areas and four in regional centres. The Communications Law Centre concluded that this latter test of a 'minimum number of commercial media groups … would not prevent the formation of virtual monopolies of the major sources of news and information in large regional centres, where broadband take-up is lower than in the cities, and the local newspaper is particularly valued'.[29] The *Sydney Morning Herald* editorialised that 'Media policy should be about improved choice … The Government has yet to explain how … consolidation could improve the consumer's choice one jot.'[30] The Act suggests that the Howard Government intended to entrench conservative opinion by reducing the range of opinion expressed in Australian media. The Digital Television Act, which was introduced at the same time, also politicises the allocation of media licences by requiring ministerial approval of new commercial digital free-to-air television licences. The reduction of opportunities for public discourse in the mainstream media represents a sinister erosion of freedom of expression.

The government's argument for all this was that it would enable the mainstream media to strengthen its competitiveness with new web-based media. Pamphleteering is certainly prospering through weblogs. New York University academic Jay Rosen argues that 'Freedom of the press belongs to those who own one, and blogging means anyone can own one', though he thinks that does not mean declining influence for professional journalists.[31] Writer Lance Knobel, former adviser to the Prime Minister's Strategy Unit in London, lists four internet innovations creating a new democratisation: blogs; Wikipedia, which depends on users to add content; Google; and Really Simple Syndication (RSS), which allows new feeds to be constructed from content on a website.[32] The estimated 8.5 million weblogs in 2005 compete for attention, but unless they are reported in mainstream media their influence is small. Television, newspapers and radio are the main source of domestic news and current affairs for over 95 per cent of the population; 3 per cent report that the internet is their main source of news. About 75 per cent currently never or rarely use the internet as their main source of news.[33] Of the quarter of the population who access the internet on a fairly regular basis for news, about 90 per cent rely on websites associated with mainstream media providers, at least partly because they are free, presumably: only 1 per cent of Australians rely on the alternatives that cost money. 'None of the new species of media will have anywhere near the power of today's proprietor-controlled media,' concludes Eric Beecher, publisher of the online daily newsletter *Crikey.com* and former editor-in-chief of the Melbourne *Herald and Weekly Times*, though (not surprisingly) he goes on to say that 'their cumulative effect could be devastating'.[34]

The assertion that competition policy will prevent undue concentration of media ownership is inherently unpersuasive, given past experience, but as well, the Trade Practices Act was weakened by amendments in October 2006 that tend to enable big business mergers and acquisitions, including those among media companies.

There is particularly strong ideological assertiveness on radio programs such as those of John Laws and Alan Jones. Hendrik Hertzberg, an editorial writer for *The New Yorker*, vividly describes US right-wing radio as:

> niche entertainment for the spiritually unattractive. It succeeds because a substantial segment of the right-wing rank and file enjoys listening, hour after hour, as smug, angry, disdainful middle-aged men spew raw contempt at reified enemies, named and unnamed. To the chronically resentful, they offer the sadistic consolation of an endless sneer.[35]

This is a cause not only for criticism, but also for regret – that so many people have lives cramped by such a sense of injustice and marginalisation. The very existence of such programs in Australia is a challenge to all who care about society to work for greater fairness and inclusiveness.[36]

As in the United States, many parts of the Australian media exaggerate threats and therefore also audience fears.[37] Most media outlets concentrate on reporting conflict, violence and destruction. They thrive during crises and scandals. Relentless negative reporting about politics undermines confidence in institutions and politicians. Non-government views receive disproportionately little space in the news programs and pages of the mainstream media.

'The commercial interests of media owners are in conflict with the interests of good journalism,' says Beecher.[38] Advertising is integrating with entertainment and even news, eliminating boundaries to such an extent that distortion and spin are becoming endemic in reporting in all sorts of areas beyond the political. Many news outlets seem more interested in entertaining their audiences than in informing them. Australian newspapers attempt to lighten their content by entertaining readers, but this makes them less useful in delivering news, so fewer people bother to read them. Celebrity is worshipped, image is celebrated and spin has become the norm. When Britney Spears shaves her head it's a leading news story. Writing about the United States, John Stacks, a former deputy managing editor of *Time* magazine, concludes that 'The democratic ideal of an informed electorate is dying before our eyes.'[39] Is that equally true of Australia?

The financial starvation of the ABC and SBS is also restricting public discourse. The government's determination to achieve ideological control is demonstrated by appointments to the ABC Board of doctrinaire critics, abandoning even the pretence of impartiality. The government's habitual vilification of the ABC has had an impact. ABC news bulletins spend more time on court cases, accidents and other local violence than on state, national or international issues. The establishment of yet another level of editorial scrutiny through the appointment of a Director of Editorial Policy risks restricting opinion and increasing self-censorship even further, so strengthening authoritarian control. Journalist and writer Margaret Simons comments, realistically, that:

> under attack, the ABC not only jumps through many, many
> accountability hoops already there, but adds a few new ones to show
> what a good dog it can be ... The Australian people certainly don't

think the ABC is biased ... But Mark Scott [the Managing Director] says public regard is not enough. There is criticism; therefore new hoops must be jumped through. 'Beat me, beat me,' he seems to be saying.'[40]

Yet even though the ABC and SBS have been assaulted and wounded, they continue to be valuable sources of intelligent analysis and cultural expression. SBS transmits the highest quality television news in the country.

The severity of these constraints on Australian journalists makes the achievements of some even more impressive. Every year the UN Association of Australia organises Media Peace Awards for reports which increase understanding of situations of conflict and deprivation. The entries cover issues relating to Aboriginal reconciliation, multiculturalism, treatment of refugees, the rights and image of older people, women and children in Australia as well as civil conflict in Sudan, Timor Leste and West Papua and the consequences of the invasions of Afghanistan and Iraq. The reports may be disturbing, but they are also moving, and they remind us that a significant number of Australian print, television and radio journalists continue to produce imaginative, high quality, intelligent and humane reports despite the organisational bias and parochialism with which they have to cope. For example, in 2006 the judges described a series by *Sydney Morning Herald* journalist Paul McGeough on *Death and Democracy: The uncertainty of life after 9/11* relating to Afghanistan, Iraq and Lebanon as 'magisterial', covering the political and the personal with such 'overwhelming power and perception that [it] sets a new standard of Australian journalism'.

Fortunately, in recent years there has been a striking growth of new and upgraded magazine publishing about public affairs, including the *Australian Quarterly Essays* series, *The Monthly*, *The Griffith Review*, *Dissent* and *Australian Book Review*, in addition to important long-standing magazines and journals such as *Arena*, *Meanjin*, *Eureka Street*, *Ecos* and *Overland*. Several publishing houses have launched series of short books, including Briefings by UNSW Press, Australia Now by Pluto Press, Small Books by Scribe and the Alfred Deakin Debate by

Miegunyah Press, an imprint of Melbourne University Publishing. Though these reach comparatively small numbers of readers, they nevertheless inform and influence opinion. Writing this book would have been far more difficult without access to the weekly emails from Australian Policy Online and On Line Opinion. Peter Browne and his colleagues working on Australian Policy Online have designed an indispensable tool for everyone involved in policy analysis and design. Others, such as *New Matilda*, the *Australian Review of Public Affairs*, and *Creative Economy* are also valuable. Community media, radio, television and newspapers can also be influential locally.

This discussion suggests some clear strategies for strengthening democratic discourse. Parliamentary responsibility for its own affairs should be strengthened. The Senate Committee system should be revitalised to enable more genuinely bipartisan and truly revelatory inquiries, such as that which concluded in 2005 on the abuse of children in institutional care. Much closer attention and increased funding for education at all levels is vital, as outlined in Chapter 4. Sharply increasing support for impartial analytical research and publication is essential. Ending the financial starvation of the ABC and SBS is crucial. All ABC and SBS Board positions should be advertised, and appointments made by an independent selection committee or an all-party parliamentary committee, as Labor is proposing to do.

An unequivocal commitment to increasing media diversity is the highest priority. If Howard's media Acts have not been implemented when the government or control of the Senate changes, the Acts should be immediately amended to the maximum extent possible. Establishment of a Commonwealth fund to which new media companies could apply for support would be a cost-effective means of facilitating growth of media diversity. (Such financial support exists in Canada.) Kerry Stokes' 14.9 per cent ownership of WA Newspapers must be rigorously reviewed, because if it is approved, it would give him control or great influence on the two principal media outlets in Perth. An independent commission or multi-party parliamentary inquiry should be swiftly set up to analyse alternatives and make recommendations.

Political mobilisation and a republic

Despite the general trend of decline in US presidential election voter turnout during recent decades, it rose from 51 per cent in 2000 to 55 per cent in 2004.[41] Both Democrats and Republicans thought that issues of life and death, reality and delusion, as well as personal wellbeing were at stake in that election. People naturally participate more actively when outcomes matter to them, when anger or hope are strong. Australians are currently neither angry enough nor hopeful enough, and without the goad of one and the promise of the other, political imagination has been stifled.[42]

The moral dimension of wider issues has been missing from Australian political debate (though issues of sexual morality have been prominent in the rhetoric of some politicians). Many politicians in both major party groupings believe that votes are determined by self-interest alone, so they appeal only to local, narrow, selfish concerns. But in fact we are all a mixture of self-interest and altruism. Voters typically want MPs who not only represent their interests but who also lead in identifying cost-effective ways of strengthening security, freedom, fairness and vitality for Australians – and often for peoples in other nations as well. As David Williamson, storyteller to the tribe, says, 'there's still some idealism left that the world should be a better place … [and recognition that] the world is unequal and unjust'.[43]

Principles matter. The overwhelming support for Cathy Freeman's gestures of commitment to the rights of Indigenous peoples was not only a reflection of the euphoria about her victory but also a strong emotional endorsement of the justice of her actions. The intensity of the grief about Steve Irwin's death was not only about the shocking loss of a man with extraordinary vitality and flair for publicity, but also reflected support for his concern for the environment. When Olympian Peter Norman died in October 2006, Australians recognised his commitment to social justice. They celebrated the moral resolve he showed in raising his fist in support of the two African-American sprinters with whom he shared the victory dais at the 1968 Mexico City Olympics.

The majority of voters have plenty of commonsense. They recognise insincerity and self-interest and take that into account when they vote. Of course many factors influence voting choices. Fear can overwhelm hope and self-interest altruism. Yet for most of the last quarter century neither major party grouping has attempted to appeal to voters' altruism or desire for truth and principle. There is considerably more courage and principle on all sides of Parliament than is generally acknowledged, but it is less often recognised and celebrated than is healthy. So unease, discontent and resentment continue to grow in different parts of the electorate. In the last couple of decades comprehensive political dialogue has been paralysed. That appearance is misleading, though: a struggle has been continuing, but many of the issues have been hidden or neglected and so have failed to ignite engagement. Any political party will increase its attractiveness when there is a moral dimension to its policies, such as commitment to integrity and social justice, and when there is a direct appeal to voters' altruism.

Participation is also greater when institutions have legitimacy. For the young, 'legitimacy based on inclusion is replacing legitimacy based on hierarchical authority', write leading American international relations scholars Professors Joseph Nye and Philip Zelikow.[44] One of the principal arguments made by supporters of an Australian republic is that it would be more inclusive, replacing a monarch living on the opposite side of the world to whom Australians not of British origin have little natural loyalty with an Australian citizen who lives here and is capable of reflecting the country's ethnic and cultural diversity. The president of an Australian republic would be a living symbol of our national uniqueness and unity. Establishment of an Australian republic would increase our sense of autonomy and could contribute to strengthening our egalitarian and democratic traditions.[45] Many supporters hoped that the debate would provide an opportunity for articulating a new political direction for Australia, reflecting the varied political and cultural traditions of our diverse countries of origin. In any renewal of the campaign for a republic the first difficulty to be overcome is reaching agreement on how to elect a president. A promising possibility would be election by all voters from a shortlist of candidates selected by a bipartisan committee. A necessary pre-condition is a Prime Minister and Leader of the Opposition united in supporting a republic.

Strengthening the effectiveness of Parliament is vital to renewing the legitimacy of political processes, for Parliament is the 'one institution in the political structure with the formal standing and authority to renew the link between the Australian community and the formal policy-making system'.[46] Many aspects of Parliament need reform, including the proceedings of the chambers, their committee systems and party functioning. For example, despite the growth in the proportion of female members and senators, the continuing macho style of parliamentary debate discredits the institution. Abuse, obstruction, contrivance, hyperbole and irrelevance characterise question time. Question time has become a debating bear pit where points are scored for the most original and memorable forms of abuse and where the intellectual persuasiveness of the argument, its historical foundations or its philosophical rigour count for little. The search for, or provision of, information is only rarely the purpose of the questioner or answerer.[47] Many listeners are repelled. Some parents said that they would not let their children attend or listen to the House because of Keating's rudeness. Children said they would be sent out of the classroom for behaving like members. Yet the journalists reward such behaviour with their admiration. The quality of debate is even poorer now than it was in Keating's time. Wit and mockery can be powerful ingredients in political repartee, but abuse has no place.

Change in the culture of Australian parliamentary debate cannot be legislated. It depends on leadership, incentives and the choices of individual members. If ministers won the warmest praise from the media and voters for the intelligence, relevance and succinctness of their answers the quality would improve. Strengthening the impartiality of the speakership, by agreement not to contest the Speaker's re-election, could increase the fairness and rigour with which question time and debates are chaired. The difference in tone of parliamentary debates in countries where proportional representation requires the formation of governing coalitions is striking, because all members know that they may have to cooperate with each other at some time. Even the House of Commons has considerably less of the personal abuse and irrelevant posturing which are so frequent in the Australian Parliament.

Many improvements in both the representational capacity of Parliament and the quality of political debate could flow from one simple but difficult change: abandonment of the Caucus solidarity rule by the Labor Party. At present Labor members can be expelled from the party for voting against a Caucus decision. Caucus dynamics normally ensures that this means the Labor leader gets his (and so far it has always been his rather than her) way. For a party which has split three times, the rule has a clear justification: it was intended to ensure members' adherence to the party platform. That was when Labor Prime Ministers still saw themselves as bound by the platform. Party discipline is very important, it's true: no member is omniscient, and collective decision-making can often better allow various interests and views to be considered. But the importance of the capacity to dissent from misguided Cabinet decisions was vividly demonstrated by the Liberals who dissented from the Howard Government's migration amendments in 2006 (they involved indefinite detention of asylum seekers without trial). Making a fetish of Caucus solidarity is a false god and the rule should be amended. Some loosening of party solidarity could make Parliament a more genuinely vigorous forum.

Parliamentary committees are a channel between the public and policy-makers. They also enable MPs and senators to focus careful attention on rigorous inquiry about high-priority issues, including major strategic questions. Until 1987 the House of Representatives had only a few committees, covering only a third of the Commonwealth's responsibilities. A comprehensive committee system was established in the Senate early in the 1970s but was resisted in the House by both major parties because both believed committees might be used to criticise the government. The Hawke Government favoured reform in principle, and after the 1987 election the writer proposed change: a Labor Party committee was elected which conducted discussions and won acceptance for the first comprehensive system of committees for the House.[48] The new system was judged a major step forward for the House.

Still further reforms are required because both governments and the public service have many ways of constraining committees and of resisting their recommendations. Subjects referred to committees have to be approved by ministers beforehand, for one. For another, governments dispense patronage through their control of committee funding and staffing and thus of the committees' capacity for analysis, research, employment of experts and travel. And for a third, neither ministers nor public servants are particularly welcoming of political review of their responsibilities, so they sometimes delay or fail to respond to committee reports. Committed members can cause embarrassment about such procrastination, but only if they are willing to make waves – and bear whatever consequences that may have. Many journalists think that committees are not normally the main game, so their work and findings deserve little attention.

Establishing a bipartisan Parliamentary Commission with responsibility for budgeting and staffing for Parliament would make Parliament independent of government control. It should have responsibility for management of all aspects of Parliament and its committees, so that a government could not immobilise work of the houses through inadequate funding and staffing. Making committees work effectively depends on members' and the public's determination.

The Australian Collaboration of peak NGO councils constructively suggests that:

Government accountability and trust in government could be strengthened by passage of a Commonwealth Act matching the Canadian Federal Accountability Act 2006. Under the Canadian Act, all corporate and union donations to political parties and candidates are banned; the amount an individual can donate has been reduced; a new Commissioner of Lobbying is created; ministerial staff and senior public servants are prohibited from lobbying for five years after leaving office; and an independent tribunal is created to increase protection for whistleblowers. In addition to these provisions, under this Act the role of the Ethics Commissioner and the Auditor General has been strengthened. The role of the Ethics Commissioner is to consider complaints from politicians and members of the public and to fine violations. The role of the Auditor General is to aid accountability

by conducting independent audits of federal government. An
Accountability Act in Australia would reduce the opportunity for
corruption and undue political influence; restrict election financing;
give Australians confidence that lobbying is done ethically; provide
protection to whistleblowers; and hold the Government accountable
for financial operations through a rigorous auditing process.[49]

Revitalising politics also requires reform of the parties. Political parties
are the least popular type of voluntary association in Australia, attracting
affiliation from only 4 per cent of respondents to a 2002 social attitudes
survey.[50] NGOs that offer the opportunity to make a difference have
much larger memberships: groups helping people with special needs
attracted 14 per cent; environment and aid organisations such as
the Australian Conservation Foundation and World Vision attracted
10 per cent; and groups that promote rights such as of women or
refugees attracted 7 per cent of respondents. Political science professor
Gerry Stoker, of the University of Manchester, writes that 'we need a
politics designed for amateurs so that citizens can engage in politics and
retain a life'; his comments are also entirely applicable to Australia.[51]

It is vital to also address the intra-party democratic deficit. Members
often feel powerless and frustrated about lack of engagement with
parliamentarians. The dominant role of factions in both the Liberal
and Labor parties undermines confidence that the best candidates will
be selected and in the possibility of reasonable policy development.
The destructiveness of factional conflict erodes party democracy and
reduces trust and accountability. Members sometimes drop out when
they find parties controlling, when they find that 'involvement is
time consuming; [that] it is all about compromises, ambiguities,
and the absence of finality', notes Michelle Grattan.[52] A change of
culture is required. An explicit commitment to help members make
a contribution by providing more opportunities for the exchange of
ideas and information is required, including through speakers and
discussions at branch meetings. The revitalisation of party branches and
committees comes principally from the membership. Party rules need
to be fairly and unflinchingly upheld so that abuses such as branch
stacking are eliminated. The American system of primary voting by

party affiliates has been suggested as a means of widening the range of candidates, but it is difficult to see where the drive for such a major reform would originate in Australia. New technologies offer possibilities for retaining and increasing party membership, improving consultation and communication, strengthening advocacy and expanding the parties' financial bases.

The parties must improve consultation with the community. Public meetings in each part of the electorate called by MPs, senators or candidates can be highly effective means of 'sustain[ing the] conversation' between the public and their representatives.[53] Carmen Lawrence describes experiments in other countries, including: citizen-initiated parliamentary committee inquiries; greater use of Royal Commissions for long-term policy development; deliberative polls, citizens' juries and consensus conferences on contentious issues where balancing expert opinion and public understanding are important; internet forums and chat rooms; and public funding of advocacy groups.[54] Lawrence reports that the Scottish Parliament describes the ability of civil society to influence policy as the cornerstone of the new Scottish Constitution, and has held a festival of politics that included many means of discourse. Following a Commission on Democracy, Sweden has developed a democracy policy and assigned responsibility for the program to a senior minister.

A code of practice for appointments to advisory committees should be prepared, agreed and implemented. The British Commissioner of Appointments, employed to monitor, regulate and report on appointments to public bodies, is an attractive precedent. Encouragement for a diversity of think-tanks is important, for as Nobel Laureate Linus Pauling said, 'The only way to have good ideas is to have lots of ideas and to discard the bad ones.'

ANU academic Ian Marsh and David Yencken argue strikingly that '[e]very wholly new domestic issue on the Australian political agenda in the past thirty years was originally championed by a social movement', and point to the impact of the environmental, women's, Indigenous, gay, anti-globalisation, republican and other movements.[55] 'Eighty-six per cent of Australians are associated with one of the 700,000 not-for-profit organisations in Australia and 48 per cent with two,' says Elizabeth Cham, 'so they must recognise their power.'[56] Many of these have an interest in being, and the capacity to be, advocates. While there has been a long-term trend of falling engagement with traditional civil society organisations – such as the established political parties and churches – there have also been surges of input to new religious, ecological and anti-corporate formations. Networks of civil society organisations and political parties over particular issues can be powerful political forces. Citizens individually and in groups can work to analyse, educate, sustain, praise, criticise, goad, influence, reform and lead.

Governments take notice of interest groups such as corporations, business groups, small business, farmers, unions and cultural institutions, churches and other civil society groups, and are subject to pressures from other governments, global business, international NGOs and multilateral agencies. For electoral reasons, they must also take notice of civil society. Politics is a competition, in which power is very unevenly distributed, but in which no one is completely powerless. Those who opt out are choosing to make it easier for other interests to increase their dominance; participation makes an outcome which takes account of all concerns more probable. Professor Mark Considine, Dean of Political Science, Criminology and Sociology at the University of Melbourne, argues persuasively that for governments, partnerships including civil society, business, unions and government representatives can be effective means of increasing policy responsiveness to all these competing interests and needs.[57]

Security, generosity, cooperation, equity, ecological responsibility, inclusiveness and intellectual and cultural vitality can all be enhanced. Everyone has some capacity to influence others. In our democracy, even with its distortions and inadequacies, powerlessness is a personal choice. If everyone who cares about an issue became more politically active, public policy would quickly evolve. Everyone can write to their MP and to the paper, attempt to speak on talkback radio, influence their community organisation, church, business or union. Those who are really concerned can join political parties and influence their policies from inside. Many community organisations have the capacity to debate issues and make proposals. Politicians are like the rest of us: they respond better to encouragement than to blame. So when a constructive policy or action is announced, sending a letter or email of support will reinforce progress. We can all contribute to a shared campaign for a more secure, fair, sustainable and vibrant Australia and a more just and peaceful world.

chapter 8

a way forward

Conception and development precedes the birth of a new entity. We must nourish the future, so that it may emerge whole and with a chance of maturation.

Nelson Mandela

Nelson Mandela, one of the world's most respected leaders, visited Australia in October 1990. Victory over apartheid was imminent, but a constitution for South Africa which would guarantee the fundamental right of one person one vote was yet to be drawn up. When addressing a parliamentary luncheon, Mandela expressed appreciation of Australia's 'unswerving respect' of sanctions against South Africa while apartheid persisted, saying, 'Your role in the Commonwealth and United Nations is further demonstration of your unequivocal and principled stand on the side of those who respect the universal values of equality, freedom, justice and peace for all.'[1] Though it was only eight months since Mandela had been released from 27 years of imprisonment, he spoke without bitterness, and with such firm authority and grace that he was given the first standing ovation by members and senators in the new Parliament House. Many Australians want leaders who speak with Mandela's authority, based on the moral integrity of strong commitment to 'the universal values of equality, freedom, justice and peace for all'. We want Mandela's style of leadership, rejecting economic, ethnic, gender and other divisions and committed to building a fairer, inclusive society.

Such political authority requires committed engagement with democratic political processes, and this includes, on the part of our parliamentarians, both attentive representation and strong leadership. Representation involves finding out what voters think. Leadership requires analysing public issues and reflecting on how to tackle them, setting priorities and preparing strategies, and then explaining them and persuading the electorate of their value. Mandela is a great leader because he so eloquently articulates the anger and the hope of the South Africans he represents. Effective leadership involves both following and leading.

Politicians are often criticised for depending too much on opinion polls and focus groups, but parliamentarians in a representative democracy have a central responsibility to be attentive to voters' wishes. Representatives must listen to the opinions expressed in focus groups – but they should not be limited by them. An active politician has many sources of opinion available, including talking to constituents and checking people's responses to surveys. An effective political process requires that these methods be used often and well. Such attentiveness to attitudes and interests immediately illuminates the diversity of opinion. Representation requires compromises between the inevitable differences of interest and attitude which characterise a diverse society, but this does not make pandering to the assertive or the powerful inevitable. Political representatives can usually choose from a range of opinions and positions, and therefore have a degree of freedom to act with imagination and decisiveness while also seeking re-election. Public opinion is not fixed. Opinions evolve, and public discourse, rhetoric, policies and decisions of political leaders can be a major force in influencing the direction of change. We would do well to remember Abraham Lincoln's words about how good leaders bring out the 'better angels of our nature'.

A popular children's story entitled *Who Sank the Boat*, by Pamela Allen, tells of a cow, a donkey, a sheep, a pig and a tiny mouse that lived beside the sea.[2] One warm sunny morning they decided to go for a row in the bay. As each of the animals stepped into the boat it rocked dangerously, but each time capsizing was avoided ... until 'the tiny little mouse' jumped in, at which point the boat sank.

Australians experienced such a tipping point during 2006, when community concern about climate change rapidly took off. For decades scientists had been publishing evidence of increasing carbon dioxide in the atmosphere and environmentalists had been calling for cuts to emissions of greenhouse gases, but change came only because of intensifying concern about the consequences – rising temperatures, deepening drought and growing climatic turbulence – combined with (if not indeed caused by) increasingly powerful analysis and skilful advocacy. Only then was the opposition of energy corporations, other interest groups and their reactionary ideological allies overcome, and only then did the concern of the whole population rapidly increase. Such an explosion of awareness does not lead to change of public policy unless political processes are working well and representatives are either leading community education or immediately acting to address community concern. If governments remain unresponsive, there will be electoral consequences.

In 2007, Australian political debate has been energised. Kevin Rudd has injected fresh energy and insight, and opinion has moved his way.

John Howard has responded by strengthening his daily campaigning even further. Greens Senator Bob Brown was encouraged by the change in opinion about global warming. The media enjoyed a livelier contest and cheered all sides on. But much more than victory at an election is at stake. The issues are whether any side will respond decisively and comprehensively to the challenges facing Australia. This book suggests that voter attitudes are giving greater scope for policy change than most parliamentarians have yet seized. The book argues for both greater responsiveness of political representatives to electoral opinion and more – and more active – leadership. It commends concerns for the wellbeing of all Australians, the common good of our society and a national contribution to global peace and justice. Such an approach involves revitalising the political process by opening many more issues for public discussion and negotiation. It involves a genuine attempt to make our representative democracy more effective by basing policy on voters' preferences while at the same time recognising the responsibility of elected representatives to be careful analysts and humane, accountable decision-makers. This is a difficult task, involving constant evaluation, flexibility, imagination, wisdom and determination.

The vision outlined in the book is for an Australia which takes seriously the threats to human civilisation from environmental damage, global poverty, injustice and intolerance, and acts accordingly. Such an Australia will: be concerned with the health and wellbeing of all its citizens; act purposefully to deal with poverty and disadvantage and to reduce the increasing divide between the rich and poor; set targets and make serious commitments to the reduction of Indigenous poverty and disadvantage; invest strongly in the future through education, training and other means; be deeply committed to the continuous enhancement of its democratic and multicultural traditions; and take the strongest actions possible to strengthen international institutions, since without them humankind will never be able to deal adequately with the serious interdependent challenges it now faces. To achieve such a vision, the following pages summarise key issues confronting Australia and its relationships with the world that need urgent attention.

Major proposals

The book identifies eleven issues.

Climate change – Climate change is at once a matter of constraining rising temperatures, climatic turbulence and drought, a survival issue, and a major issue of social justice, because the poorest communities will suffer the most. As the country with the largest average GHG emissions per person, Australia has a physical, political and moral responsibility to swiftly and dramatically reduce those emissions. Three immediate actions are essential. First, we must ratify the Kyoto Protocol, to signal the start of our cooperation with the existing global strategy. Second, we must prepare, adopt and implement a national strategy listing ambitious short time-based targets for reduction of GHG emissions and the means for achieving them, which should include a comprehensive tax on carbon emissions and emissions trading. Third, and simultaneously, we must greatly strengthen our programs for reducing energy use and adopting renewable energy technologies. Increased support for R&D of renewable energy technologies is essential. The introduction of nuclear energy would be a wasteful means of producing electricity because of the enormous capital cost (which would be a major reason for needing a large public subsidy), uncertainties about pricing the output, the unsolved problem of waste disposal, and the risks of accidents or misuse in the manufacture of nuclear weapons.

Education – Preschool experiences are potent influences in determining social, intellectual and emotional development, yet Australia spends barely half the *average* proportion of national income of other developed countries on preschool education and support. Correcting this anomaly is arguably the highest priority for social policy. Investing in the physical infrastructure of primary and secondary public schools, vocational education and training institutions and universities to make up for the last decade of reductions and restrictions and to move forward is essential. Setting a target and timeline to cut child poverty would assist, as would expanding investment in early childhood services, particularly for children in needy households, plus increasing the funding of support for parents and the avenues parents can use to access that support, and sharply boosting intakes to quality trade apprenticeships and other forms of vocational and professional education. Major upgrading of opportunities for lifelong learning is also vital, to boost the civilising – as well as the economic – contributions of education to the expansion of human capability.

Employment – The claim made repeatedly by the Federal Government and the media that Australia now has virtually full employment is false. Unemployment persists after 15 years of economic expansion, and prevents one in twenty of the official labour force having the work which is essential to supporting themselves and their families, to making a contribution to the community, and to having dignified lives. The many more who are pushed out of the labour force, and the further 700,000 people who are underemployed through being unable to find all the paid work they want, are barely recognised. A goal of full employment would mean aiming to reduce unemployment to 2 per cent, and to produce sufficient employment growth to eliminate underemployment. Paying more, and more thoughtful, attention to reducing underemployment through skills training, work experience programs and reductions in educational fees, and to supporting all those who want additional work in their preparation and search for jobs, is vital. Economic policy must give the same attention to the growth of employment as to other macroeconomic goals, such as low inflation and external balance. At least $1 billion is required over the next three years for appropriately designed training and service sector jobs, especially in regions of particularly high joblessness.

The workplace – The Howard Government's workplace relations policy abolished the structure of fair industrial relations that had been operating in Australia for a century (and that had been globally affirmed by ILO conventions). By undermining trade unions, collective bargaining and minimum employment conditions, the workplace relations legislation abandons the goal of security and equity at work. Employer power is dramatically strengthened, which means that the young, ageing, semiskilled and otherwise vulnerable are opened to exploitation and to having their family life subjected to management whims. Restoration of an equitable framework of industrial relations is essential for personal wellbeing and national fair play. Repeal of the falsely named 'WorkChoices' Act and abolishing the system of individual contracts known as Australian Workplace Agreements is essential. This would enable introduction of more family-friendly working practices and allow application of those ILO conventions which Australia has ratified.

Health – Australia urgently needs increased capacity for the treatment of depression and anxiety, for the promotion of understanding of mental health issues in the community, and for better integration of the mental health workforce with the health care system. Reducing the private health insurance tax rebate would release resources which are urgently needed to repair the public health system. The government should also set targets to reduce health inequalities and support a program to assist the many low-income Australians needing basic dental health care.

Housing – Rapidly rising house prices and increasing interest rates have reduced housing affordability, and consequently human security. Homelessness is widespread, and some waiting lists for public housing are a decade long. Increased rent assistance to low-income earners is vital. The Commonwealth and state governments must act cooperatively to make housing more accessible and affordable by rapidly building much more public housing, and by buying new houses to be rented on limited-term tenancies to people whose income is currently too high to obtain public housing but too low to rent at market rates.

Justice for original Australians – A renewed commitment to justice for Indigenous people is essential. It could be expressed at least in part through concerted negotiations for reconciliation between Indigenous and other Australians. One necessary condition for reconciliation is ensuring that Indigenous people enjoy the same access as other Australians to human services such as education, health, water, waste disposal and support for young children, older people and people with disabilities. A second condition is ensuring a rapid expansion of employment opportunities. A third is creating new opportunities for regional and national political representation by Indigenous peoples – to replace the abolished Aboriginal and Torres Strait Islander

Commission. One option that could be explored is establishment of seats in the House of Representatives for election by Indigenous people, as happens in New Zealand.

Reinvigorated multiculturalism – Since governments continue to approve large migration programs, renewal of the policy of multiculturalism is essential so that we effectively include those arriving in our communities. Decency, humanity and recognition of human rights suggest that Australia should honour its commitments through the Universal Declaration of Human Rights to welcome refugees. Effective commitment to multiculturalism also requires political leadership, comprehensive arrangements for welcoming migrants, explicit opposition to discrimination and the upgrading of educational and community development programs.

Investing in the future – About 1.2 million people are unable to find all the paid work they want, while at the same time there is a skills shortage. Investing in the future requires immediate initiation of a sustained program of upgrading physical and social capital, including education and vocational training at all levels, funded in part by recognising that investment benefits future generations and can therefore be properly financed through borrowing. Access to business credit must be accessible and interest rates kept as low as possible in order to provide conditions conducive to entrepreneurship and enterprise expansion. Renewed commitment to stimulating innovation through research, development and demonstration is vital to the dynamism of Australian manufacturing and services, as is reducing dependence on mineral exports. Increased support for research and innovation is crucial to Australia's economic vitality.

Global security and justice – International security and development have been undermined by the Bush Administration's unilateral aggression and contempt for international law. As a consequence, the world has become more insecure, violent, inequitable and climatically unstable. Obedience to such a regime has damaged Australia's security and international standing, and limited the scope for independent responses to threats to global wellbeing. Strengthening international security requires renewed commitment to the international rule of law based on the United Nations Charter. Australian security involves seeking peaceful solutions to conflicts through diplomatic negotiation, abandoning support for symptoms of American hubris such as pre-emptive aggression, reducing wasteful and provocative military expenditure, and engaging in efforts to strengthen UN forums. Improvement of global economic governance is essential. Extension of the range and depth of global public goods – such as international cooperation to reduce GHG emissions and curtail tax avoidance – is essential, as are rapid increases in finance for development. Equitable economic and social development requires major increases in aid, especially by the least generous donors, such as Australia. The rights of developing countries to decide their own economic and social strategies must be recognised, without imposition of the doctrinaire conditions habitually required by the IMF and the World Bank. Impediments to development such as agricultural protection and subsidies in rich countries need to be removed.

Enhancing a democratic Australia – Politics is a focus for resolving conflicts over competing interests. In recent years many interests and issues crucial to a harmonious, socially just, and environmentally sustainable society have been neglected or repressed. Revitalising Australian political processes involves replacing authoritarian tendencies with inclusive, participatory opportunities for dialogue and consultative engagement. Parliament's role would be enhanced by independent funding, increased staffing, greater involvement in decision-making about major issues and strengthening of committees. Mobilising political imagination requires enlivening public discussion and party organisations, and renewal of communication and accountability amongst ministers, parliamentarians, party members, community organisations and voters. Accountability legislation could set limits to donations to political parties, and to the amounts governments spend on so-called public information campaigns, and set ethical standards for politicians and their staff. The inhibition of public discourse caused by the narrowing concentration of media ownership should be addressed immediately by the establishment of an independent inquiry.

A viable path

To reach these goals and take these actions, strong leadership from government will be required. Political leaders, especially the Prime Minister and the national government, have to set out clearly and specifically the standards required in a decent society. When they do, citizens respond very positively. When they don't, they give licence to antisocial and divisive behaviour. Political leaders must have the determination – and the intestinal fortitude – to tackle the major problems we now face. New Zealand Prime Minister Helen Clark is a good example of the courage and foresight needed: she has, for example, committed to making New Zealand the first carbon-neutral country in the world.

Economic policies and ideology will have to change. Climate change is an example of massive market failure that cannot be dealt with unless there is substantial government intervention. An appropriate balance between environmental protection, personal wellbeing, economic development and social justice cannot be achieved without active engagement and action by governments. Several examples of approaches in other countries which have achieved greater overall success are described in earlier chapters.

The policies described in this book are both politically and economically feasible. Attitude and opinion surveys show that the issues of greatest concern to voters include: economic competence; security at work and work–family balance; climate change; health; education; and opposition to the Iraq War. A party with a strong commitment to economic security, to enhancing employment opportunities, to reducing GHG emissions, to improving the quality and accessibility of health and education services in all their aspects, and to a foreign policy aiming at international cooperation to reduce the threat of violent conflict would be politically attractive, providing it has credible policies for achieving these goals. Dissatisfaction with current values, and with the balance between work and the rest of life, and growing public discussion about these values and policies, suggest that Australia may be close to a turning point.

Economic feasibility for this alternative strategy derives from many aspects of the recommended policies, including increasing opportunities for paid work, which both reduces public outlays and increases taxation revenue, and constraining expenditure in areas where it is not needed. Wasteful public spending includes irrelevant weapons systems, ineffective attempts to protect people and buildings against exaggerated terrorist threats, detention centres for asylum seekers, ineffective and unfair taxation allowances for corporations and high income earners and excessive allowances for MPs. Funds for long-term economic and social investment can responsibly be increased by borrowing. Improvements in human wellbeing would reduce the rate of growth in demand for services. Gradual application of such a changed approach would itself be attractive through avoiding the policy turbulence which has characterised the economic policies of the last quarter century. The decade and a half of sustained economic growth gives us an opportunity now to move to firmer ground by balancing economic and social policy so as to improve both efficiency and equity, and thus strengthen security for all Australians.

A paradigm shift depends on both leadership and community action. Leaders can inspire and enlarge our vision. People respond enthusiastically to the hope offered by leaders who dare to be innovative, take risks, and explain fully why specific policies are desirable. A fine start would be to affirm the qualities of equality, freedom, justice and peace for all advocated by Nelson Mandela when he visited Australia. Renewal requires a strong moral commitment: or as leading British intellectual Geoff Mulgan writes, 'that sense of compelling mission and moral purpose that marks out true leaders and truly transformational administrations'.[3] Such bases offer a gateway to a viable path along which Australia could gradually become a more secure, sustainable, socially just and vibrant society.

We can't just rely on inspiring leaders, though. Each of us can act responsibly and in so doing contribute to inspiring others. Some years ago Peter Nicholson published a cartoon in the first frame of which a young couple is watching the first moon landing on television and one remarks, 'There's nothing we can't do'. In the second, contemporary frame, an old couple is watching a news report of a current disaster and one says, 'There's nothing we can do'. This feeling of powerlessness is widespread. It is seductive, but it is self-fulfilling. If we despair, we simply give up. If we retain hope and take the initiative, we can make a difference. Those people with clear aims, determination and persistence can and do influence outcomes. Robert Kennedy said in a famous speech in Cape Town in 1966:

> It is from numberless diverse acts of courage and belief that human history is shaped. Each time a [person] stands up for an ideal or acts to improve the lot of others, or strikes out against injustice, they send a tiny ripple of hope, and crossing each other from a million centres of energy and daring, these ripples will build a current which can sweep down the mightiest walls of oppression and resistance.

notes

CHAPTER 1

1 Published in Les Murray (ed.), *The Best Australian Poems of 2005*, Black Inc., Melbourne, 2005, p. 173.

2 Irving Saulwick and Denis Muller, *Fearless and Flexible: Views of Gen Y*, Report prepared for the Dusseldorp Skills Forum by Saulwick Muller Social Research, October 2006, p. 6.

3 Pamela Bone, 'Amid the comfort of friends and kindness of strangers, adieu', *The Age*, 19 December 2005, p. 13.

4 Real net national income per capita from Australian Bureau of Statistics (ABS), *Australian System of National Accounts*, 1 November 2006, Cat. No. 5204.0.

5 International Monetary Fund (IMF), *World Economic Outlook*, Washington DC, April 2006. Comparisons of gross national income (GNI) show the same relationship with Australia, at about the median for OECD countries. In 2003, Australia's GNI was US$29,200 compared with France US$29,300, Finland US$29,600 and Sweden US$29,800: ABS *Measures of Australia's Progress 2006 (MAP)*, 24 May 2006, Cat. No. 1370.0, p. 64.

6 Andrew Leigh, 'Three ideas on tax reform', *Progressive Essays*, February 2006, <http://andrewleigh.com>

7 ABS, *MAP*, 2006, p. 61.

8 Dennis Trewin, 'Forward', ABS, *MAP*, 2006.

9 All these and the following figures are from ABS, *Labour Market Statistics*, Cat. No. 6105.0, *Labour Force, Australia*, Cat. No. 6202.0 and *Labour Force, Australia*, Cat. No. 6224.0.55.001.

10 ABS, *MAP*, 2006, p. 189.

11 ABS, *Deaths, Australia, 2005*, 30 November 2006, Cat. No. 3202.0.

12 ABS, *MAP*, 2006, p. 178. The disaggregated figures are interesting. The proportions of people over 18 years with the highest life satisfaction included those who were married, whose life satisfaction averaged 81 per cent; and those with no long-term health condition (83 per cent). Those whose average life satisfaction was lowest included the separated or divorced (63 per cent); lone parents (60 per cent); those with mental and behavioural problems (46 per cent); those with high or very high levels of psychological distress (34 per cent); and the unemployed (56 per cent). Psychological research has found that such personal characteristics as optimism, high self-esteem, the ability to set compatible goals and progress towards them, the ability to understand and interpret the world, a sense of meaning in life (or spirituality), and a sense of personal control correlate with high levels of life satisfaction.

13 R. Veenhoven, 'States of nations', World Database of Happiness, <http://worlddatabaseofhappiness.eur.nl 2006>.

14 Rodney Tiffen and Ross Gittins, *How Australia Compares*, Cambridge University Press (CUP), Cambridge, 2004.

15 John Hooker, 'Australian values: Living down under', *New Matilda*, 14 June 2006.

16 Judith Wright, 'Child and Wattle-tree', *Collected Poems, 1942–1985*, Angus & Robertson, Sydney, 1994, p. 31.

17 James Jupp, *From White Australia to Woomera: The story of Australian*

immigration, CUP, Cambridge, 2002, p. 117.

18   Richard Alley, quoted by Fred Pearce, 'Global meltdown', *The Guardian*, Society section, 30 August 2006, p. 8.

19   Bill McKibben, 'How close to catastrophe?', *New York Review of Books* (*NYRB*), 16 November 2006, p. 23.

20   Barry Pittock, 'Are scientists under-estimating climate change?', reported in *The Age*, 22 August 2006, p. 4 .

21   Tim Colebatch, 'Canberra critics bulldozed: ACF head', *The Age*, 31 August 2006.

22   ABS, *MAP*, 2006, p. 98.

23   Chandra Shah and Gerald Burke, *Qualifications and the future labour market in Australia*, Report prepared for the National Training Reform Taskforce, Centre for the Economics of Education and Training, Monash University, November 2006.

24   ABS, *Research and Experimental Development: Government and Private Non-Profit Organisations, 2004–05*, 6 October 2006, Cat. No. 8109.0.

25   Lynne Chester and Michael Johnson, 'A new approach needed for Australia's infrastructure', in Peter Kreisler, Michael Johnson and John Lodewijks (eds), *Essays in Heterodox Economics, Proceedings of the Fifth Australian Society of Heterodox Economists Conference*, 11–12 December 2006.

26   *The Ipsos Mackay Report: Mind and mood*, No. 120, June 2006, Ipsos Australia P/L, Sydney, p. 8.

27   British Commission on Urban Life and Faith, 'Faithful cities', London, 2006, <http://www.culf.org.uk>

28   Anne Turley, 'Bright job figures hide darker picture', *The Age Business Day*, 24 April 2007, p. 12.

29   ABS, *Australian Labour Market Statistics*, January 2007, Cat. No. 6105.0, p. 64.

30   Joanna Abhayaratna and Ralph Lattimore, *Workforce participation rates – How does Australia compare?*, Staff Working Paper, Productivity Commission, December 2006.

31   Fred Argy, *Australia at the Crossroads: Radical free market or a progressive liberalism?*, Allen & Unwin, Sydney, 1998; Fred Argy, *Where to from here? The retreat of egalitarianism in Australia?*, Allen & Unwin, Sydney, 2001; Fred Argy, *Equality of opportunity in Australia: Myth and reality*, Discussion Paper No. 85, The Australia Institute, Canberra, April 2006.

32   Argy, *Equality of opportunity in Australia*, 2006, p. 83.

33   Deborah Gough, 'Australians value a "fair go" highest', *The Sunday Age*, 12 November 2006.

34   Peter Saunders and Bruce Bradbury, 'Monitoring trends in poverty and inequality: Data, methodology and measurement', *The Economic Record*, 2006.

35   ABS, *MAP*, 2006.

36   Melbourne Institute of Applied Economic and Social Research, *Poverty lines: Australia, March Quarter 2006*.

37   Tony Vinson, *Dropping off the edge: The distribution of disadvantage in Australia*, Report for Jesuit Social Services and Catholic Social Services Australia, February 2007.

38   Peter Saunders, 'Income distribution and redistribution', in Ian McAllister, Steve

Dowrick and Riaz Hassan (eds), *The Cambridge Handbook of Social Sciences in Australia*, CUP, Cambridge, 2003, pp. 131–32.

39   The ratio of the income of the 90th percentile to the 10th rose from 4.02 to 4.24. Andrew Leigh, 'What they are saying about us in Luxembourg', Andrew Leigh's web page, 23 September 2006. Another indicator is the inequitable growth of disposable family income during the Howard years: incomes at the 10th percentile rose by 7 per cent between 1995 and 1996 and 2003 and 2004, while those at the 90th rose by 17 per cent.

40   AB Atkinson and Andrew Leigh, *The distribution of top incomes in Australia*, ANU Centre for Economic Policy Research, Discussion Paper No. 514, March 2006.

41   *Ibid.*, p. 9.

42   John Collett, 'Company chiefs strike it rich', quoting remuneration consultant Mercer, in *Sydney Morning Herald* (*SMH*), *Money* section, 30 August 2006, p. 10.

43   The gaps between the salaries of university CEOs and staff have also widened. Even the Vice-Chancellors of the universities of New South Wales and Sydney receive total packages of $750,000 and over $1 million respectively: *SMH*, 29 August 2006, p. 4.

44   ABS, *Australian System of National Accounts 2005–06*, 1 November 2006, Cat. No. 5204.0.

45   *Ibid.*, p. 146.

46   ABS, *Australian Economic Indicators*, September 2006, Cat. No. 1350.0, p. 14.

47   Interest on mortgage and consumer debt rose to 11.4 per cent of Australians' disposable income in June 2006, compared with 9 per cent in 1989–90: *The Age*, 12 September 2006.

48   Tim Colebatch, *The Age*, 26 August 2006.

49   Carmen Lawrence, *Fear and Politics*, Scribe, Melbourne, 2006, pp. 2–5.

50   ABS, *Mental Health in Australia: A Snapshot, 2004–05*, 30 August 2006, Cat. No. 4824.0.55.001.

51   Martina Boese and Rosanna Scutella, *The Brotherhood's Social Barometer: Challenges facing Australian youth*, Brotherhood of St Laurence, Melbourne, August 2006, p. 32.

52   ABS, *Personal Safety Survey, Australia*, 21 August 2006, Cat. No. 4906.0, p. 6.

53   *Ibid.*, pp. 158–63.

54   ABS, *MAP*, 2006, p. 171.

55   Jupp, *From White Australia to Woomera: The story of Australian immigration*, 2002, p. 101.

56   *Ibid.*, p. 86.

57   Douw Kruger, 'Count your blessings, Australia', *The Age*, 25 January 2007.

58   Caroline Moorehead, 'Amnesia in Australia, *NYRB*, 16 November 2006, p. 14.

59   Quoted in Alison Broinowski, *Howard's War*, Scribe, Melbourne, 2003.

60   Katherine Betts, 'The ageing of the population and attitudes to immigration', *People and Place*, vol. 14, no. 2, 2006.

CHAPTER 2

1   *The Ipsos Mackay Report: Mind and mood*, No. 116, June 2005, Ipsos Australia P/L, Sydney, p. 6.

2   *Ibid.*, p. 3.

3   Irving Saulwick and Associates (in collaboration with Denis Muller and Associates), *The Howard Decade: A Saulwick Age poll study of voter attitudes to the Howard years*, Melbourne, February 2006.

4   These are comprehensively reported in S. Wilson, G. Meagher, R. Gibson, D. Denemark and M. Western (eds), *Australian Social Attitudes: The first report*, UNSW Press, Sydney, 2005.

5   *Ibid.*, p. 105.

6   *Ibid.*, p. 109.

7   P. Raskall, 'Tax reforms: An unfinished agenda or finishing the agenda', *Australian Options*, Summer 2005, p. 5.

8   Richard Eckersley, 'Losing faith in the official future', *Australia Institute News*, no. 47, June 2006, pp. 6, 7. Eckersley has consolidated his important, well-developed work in this area in a book entitled *Well and Good: Morality, meaning and happiness* (Text, Melbourne, 2004).

9   *The Ipsos Mackay Report*, June 2006, p. 32.

10   This follows John Quiggin, 'Economic liberalism: Fall, revival and resistance', in Peter Saunders and James Walter (eds), *Ideas and Influence: Social science and public policy in Australia*, UNSW Press, Sydney, 2005, p. 21.

11   The *Australian Financial Review* (*AFR*) provides plenty of evidence that Australia is being run by the income maximisers. It is generally written as though increasing income is the ultimate goal of productive life. The tone of the newspaper is unrelentingly acquisitive. In contrast to the *Financial Times*, there is negligible comment about wider issues.

12   Barry Jones, *A Thinking Reed*, Allen & Unwin, Sydney, 2006, p. 524.

13   James Walter, *Tunnel Vision: The failure of political imagination*, Allen & Unwin, Sydney, 1996, p. 52.

14   H.C. Coombs, 'A call to regain lost independence', *National Graduate*, Autumn 1993, p. 9.

15   Dean Drayton, to the national conference of the Uniting Church of Australia, 6 July 2006.

16   Richard Eckersley, 'The quality of life', in Saunders and Walter (eds), *Ideas and Influence*, 2005, p. 206. A particularly clear example of this is the change in values of American students who study liberal economics. Comparisons of the values of students before and after conventional courses in liberal economics show that there is a marked increase in their self-interestedness: the values implicit in their technical courses change their world view and they become more selfish and sceptical of altruism. Anecdotal experience suggests that the same change happens to many students in Australian neo-classical economics departments.

17   Michael Pusey, *The Experience of Middle Australia: The dark side of economic reform*, CUP, Cambridge, 2003.

18   John Elder, 'In search of the dinkum way', *The Sunday Age*, 17 September 2006.

19   This paragraph is adapted from John Langmore, 'Howard's end', in Barry Jones (ed.), *Coming to the Party*, Melbourne University Press (MUP), Melbourne, 2006.

20   Hugh Mackay, 'Howard: An ordinary bloke who feeds a nation's prejudices', *The Age*, 21 February 2006.

21   Robert H. Frank, Thomas Gilovich and Dennis Regan, 'Does studying economics inhibit cooperation?', *Economic Perspectives*, vol. 7, no. 2, Spring 1993.

22   Pilita Clark, 'A subject worth taking seriously', *Financial Times, Weekend*, 22–23 July 2006, p. 4.

23   Richard Layard, *Happiness: Lessons from a new science*, Penguin, New York, 2005, pp. 24–26.

24   *Ibid.*, p. 21.

25   Michael Leunig, *A Common Prayer*, Collins Dove, Melbourne, 1990.

26   Alexander Pope, *An Essay on Man*, Ep. iii, l. 303.

27   For example Carol Ryff, in F. Huppert et al., *The Science of Well-being*, Oxford University Press (OUP), Oxford, 2005.

28   Eckersley, 'The quality of life', p. 198.

29   Bentham based his idea on Francis Hutcheson's statement, 'That action is best, which procures the greatest happiness for the greatest numbers', in *Inquiry into the original of our ideas of beauty and virtue*, Treatise I, sec. v, para 18, 1725.

30   Hugh Collins, 'Political ideology in Australia: The distinctiveness of Benthamite society', *Daedalus*, Winter 1985, p. 148.

31   Keith Hancock, *Australia,* Australian Publishing Co. Ltd, Sydney, 1945.

32   Paul Ormerod and Helen Jones, 'Measuring happiness is flawed, legislating for it, madness', *AFR, Weekend*, 5–9 April 2007, pp. 6, 7.

33   *Ibid.*, p. 7.

34   The Universal Declaration of Human Rights, which was approved unanimously in the United Nations General Assembly while the Australian Dr Evatt was President in December 1948, sets a fine minimum global standard by providing a useful guide to such goals and their implications for policy.

35   See Brian Howe, *Weighing up Australian Values: Balancing transitions and risks to work and family in modern Australia*, UNSW Press, Sydney, 2007.

36   The Centre for Public Policy, *From welfare to social investment: Re-imagining social policy for the life course*, Conference Background Paper, 21–22 February 2007.

37   Tony Atkinson, 'EU social policy, the Lisbon Agenda and re-imagining social policy', *Henderson Oration*, presented to the conference From Welfare to Social Investment, Centre for Public Policy, University of Melbourne, 21 February 2007.

38   *Ibid.*, p. 16.

39   <http://ec.europa.eu/publications/booklets/move/55/index_en.htm>.

40   Clive Hamilton and Emma Rush, *The attitudes of Australians to happiness and social well-being*, The Australia Institute, Webpaper, September 2006.

41   Ian Lowe, Address to the Conservation Council of Victoria, 1993, p. 12.

42   Larissa Behrendt, *Achieving Social Justice: Indigenous rights and Australia's future*, The Federation Press, Sydney, 2003.

43   Cited in David Hollinsworth, *Race and Racism in Australia* (2nd edition), Social Science Press, Katoomba (NSW), 1998, p. 207.

44   The National Aboriginal Community Controlled Health Organisation and Oxfam Australia, *Close the Gap: Solutions to the Indigenous health crisis facing Australia*, April 2007: <http://www.oxfam.org.au/media/files/CTG.pdf>.

45   *Ibid.*, p. 3.

46   *Ibid.*

47   ABS, *National Aboriginal and Torres Strait Islander Social Survey, 2002*, available through <http://www.ausstats.abs.gov.au/Ausstats>; ABS, *The health and welfare of Australia's Aboriginal and Torres Strait Islander people 2005*: <http://www.ausstats.abs.gov.au/Ausstats/subscriber.nsf/Lookup/F54883AEE4071013CA25706800757A2E/$File/47040_2005.pdf>.

48   The National Drug Research Institute, 'Alcohol killed 1145 Indigenous Australians in five years: "One-size-fits all" doesn't work', Media Release, 12 February 2007: <http://db.ndri.curtin.edu.au/media.asp?mediarelid=83>.

49   Mark Leibler, cited in ABC (Australian Broadcasting Corporation) News Online, 'Indigenous communities being defamed: Lawyer', 30 May 2006, <http://www.abc.net.au/news/newsitems/200605/s1650383.htm>.

50   See Australians for Native Title and Reconciliation (ANTaR), '"Mainstreaming" Indigenous Affairs', 2005: <http://www.antar.org.au/content/view/95/292>.

51   *Ibid.*

52   Michael Morrissey, 'The Australian state and Indigenous people 1990–2006', *Journal of Sociology*, vol. 42, no. 4, pp. 347–54, p. 352.

53   David Cooper, 'Shared responsibility agreements: Whitewashing Indigenous service delivery', *Indigenous Law Bulletin*, 2005: <http://beta.austlii.edu.au/au/journals/ILB/2005/61.html>.

54   Australians for Native Title and Reconciliation (ANTaR), 'Federal budget: An opportunity squandered', Media Release, 10 May 2006: <http://www.antar.org.au/content/view/226/127/>.

55   Jon C. Altman, 'Economic development and Indigenous Australia: Contestations over property, institutions and ideology', *The Australian Journal of Agricultural and Resource Economics*, vol. 48, no. 3, pp. 513–34.

56   *Ibid.*, p. 518.

57   *Ibid.*

58   Susanna Dunkerley, 'Native title claims could be shortened under proposed laws', *National Indigenous Times*, 14 February 2007: <http://www.nit.com.au/breakingNews/story.aspx?id=9404>.

59   ABC, 'Study finds Indigenous communities losing out in land use agreements', 30 January 2007, transcript: <http://www.abc.net.au/am/content/2007/s1836293.htm>.

60   Jackie Huggins, 'The figures seem to confirm that practical reconciliation is not enough', *Online Opinion*, 19 November 2003: <http://www.onlineopinion.com.au/view.asp?article=872>.

61   Robert Manne, 'The stolen generations', in Michelle Grattan (ed.), *Essays on Australian Reconciliation,* Black Inc., Melbourne, 2000, p. 130.

62   John Howard, 'Address to the National Press Club in the Great Hall, Parliament House, Canberra', 25 January 2006, transcript: <http://www.australianpolitics.com/news/2006/01/06-01-25_howard.shtml>.

CHAPTER 3

1   Dr Mae-Wan Ho, cited in Institute of Science in Society, 'Shutting down the oceans Act III: Global warming and plankton; snuffing out the green fuse', ISIS Press Release, 23 August 2006.

2   P.M Cox, R.A. Betts, M. Collins, P.P. Harris, C. Huntingford and C.D. Jones, 'Amazonian forest dieback under climate-carbon cycle projections for the 21st century', *Theoretical Applied Climatology*, vol. 78, nos 1–3, June 2004, pp. 137–56, p. 149.

3   Andrew E. Dessler and Edward A. Parson, *The Science and Politics of Global Climate Change*, CUP, Cambridge, 2006; Tim Flannery, *The Weathermakers: The history and future impact of climate change*, Text Publishing, Melbourne, 2005; Elizabeth Kolbert, *Field Notes from a Catastrophe*, Bloomsbury, New York, 2006; P.H. Liotta and Allan W. Shearer, *Gaia's Revenge: Climate change and humanity's loss*, Praeger Publishers, Westport CN, 2007; George Monbiot, *Heat: How to stop the planet burning*, Penguin, London, 2006; A. Barrie Pittock, *Climate Change: Turning up the heat*, CSIRO Publishing, Melbourne, 2005.

4   The Intergovernmental Panel on Climate Change (IPCC) was established in 1998 by the World Meteorological Organization (WMO) and the United Nations Environment Programme (UNEP) to assess the 'the scientific, technical and socio-economic information relevant to understanding the scientific basis of risk of human-induced climate change, its potential impacts and options for adaptation and mitigation'. The IPCC views have been confirmed by the Royal Society, the US National Academy of Sciences, the American Meteorological Society, the American Geophysical Union and the American Association for the Advancement of Science. For the three latest reports (released in February 2007, April 2007 and May 2007), see IPCC, 'Climate change 2007: The physical science basis – summary for policymakers', Contribution of Working Group I to the Fourth Assessment Report of the IPCC, 2007; IPCC, 'Impacts, adaptation and vulnerability – summary for policymakers', Contribution of Working Group II to the Fourth Assessment Report of the IPCC, 2007; and 'Mitigation of climate change – summary for policymakers', Contribution of Working Group III to the Fourth Assessment Report of the IPCC, 2007.

5   IPCC, 'Climate change 2007: The physical science basis', 2007.

6   David A. King, 'Climate change science: Adapt, mitigate, or ignore?', *Science*, vol. 303, no. 5655, 2004, pp.176–77.

7   IPCC, 'IPCC second assessment – Climate change 1995', A Report of the Intergovernmental Panel on Climate Change, 1995.

8   IPCC, 'Climate change 2001: The scientific basis – summary for policymakers', Contribution of Working Group I to the Third Assessment Report of the Intergovernmental Panel on Climate Change, 2001.

9   The IPCC uses the following terms to indicate the assessed likelihood of an outcome or a result: Virtually certain > 99% probability of occurrence; Extremely likely > 95%; Very likely > 90%; Likely > 66%; More likely than not > 50%; Unlikely < 33%; Very unlikely < 10%; Extremely unlikely < 5%.

10   Tim Flannery argues, 'The outcome is that the pronouncements of the IPCC do not represent mainstream science, nor even good science, but lowest common

denominator science ... Yet in spite of its faults, the IPCC's assessment reports, which are issued every five years, carry weight with the media and government precisely because they represent a consensus view': *The Weathermakers*, 2005, p. 246.

11   Global dimming occurs when visible air pollution reflects sunlight back into space, creating a cooling effect which scientists claim masks the full effects of global warming. See Gerry Stanhill and Shabtai Cohen, 'Global dimming: A review of the evidence for a widespread and significant reduction in global radiation with discussion of its probable causes and possible agricultural consequences', *Agricultural and Forest Meteorology*, vol. 107, no. 4, 2001, pp. 255–78.

12   James Owen, 'Global warming preserved "mass kill" fossils, study says', *National Geographic News*, 18 October 2005.

13   World Health Organization (WHO), 'Climate change and human health – risks and responses', Geneva, 2001.

14   'New climate report warns of droughts', *The Age*, 11 March 2007.

15   IPCC, 'Climate change 2001: The scientific basis', 2001.

16   Saufatu Sopoanga, Prime Minister of Tuvalu at the 58th Session of the United Nations General Assembly, New York, 24 September 2003.

17   See Graeme Pearman and Alan Dupont, 'Heating up the planet: Climate change and security', Lowy Institute for International Policy, Sydney, Paper 12, 2006.

18   Nicholas H. Stern, *The Economics of Climate Change: The Stern Review*, CUP, Cambridge, 2007.

19   *Ibid.*

20   *Ibid.*

21   Ian Sample, 'Scientists offered cash to dispute climate study', *The Guardian*, 2 February 2007.

22   Jennifer Lee, 'Exxon backs groups that question global warming', *The New York Times*, 28 May 2003.

23   See ABC, *Four Corners*, 'The greenhouse mafia', broadcast 13 February 2006.

24   Robert Manne, 'The nation reviewed: Comment', *The Monthly*, February 2006, p. 15.

25   Kevin A. Baumert, Timothy Herzog and Jonathan Pershing, *Navigating the Numbers: Greenhouse gas data and international climate policy*, World Resources Institute (WRI), 2005.

26   Bureau of Meteorology (BoM), 'Australia's hottest year on record', Annual Australian Climate Statement 2005, 4 January 2006. The nation's annual mean temperature for 2005 was 1.09°C above the standard 1961–90 average; 2006 was the 6th hottest year on record (0.47°C above the standard 1961–90 average).

27   CSIRO, 'Climate change projections for Australia', CSIRO Atmospheric Research, Melbourne, 2001.

28   *Ibid.*

29   *Ibid.*

30   IPCC, 'Impacts, adaptation and vulnerability', 2007.

31   The United Nations Framework Convention on Climate Change (UNFCCC) is an international environmental treaty that emerged from the United Nations

Conference on Environment and Development (UNCED) held in Rio de Janeiro in 1992, also known as the Earth Summit.

32   As an 'alternative' to Kyoto, in July 2005 Australia adopted an international non-treaty agreement with China, India, Japan, the Republic of Korea and the United States. The agreement is called the Asia-Pacific Partnership on Clean Development and Climate, also known as AP6. The member countries, accounting for approximately 40 per cent of the world's carbon dioxide emissions, agreed to a model 'for private and public taskforces to address climate change, energy security and air pollution'. The partner countries agreed to cooperate on development and transfer of technology in order to reduce GHG emissions, but within a paradigm of economic development. Arrangements under AP6 enable countries to set their own goals for reducing GHG emissions but with no mandatory enforcement mechanisms. The lack of specific targets or timetables for reducing emissions, as well as the reaffirmation that 'fossil fuels underpin our economies and will be an enduring reality for our lifetimes and beyond', is highly problematic for addressing climate change on the scale that is required.

33   See Australian Greenhouse Office, Department of the Environment and Water Resources: <http://www.greenhouse.gov.au/international/index.html>.

34   Robin Eckersley, 'PM's stance on climate change immoral', *The Age*, 8 November 2006.

35   *Ibid.*

36   Australian Government, 'National Greenhouse Gas Inventory 2004: Accounting for the 108% target', Australian Greenhouse Office, Department of the Environment and Heritage, Canberra, 2006.

37   Jonathan Pershing and Fernando Tudela, 'A long-term target: Framing the climate effort', in Joseph E. Ady et al., *Beyond Kyoto: Advancing the international effort against climate change*, Pew Center on Global Climate Change, Arlington VA, 2003.

38   IPCC, 'Mitigation of climate change', 2007.

39   Australian Government, '2006: Tracking to the Kyoto Protocol', Australian Greenhouse Office, Department of the Environment and Heritage, Canberra, 2006.

40   Australian Conservation Foundation (ACF), 'Emissions trading – test for an effective scheme', 6 February 2007.

41   Department of Prime Minister and Cabinet, 'Prime Ministerial Task Group on Emissions Trading – Final Report', 2007.

42   Australian Government, 'Securing Australia's Energy Future', Department of Prime Minister and Cabinet, Canberra, 2006.

43   Peter Kinrade, 'Toward a sustainable energy future in Australia', *Futures*, vol. 39, nos 2–3, 2007, pp. 230–52, p. 247.

44   Australian Government, '2006: Tracking to the Kyoto Protocol', 2006.

45   Clive Hamilton, *Running from the Storm: The development of climate change policy in Australia*, UNSW Press, Sydney, 2001, p. 1.

46   ABC, 'Australia to debate prospect of nuclear power', 21 November 2006, program transcript.

47   Hugh Saddler, Mark Diesendorf and Richard Dennis, 'A clean energy future for

Australia: A study by energy strategies for the clean energy future group', World
Wildlife Fund Australia, 2004.

48   Australia Bureau of Agricultural and Resource Economics (ABARE), *Energy
Update 2006.*

49   In December 2006, the Federal Government awarded $13 million for eight
renewable energy projects under Australian Government's Renewable Energy
Development Initiative (REDI). The funded projects include: research into
cloud seeding to increase natural snowfalls and inflows to storages of the
Snowy Mountains Scheme; funds for the development of a waste recycling
system demonstration plant; a new yeast technology to convert plant waste
into ethanol; the development of photovoltaic cell process for improving the
yield from silicon for solar power; a regenerator for adapting supercritical cycles
to geothermal power applications; the development of a special vertical axis
wind turbine; turbulence mapping at wind energy sites; and funds for a new
generation modular biomass power plant.

50   Climate Action Network (CAN) Australia, 'Position paper on emissions
trading', 5 October 2005.

51   New South Wales announced a renewable energy target of 10 per cent by 2010
and 15 per cent by 2020 if elected in 2007. Other states have made similar
commitments, including Victoria, with a 10 per cent target by 2016; South
Australia, with a 20 per cent target by 2014; and Western Australia, with a 6 per
cent target by 2010. The European Union has committed to a 21 per cent target
by 2010, China to 15 per cent by 2015, and California to 20 per cent by 2010,
33 per cent by 2020 and 80 per cent by 2050.

52   Saddler, Diesendorf and Dennis, 'A clean energy future for Australia', 2004.

53   Department of Prime Minister and Cabinet, 'Uranium mining, processing and
nuclear energy – opportunities for Australia?' Canberra, 2006.

54   *Ibid.*

55   Stern, *The Economics of Climate Change*, 2007.

56   'Climate change: The year of living responsibly', *The Age*, 8 January 2007.

57   *Ibid.*

58   National Land and Water Resources Audit (NLWRA) 2002, 'Australian
catchment, river and estuary assessment 2002', Land and Water Australia,
Canberra, 2002.

59   Australian State of the Environment Committee (SOE), 'Australia State of the
Environment (SOE) 2006', independent report to the Australian Government
Minister for the Environment and Heritage, Canberra, 2006, p. 66.

60   Mike Young, cited in Rosslyn Beeby, 'Bid to take water power: Scientists called
in for crisis meeting', *The Canberra Times*, 21 October 2006.

61   ACF, 'Water crisis – govts must buy back water from irrigators', 12 January
2007.

62   National Water Commission, 'Australian Water Resources 2005 Fact Sheet',
2005.

63   Peter Cullen, 'Facing up to the water crisis in the Murray-Darling Basin', Speech
presented to the Brisbane Institute, 13 March 2007.

64   Water Services Association of Australia (WSAA), 'Testing the water: Urban
water in our growing cities', WSAA Position Paper No. 1, October 2005.

65   ABS, 'Drought drives down water consumption', Media release, 28 November 2006.

66   Quentin Grafton, cited in Australian National University (ANU), '"Living Murray" strategy needs rethink: Study', Media release, 6 November 2006.

67   Roy Morgan Poll, 'Australians still believe government should be doing more about water conservation', Finding No. 3985, 1 March 2006.

68   SOE, 'Australia State of the Environment (SOE) 2006', 2006.

69   Chris D. Thomas et al., 'Extinction risk from climate change', *Nature*, vol. 427, no. 6970, 2004, pp. 145–48.

70   Flannery, *The Weathermakers*, 2005, p. 183.

71   IPCC, 'Impacts, adaptation and vulnerability', 2007.

72   SOE, 'Australia State of the Environment (SOE) 2006', 2006.

73   IPCC, 'Climate change 2001: The scientific basis', 2001.

74   Flannery, *The Weathermakers*, 2005, p. 177.

75   SOE, 'Australia State of the Environment (SOE) 2006', 2006.

76   *Ibid.*

77   *Ibid.*

78   *Ibid.*

79   Rachel Carson, *Silent Spring*, Riverside Press MA; Houghton Mifflin, Cambridge MA, 1962.

80   Jim Woodhill and Niels G. Röling, 'The second-wing of the eagle: The human dimension in learning our way to more sustainable futures', in N.G. Röling and M.A.E. Wagemakers (eds), *Facilitating Sustainable Agriculture: Participatory learning and adaptive management in times of environmental uncertainty*, CUP, Cambridge, 1998, pp. 46–71.

CHAPTER 4

1   See Fiona Stanley, Margot Prior and Sue Richardson, *Children of the Lucky Country? How Australian society has turned its back on children and why children matter*, Macmillan, Sydney, 2005.

2   *Ibid.*, pp. 48–54, p. 75.

3   Rosanna Scutella and Paul Smyth, *The Brotherhood's Social Barometer: Monitoring children's chances*, Brotherhood of St Laurence, Melbourne, December 2005, p. 27.

4   Tony Nicholson, 'It's time to share the spoils', *The Age*, 14 July 2006.

5   National Academy Press, Washington DC, 2000.

6   Jo Chandler, 'Spare the early education dollar … spoil the child', *The Age*, 3 March 2006.

7   See James Heckman, 'Invest in the very young', in R.E. Tremblay, R.G. Barr and R. De V. Peters (eds) *Encyclopaedia on Early Childhood Development* [online], Centre of Excellence for Early Childhood Development, Montreal, 2004, pp. 1–2; <http://www.excellence-earlychildhood.ca/documents/HeckmanANG.pdf>.

8   Victorian Government, *A Fairer Victoria: Creating opportunity and addressing disadvantage*, Melbourne, 2005, pp. 9, 14, 16, 17.

9   Simon Marginson, 'Education and human capital', in Saunders and Walter (eds), *Ideas and influence*, 2005, p. 69.

10   See OECD, *Starting Strong II: Early childhood education and care*, Paris, 2006, p. 105; <http://www.oecd.org/dataoecd/14/32/37425999.pdf>.

11   Scutella and Smyth, *The Brotherhood's Social Barometer*, 2005, p. 27.

12   UNICEF, 'Child poverty in rich countries, 2005', UNICEF Innocenti Research Centre Report Card No. 6, Florence, 2005, p. 4.

13   *Ibid.*

14   *Ibid.*, pp. 20–23.

15   Richard Teese, 'Federal funding favours the elite', *The Age*, *Education* section, 1 November 2004, p. 10.

16   Andrew Macintosh and Deb Wilkinson, 'School vouchers and educational equity', *The Australia Institute Newsletter*, no. 47 June 2006.

17   George Megalogenis, *The Longest Decade*, Scribe, Melbourne, 2006, pp. 204–05.

18   Marginson, 'Education and human capital', 2005, pp. 69–70.

19   Simon Marginson, 'Higher education', in Manne (ed.), *The Howard Years*, Black Inc., Melbourne, 2004, p. 239.

20   OECD, *Education at a Glance 2006*, Paris, 2006, Table B.3.3 (data is for 2003), at: <http://www.oecd.org/datoecd/7/33/37344676.xls>.

21   Tim Colebatch, 'Wage cuts won't boost jobs', *The Age*, 20 June 2006.

22   Mark Coultan, 'Australia's tech sector lags world', *The Age*, 28 September 2006.

23   Marginson, 'Higher education', 2004, p. 223.

24   *Ibid.*, p. 224.

25   Marginson, 'Education and human capital', 2005, p. 80.

26   *Ibid.*, p. 226.

27   *The Age*, 13 September 2006.

28   See Dusseldorp Skills Forum, 'How young people are faring 2006: Key indicators – An update about the learning and work situation of young Australians', Sydney, 2006: <http://www.dsf.org.au>.

29   Marginson, 'Higher education', 2004, p. 239.

30   *Ibid.*, p. 241.

31   ALP, 'Australia's universities: Building our future in the world – A White Paper on higher education, research and innovation', Canberra, July 2006, pp. 67, 64.

32   ALP, 'Teaching standards: Recognising and rewarding quality teaching in public schools', Canberra, October 2006.

33   The Hon. Julie Bishop MP, Speech to the Curtin Institute Public Policy Forum, 24 July 2006, typescript.

34   The Hon. Julie Bishop MP, Inaugural Murdoch University Banksia Association Lecture, 3 October 2006, typescript.

35   See Louise Brooks, 'Trends in "traditional apprenticeships"', National Centre for Vocational Education and Research, Adelaide, 2004, Figure 1.

36   Dr Peter Kell, *TAFE Futures: An inquiry into the future of Technical and Further Education in Australia*, Report commissioned by the Australian Education Union, July–October 2006.

37   TAFE Directors Australia, 'An innovation platform for TAFE', Discussion Paper, September 2006.

38   This follows the Australian Research Council's award of funding to University of

Melbourne academics John Polesel, Jack Keating and Richard Teese for a two-year project commencing in 2007.

39   The Hon. John Howard MP, 'Skills for the future, Statement to Parliament', 12 October 2006.

40   Australian Industry Group, *The Australian Skills Fund: An Australian industry group initiative to support Australia's development as a more skilful global competitor*, Sydney, 2006.

41   Fred Argy, 'An analysis of joblessness in Australia', *Economic Papers*, vol. 24, no. 1, March 2005, pp. 75, 80, 77.

42   As calculated by the Centre of Full Employment and Equity (CofFEE) at the University of Newcastle.

43   See discussion of various estimates in Argy, 'An analysis of joblessness in Australia', 2005, p. 77 and on the CofFEE website, <http://e1newcastle.edu.au/coffee/>.

44   Paul Frijters and Robert Gregory, 'From golden age to golden age: Australia's "great leap forward"?', 2006, pp. 8–9: <http://econrsss.anu.edu.au/Staff/gregory/pdf/greatleapforward.pdf>.

45   Tiffen and Gittins, *How Australia Compares*, 2004, Tables 4.3 and 4.4.

46   See Parliament of Australia Joint Standing Committee on Migration, 'Negotiating the maze: Review of arrangements for overseas skills recognition, upgrading and licensing', Canberra, 2006.

47   Bill Mitchell, 'Full employment: Not even close', *Commentary*, 11 December 2006: <http://e1.newcastle.edu.au/coffee/pubs/oped/2006/cofFEE_Conference_Newcastle_11_12_2006.pdf>.

48   Megalogenis, *The Longest Decade*, 2006, p. 192.

49   For example, 60 per cent of young women want to be in full-time employment at the age of 35 whereas only 4 per cent want to be full-time homemakers, according to a large-scale longitudinal study cited by Belinda Probert, 'Introduction', in Patricia Grimshaw, John Murphy and Belinda Probert (eds), *Double Shift: Working mothers and social change in Australia*, Circa, Melbourne, 2005, p. 1.

50   An excellent recent study of why these changes are inappropriate is Michael Horn and Lucinda Jordan, *'Give me a break!' Welfare to work – A lost opportunity*, Research and Social Policy Unit, Melbourne Citymission, Melbourne, June 2006.

51   *OECD Employment Outlook 2004*, as cited by Barbara Pocock, 'Work, family and the shy social scientist', in Saunders and Walter (eds), *Ideas and influence*, 2005, p. 128.

52   ABS, *The Labour Force, Australia*, Cat. No. 6202.0, ABS, Canberra, as cited by Pocock in Saunders and Walter (eds), *Ideas and influence*, 2005, p. 127.

53   Tiffen and Gittins, *How Australia Compares*, Table 4.22.

54   Horn and Jordan, *'Give me a break!'*, 2006, p. 36.

55   *Ibid.*, p. 21.

56   Argy, 'An analysis of joblessness in Australia', 2005, p. 79.

57   Tiffen and Gittins, *How Australia compares*, 2004, Table 3.14.

58   ABS, *MAP*, 2006, p. 93.

59   'The state of Australian manufacturing: Summary report', Report for the

Australian Manufacturing Workers' Union prepared by the National Institute of Economic and Industry Research (NIEIR), Melbourne, July 2006.

60   *Ibid.*, p. vii.

61   Business Council of Australia, *New Pathways to Prosperity: A national innovation framework for Australia*, Melbourne, 2006, p. 4.

62   Jay Rutovitz, Mark Wakeham and Monica Richter, 'A bright future: 25% renewable energy for Australia by 2020', Report by the ACF, Greenpeace Australia Pacific, and CAN Australia, Melbourne, April 2007, p. 19.

63   See David Peetz, *Brave New Workplace: How individual contracts are changing our jobs*, Allen & Unwin, Sydney, 2006.

64   Andrew Fenton, 'Fight IR with fire', *Melbourne Times*, 28 February 2007.

65   Mark Davis, 'Revealed: How AWAs strip work rights', *SMH*, 17 April 2007.

66   Speech by Sharan Burrow, ACTU and ICFTU President, ILO Conference, Geneva, 6 June 2006.

67   'Research evidence about the effects of the 'WorkChoices' Bill', a submission to the Inquiry into the Workplace Relations Amendment (Work Choices) Bill 2005 by a group of 151 Australian industrial relations, labour market, and legal academics, 1 November 2005, typescript, p. 43.

68   This discussion has drawn on – in addition to the Senate submission by the 151 academics – Professor Joseph Isaac's Foenander Lecture, 'Reforming Australian industrial relations?', delivered at the University of Melbourne, 28 August 2006, and on Tim Battin, 'Choice for whom? A discussion of the new industrial relations laws', Australian Catholic Social Justice Council, Sydney, 2006.

69   See Professor George Williams' article in *The Age*, 25 August 2006. The ACTU Congress of 2006 endorsed using the corporations power for a new national industrial relations system, according to a report in *The Age*, 26 October 2006.

70   Human Rights and Equal Opportunity Commission (HREOC), 'It's about time: Women, men, work and family, Final Paper 2007', Sydney, 2007, pp. 75, 93.

71   *The Australian*, 17 January 2006.

72   'Care for kids – Labor's early childhood blueprint', Sydney, 28 July 2006, pp. 8–10.

73   See Media Release of 21 January 2007: <http://economics.hia.com.au/media/National%20Release%20AR%20Dec%202006%20HIA%20VERSION.pdf>.

74   *The Age*, 9 November 2006.

75   Hugh Stretton, *Australia Fair*, UNSW Press, Sydney, 2005, p. 127.

76   Julian Disney, 'Affordable housing in modern Australia: Over our heads – housing costs and Australian families', Paper (no. 142) presented at Australian Council of Social Service 2005 Congress, 'Re-imagining Australian society: Visions and solutions', Sydney, March 2006, pp. 67–75.

77   *Ibid.*, p. 72.

78   *Ibid.*

79   *Ibid.*

80   *Ibid.*, p. 74.

81   This and other parts of this discussion of health policy draw on my notes from an excellent presentation given by Dr Jenny Lewis to the New Directions in Australian Public Policy symposium, Centre for Public Policy, University of

Melbourne, 21 August 2006.

82   Gwendolyn Gray, *The Politics of Medicare: Who gets what, when and how*, UNSW Press, Sydney, 2004.

83   Access Economics, *The Economic Costs of Obesity: Executive summary of a report by Access Economics Pty Limited to Diabetes Australia*, Canberra, October 2006, p. v.

84   Australian Institute of Health and Welfare (AIHW), *Australia's Health 2006*, Canberra, 2006, p. 187.

85   Jenny Lewis presentation.

86   Industry Economics and Economic Forecasting, Commonwealth Department of Health and Aged Care, *Returns on Investment in Public Health: An epidemiological and economic analysis*, Canberra, 2003.

87   Jenny Lewis presentation.

88   Jenny M. Lewis, *Health Policy and Politics: Networks, ideas and power*, IP Communications, Melbourne, 2005, pp. 35–36.

89   *Ibid.*, p. 46; AIHW, *Australia's Health 2006*, pp. 394–95.

90   Accessible at: <http://www.budget.gov.au/2002-03/bp5/html/index.html>.

91   The principal diagnoses of mental ill-health, based on hospital separations, are depressive disorders (36 per cent), neurotic and stress-related disorders (17 per cent), alcohol-related disorders (12 per cent), and schizophrenia (11 per cent): ABS, 'Mental health in Australia: A snapshot, 2004–05', Cat. no. 4824.0.55.001, p. 2.

92   Mental Health Council of Australia, 'Time for service: Solving Australia's mental health crisis', Canberra, June 2006, p. 1.

93   *Ibid.*

94   London School of Economics, Centre for Economic Performance's Mental Health Policy Group, *The Depression Report – A new deal for depression and anxiety disorders*, June 2006.

95   Australian Council of Social Service (ACOSS), 'Fair dental care for low income earners: National report on the state of dental care', ACOSS Info Paper, Sydney, October 2006, p. 3.

96   *Ibid.*, p. 2.

97   *Ibid.*, p. 25.

98   Jenny Andersson, *Between Growth and Security: Swedish social democracy from a strong society to a third way*, Manchester University Press, Manchester, 2006, p. 9.

99   *Ibid.*, p. 132.

100 Tiffen and Gittins, *How Australia Compares*, 2004, Table 4.4.

101 *Ibid.*, Table 4.1.

CHAPTER 5

1   Stewart Firth, *Australia in International Politics: An introduction to Australian foreign policy*, Allen & Unwin, Sydney, 2005.

2   This and the following paragraphs are based on an entry by John Langmore in the forthcoming *Oxford Companion to Australian Politics*, OUP, Melbourne, 2007.

3   David Morgan, interviewed in the ABC TV series *Labor in Power*, broadcast June–July 1993.

4   See John Langmore and John Quiggin, *Work for All*, MUP, 1994, for a long critique of economic fundamentalism.

5   Treasury, *Pocket Guide to the Australian Taxation System*, Canberra, 2006.

6   ABS, *Australian conomic Indicators*, January 2007, Cat. No. 1350.0, is the source of this and the following statistics.

7   *Ibid.*, pp. 41–42.

8   Firth, *Australia in International Politics*, 2005.

9   Michael Lind, 'The unmourned end of libertarian politics', *Financial Times*, 17 August 2006, p. 11.

10 Alan Larrson, 'How can Europe create jobs? The development of the European Employment Strategy', lecture to the European Studies Centre, St Antony's College, Oxford, 30 April 2002.

11 These estimates are from ABS, *ABS Population Projections, Australia, 2004 to 2101*, 2006, Cat. No. 3222.0.

12 This would be a quite limited commitment, because the convention applies only to a refugee who has 'a well founded fear of being persecuted for reasons of race, religion, nationality, membership of a particular social group or political opinion, is outside the country of his nationality and is unable or, owing to such fear, is unwilling to avail itself of the protection of that country'.

13 From answers to questions in a Senate Estimates Committee reported in '"Creative" figures skew aid picture', *The Age*, 5 February 2007.

14 ACOSS, 'The bare necessities: Poverty and deprivation in Australia today', Submission to the Senate Inquiry into Poverty and Financial Hardship, Paper 127, June 2003.

15 Peter Saunders and Bruce Bradbury, 'Monitoring trends in poverty and income distribution: Data, methodology and measurement', *The Economic Record*, vol. 82, no. 258, September 2006, pp. 341–64.

16 'Disability case study', prepared by Margaret Clausen for the 2007 Anti-Poverty Coalition in South Eastern Melbourne.

17 John Langmore, 'Reducing poverty: The implications of the 1995 Copenhagen Agreement for research on poverty', in David Gordon and Peter Townsend (eds), *Breadline Europe: The measurement of poverty*, The Policy Press, Bristol, 2000. For the detailed report of action taken see UN Secretary-General, *Comprehensive report on the implementation of the outcome of the World Summit for Social Development*, A/AC.253/13, 14 December 1999.

18 Senate Community Affairs Committee, *Funding and operation of the Commonwealth – State and Territories Disability Agreement*, Canberra, February 2007.

19 Several OECD countries are raising retirement ages: for example, Germany is raising it from 65 to 67 over a couple of decades.

20 Atkinson, 'EU social policy, the Lisbon Agenda and re-imagining social policy', 2007, pp. 25–27.

21 Joan Hughes, 'Where to now? Income support and workforce participation for carers', from Welfare to Social Investment Conference, Centre for Public Policy, University of Melbourne, 22 February 2007.

22   *Ibid.*, p. 27.

23   OECD, *Economic Survey of Australia*, Paris, July 2006, p. 5.

24   Gerard Caprio and Daniela Klingebel, 'Episodes of systemic and borderline financial crises,' World Bank Discussion Paper, 1999.

25   Joe Stiglitz, 'Employment, social justice, and societal well-being', *International Labour Review*, 2002, pp. 1–2.

26   Peter Auer, *Employment Revival in Europe: Labour market success in Austria, Denmark, Ireland and the Netherlands*, ILO, Geneva, 2000; John Langmore, 'Some background context to the origins of the Accord', in K. Wilson et al. (eds), *Australia in Accord: An evaluation of the prices and incomes policies in the Hawke and Keating years*, Victoria University, Melbourne, 2000; Ralph Willis and Kenneth Wilson, 'Introduction', in Wilson et al. (eds), *Australia in Accord*, 2000.

27   Neil Warren, *Tax: Facts, fiction and reform*, Australian Tax Research Foundation, Research Study 41, 2004, p. 17.

28   Patricia Apps, 'The high taxation of working families', *Australian Review of Public Affairs*, vol. 5, no. 1, December 2004, pp. 1, 2.

29   AMP.NATSEM, 'Trends in effective marginal tax rates 1996–97 to 2006–07', *Income and Wealth Report*, Issue 14, September 2006, p. 7.

30   CEDA, 'Tax cuts for growth: The impact of marginal tax rates on Australia's labour supply', CEDA Information Paper 84, Melbourne, 2006, p. 1.

31   Shaun Wilson and Gabrielle Meagher, 'Howard's welfare state: How popular is the new social policy agenda?', in D. Denemark, Gabrielle Meagher, Shaun Wilson, Mark Western and Timothy Phillips (eds), *Australian Social Attitudes 2: Citizenship, work and aspirations*, UNSW Press, Sydney, 2007; Shaun Wilson, 'Not my taxes! Explaining tax resistance and its implications for Australia's welfare state', *Australian Journal of Political Science*, vol. 41, no. 4, December 2006, p. 533.

32   Bill McKibben, quoting Travis Bradford, *Solar Revolution: The economic transformation of the global energy industry*, MIT Press, Boston MA, 2006.

33   For example, Julian Disney, 'Tax distortions in the gun sights', *The Age*, 25 May 2006.

34   The OECD is undertaking significant work, and an international tax dialogue has been established amongst the OECD, IMF, World Bank, the UN and the Committee of International Tax Organizations. There was agreement at the UN in 2004 to upgrade the Committee of Experts on International Cooperation in Tax Matters.

35   The functions of an international taxation organisation could include: provision of a forum for discussion of tax matters including sharing of national taxation experience; the development of definitions, standards and norms for tax policy and administration; identification of international tax trends and problems; gathering and publication of statistical information; production of a periodical world tax report; and technical assistance to national tax authorities. Such an organisation would typically have a governing body representative of the members and responsible for drawing up broad objectives and major issues of policy, and a highly competent staff, and would hold regular meetings and issue technical publications.

36   John Quiggin, 'The end of the public sector debate', *The State of the Public Sector: The state of the States 2006*, Evatt Foundation, UNSW, Sydney, 2006, p. 52.

37   J. Mohan Rao, Lecture, UN Division of Social Policy and Development, New York, 1999.

38   Fred Argy, 'Fiscal policy for the future', *The State of the Public Sector*, 2006, p. 87.

39   Peter Sheehan, 'Accounting for government activities in Australia: The state of the budgets', Neil Walker Memorial Lecture, 2004.

40   Alan Kohler, 'Ignore Telstra's tantrum, we can manage', *SMH*, 9 August 2006, p. 24.

41   Argy, 'Fiscal policy for the future', 2006, p. 70.

42   Warren, *Tax: Facts fiction and reform*, 2004, p. 17.

43   Quiggin, 'The end of the public sector debate', 2006, p. 60.

44   Productivity Commission, 'Public support for science and innovation', Draft Research Report, 2006, p. xix.

45   All figures in this paragraph and the conclusion are from 'Investing in the economy's knowledge base', Research Note No. 24, Parliamentary Library, Canberra, 29 November 2004.

46   ABS, *Research and Experimental Development: Businesses 2004–05*, 28 August 2006, Cat. No. 8104.0.

47   ABS, *Research and Experimental Development: Higher education organisations, 2004*, 28 July 2006, Cat. No. 8111.0.

48   Greg Combet, 'Repositioning Australian manufacturing in the global economy', address to the National Manufacturing Summit, 12 December 2005.

49   ILO, *Global Employment Trends 2007*, Geneva, 25 January 2007.

50   Stephen Bartos, *Against the Grain: The AWB scandal and why it happened*, UNSW Press Briefings Series, Sydney, 2006, p. 9.

51   Lindsay Tanner, 'Hypocritical champions of competition', *AFR*, 20 July 2006, p. 79.

52   Enterprise Strategy Group, *Ahead of the Curve*, Forfás, Dublin, 2004

53   *Ibid.*

CHAPTER 6

1   Sir Brian Barder's website, <http://www.barder.com/brian/1pointofview/Q14May03.htm>.

2   'The Iraq deaths study was valid and correct', article signed by 27 medical scholars and practitioners in *The Age*, 24 October 2006.

3   Louis Uchitelle, 'When talk of guns and butter includes lives lost', *New York Times*, 15 January 2006.

4   Jürgen Habermas, *The Divided West*, The Polity Press, Cambridge, 2006.

5   Max Rodenbeck, 'How terrible is it?', *NYRB*, 30 November 2006, p. 34.

6   Brian Urquhart, *NYRB*, 11 May 2006.

7   Editorial, *New York Times*, 8 May 06.

8   Schlesinger, quoted by Brian Urquhart in 'World order and Mr Bush', *NYRB*, 9 October 2003. For a fuller discussion of the argument of this paragraph and

other sources see John Langmore, *Dealing with America: The UN, the US and Australia*, UNSW Press, Sydney, 2005.

9   Rodenbeck, 'How terrible is it?', 2006, p. 34.

10 *Ibid.*, p. 35.

11 This section is based on Langmore, *Dealing with America*, 2005.

12 Stuart Harris and Amin Saikal, 'Alliance can bear differences on details', *AFR*, 17 June 2004.

13 Paul Monk, 'Threats to Australia's future security and prosperity', Paper prepared for Australia 21, July 2006, p. 21.

14 Paul Kennedy, *The Parliament of Man: The past, present, and future of the United Nations*, Random House, New York, 2006, p. 29.

15 Benjamin R. Barber, *Fear's Empire*, Norton, New York, 2003.

16 Geoffrey Barker, *AFR*, 12 March 2007, p. 62.

17 Geoffrey Barker, 'Sudden switch in battle plans', *AFR*, 19 December 2005.

18 Alex Tewes, 'National security of just defence? The next White Paper', Parliamentary Library Research Note, 10 May 2005.

19 The Weapons of Mass Destruction Commission, *Weapons of Terror: Freeing the world of nuclear, biological and chemical arms* (The Blix Report), Stockholm, 1 June 2006.

20 Jeffrey D. Sachs, 'How aid can work', *NYRB*, 21 December 2006, p. 97.

21 See, for example, Anthony Clunies-Ross and John Langmore, 'Political economy of additional development finance', *UNU-WIDER Discussion Paper 2006/09*, UN University World Institute for Development Economic Research, Helsinki, September 2006.

22 The formation of the Group of 20, an international forum of finance ministers and central bank governors, in 1999 (which met in Melbourne in November 2006) was one attempt to fill the gap. Its purpose is to promote international financial and economic stability and to address the challenges posed by increasing globalisation. Though its membership includes both major developed and developing countries, it is unelected, there is no process for changing the membership, the group does not have a global mandate and it has no secretariat and no powers. The G20 communiqués suggest that its working arrangements give too much influence to the host country, and if the host is ill-informed about contemporary issues and trends in economic, social and environmental thinking, as was the Australian Treasury at the time of the Melbourne meeting, the published outcome may have little significance.

23 Ernesto Zedillo (Chair), *Report of the High-level Panel on Financing for Development*, UN, 2001.

24 *Ibid.*

25 As an aside, the IMF also makes extraordinarily politically loaded intrusions into Australian policy formation. Hugh Stretton gives a stunning example of the IMF's perversity in his important book *Australia Fair*. He writes: 'The IMF would like to make our poorest people poorer with a permanently declining share of national income, and our richest people richer. You doubt that? Its March 2001 report on Australia urged the government to "take early action to delink pension and disability payments from wage growth, while substantially increasing participation requirements for welfare recipients".' The IMF also

advised the government to abolish the arbitration system of awards for pay and conditions, except for a safety net for the lowest paid, advice which of course the Howard Government is taking. The same report also recommended a cut in the top rate of income tax and an increase in the income level at which it sets in. So the IMF proposed a continuous shift of resources from the poorest Australians – specifically including people with disabilities – to the already well off. The IMF confuses ends and means, and rejects the importance of political processes.

26   Human Security Centre, *Human Security Report 2005*, University of British Columbia, OUP, New York, 2005.

CHAPTER 7

1   Carmen Lawrence MP, 'The democratic project', November 2005, Paper circulated by her office, p. 1.

2   Anthony Arblaster, *Democracy* (3rd edn), Open University Press, Buckingham, 2002, Ch. 8.

3   Gianni Zapallà and Marion Sawer, 'Conclusion: Representation – Problems and prospects', in Gianni Zapallà and Marion Sawer (eds), *Speaking for the People: Representation in Australian politics*, MUP, Melbourne, 2001, p. 292.

3   Bernard Crick, *In Defence of Politics*, Penguin, London, 1993.

4   Arblaster, *Democracy*, 2002, p. 83.

5   *Ibid.*, p. 84.

6   Saulwick and Muller, *Fearless and Flexible*, October 2006, p. 9.

7   Bean in Wilson et al., *Australian Social Attitudes*, 2005, p. 127.

8   Walter, *Tunnel Vision*, 1996.

9   Bean, in Wilson et al., *Australian Social Attitudes*, 2005, p. 131.

10   *Ipsos Mackay Report 2006*, p. 3.

11   Quoted from a paper by Aaron Martin, 'Voter disengagement in the industrialized world', who in turn quotes Putnam, Pharr and Dalton, 'Introduction: What's troubling the trilateral democracies?' in Susan Pharr and Robert Putnam, *Disaffected Democracies*, Princeton University Press, Princeton NJ, 2000, p. 11.

12   ABS, *MAP*, 2006, p. 192.

13   David Lovell, *The sausage makers? Parliamentarians as legislators*, Department of the Parliamentary Library Monograph, AGPS, Canberra, 2004.

14   Norm Kelly, 'MPs incumbency benefits keep growing', *Democratic Audit of Australia*, ANU, Discussion Paper 27/06, August 2006.

15   Colin A. Hughes and Brian Costar, *Limiting Democracy: The erosion of electoral rights in Australia*, UNSW Press, Sydney, 2006, p. 8.

16   Norm Kelly, 'Electoral reforms a threat to democracy', 3 August 2006, accessed from <http://www.brisinst.org.au/resources/kelly_norm_electoral.html>.

17   Graeme Orr, 'Australian electoral systems: How well do they serve political equality?', *Democratic Audit of Australia*, ANU, Canberra, 2004, p. vii.

18   *Ibid.*, p. 12.

19   Lawrence, 'The democratic project', 2005.

20   Published by Reporters Without Borders.

21   Geoffrey Barker, 'Safer, but at what cost?', *Weekend Australian Financial Review*,

12–13 August 2006, p. 23.

22   See the online magazine *New Matilda* for information about a campaign for an Australian Bill of Rights.

23   Fiona Childs, 'Federal government advertising 2004–05', Research Note No. 2, Parliamentary Library, 20 July 2006; Hughes and Costar, *Limiting Democracy*, 2006, p. 63.

24   Civil society is defined by the World Bank as 'the non-government and not for profit groups and organisations that have a presence in public life, expressing the interests of their members and others in society': quoted in ABS, *MAP*, 2006, p. 173.

25   Margo Kingston, *Not Happy, John: Defending our democracy*, Penguin, Melbourne, 2004.

26   Saulwick and Muller, *Fearless and Flexible*, 2006.

27   John Cassidy, 'Murdoch's game', *The New Yorker*, 16 October 2006, p. 68.

28   Manne, 'The nation reviewed: Comment', 2006.

29   Tim Dwyer, Derek Wilding, Helen Wilson and Simon Curtis, *Content, Consolidation and Clout: How will regional Australia be affected by media ownership changes?*, Communications Law Centre, Melbourne, 2006, p. 170.

30   Editorial, 'A change for the worse: Canberra's media muddle', *SMH*, 12 October 2006.

31   Jay Rosen, 'Each nation its own press', in Jonathon Mills (ed.), *Barons to Bloggers: Confronting media power*, The Miegunyah Press, Melbourne, 2005, p. 27.

32   Lance Knobel, '*Nullius in verba*: Navigating through the new media democracy', in Mills, *ibid.*, p. 45.

33   Quoted by Christian Downie and Andrew Macintosh, in *New media or more the same? The cross-media ownership debate*, Australia Institute, May 2006.

34   Eric Beecher, 'The end of serious journalism?', in Mills (ed.), *Barons to Bloggers*, 2005, p. 75.

35   *The New Yorker*, 8 August 2003.

36   See, for example, Clive Hamilton, *Who listens to Alan Jones?*, Australia Institute Webpaper, July 2006.

37   Barry Glassner, *The Culture of Fear: Why Americans are afraid of the wrong things*, Basic Books, New York, 1999.

38   Beecher, 'The end of serious journalism?', 2005, pp. 69–70.

39   John F. Stacks, 'Hard times for hard news', *World Policy Journal*, Winter 2003/04, p. 14.

40   Margaret Simons, *Crikey*, 17 October 2006.

41   US Federal Election Commission.

42   To paraphrase James Walter, *Tunnel Vision*, 1996, p. x.

43   Andrew West, *Inside the Lifestyles of the Rich and Tasteful*, Pluto Press, Melbourne, 2006, p. 11.

44   Joseph S. Nye Jr and Philip D. Zelikow, 'Conclusion: Reflections, conjectures and puzzles', in Nye, Zelikow and King (eds), *Why People Don't Trust Government*, Harvard University Press, Cambridge MA, 1997, p. 263.

45   Greg Barns and Anna Krawec-Wheaton, *An Australian Republic*, Scribe Short Books, Melbourne, 2006.

46   Ian Marsh and David Yencken, *Into the Future: The neglect of the long term in*

Australian politics, The Australian Collaboration and Black Inc., Melbourne, 2004.

47   John Langmore, 'Parliamentarians, econocrats and the people', in Julian Disney and J.R. Nethercote (eds), *The House on Capital Hill*, The Federation Press, Sydney, 1996, p. 96.

48   See Langmore, *ibid.*, for a detailed description of the process and a discussion about it.

49   This paragraph is taken from *Democracy Watch*, published online by The Australian Collaboration.

50   Andrew Passey and Mark Lyons, 'Voluntary associations and political participation', in Wilson et al., *Australian Social Attitudes*, 2005.

51   Quoted by Michelle Grattan, 'The new political crisis', *The Age A2*, 7 October 2006, p. 21, from Gerry Stoker, *Why Politics Matters*, Palgrave Macmillan, Houndmills (Basingstoke, UK) 2006.

52   Grattan, 'The new political crisis', 2006, p. 21.

53   Quoted in Grattan, *ibid.*

54   Lawrence, 'The democratic project', 2005, p. 3.

55   Marsh and Yencken, *Into the Future*, 2004, p. 24.

56   Elizabeth Cham, 'Strategic challenges for the Australian not-for-profit organizations', Address to Centre for Public Policy, University of Melbourne, 6 June 2006.

57   Mark Considine, 'The power of partnerships: States and solidarities in the global era', Keynote address, Governments and Communities in Partnership Conference, Centre for Public Policy, University of Melbourne, 25 September 2006.

CHAPTER 8

1   Statement of Nelson Mandela, Deputy President of the African National Congress, at a luncheon hosted by Bob Hawke, Prime Minister of Australia, Canberra, 22 October 1990.

2   Pamela Allen, *Who Sank the Boat?*, Puffin Books, Melbourne, 1982.

3   Geoff Mulgan, *Financial Times*, 29 May 2006.

index

'457' visas 96

A Fairer Victoria 89
A more secure world 159
ABC 192–93
Abelson report 112
Aboriginal and Torres Strait Islander
    Commission 48
Aboriginals, *see* Indigenous Australians
accommodation 4, 107–10, 143–44,
    210
Accord with union movement 122–23,
    140
accountability of Parliament 199–200,
    212
ACOSS 115–16, 133–34
acquisitiveness 29
Action Against Hunger and Poverty
    170
ADF 172, *see also* military spending;
    security issues
advertising 186, 192
Age, The 73–74
ageing population 14, 136–37
Agenda for the Knowledge Nation 150
air travel 68
alcohol misuse 16, 48
Allen, Pamela 206
allowances, *see* welfare
ALP, *see* Labor Party
al-Qaeda 163
Altman, Jon 50
Americanisation of policy 21, 184
amphibians, declining numbers 82–83
'Amy' 134–35
An Inconvenient Truth 59–60
Anderson, Paul 65
Andersson, Jenny 119
Anglican Book of Common Prayer 35
Annan, Kofi 156–59, 168
Anti-Poverty Commission proposed
    135
anti-terrorism legislation 185
ANU Survey of Social Attitudes 24,
    34, 142
ANZUS Treaty 164
APEC forum 177

apprenticeships 96
Apps, Patricia 141
Arblaster, Anthony 180
Argy, Fred 12, 147
Asia Pacific Economic Cooperation
    forum 177
asylum seekers 19–21, 131–32, 211,
    see also immigration to Australia
Atkinson, Sir Anthony (Tony) 13,
    38–39, 137–38
ATSIC 48
AusAID 132–33
Australia
    alliance with US 163–67
    carrying capacity 131
    challenges to 7–22
    competitiveness 92
    current status 1–22
    democracy in 179–203, 212
    federal system 147–48
    foreign aid from 174–75
    greenhouse gas emissions 60–72
    water use 74–80
Australian Citizenship Council 31–32
Australian Collaboration of peak NGOs
    199–200
Australian Competition and Consumer
    Commission 152
Australian Conservation Foundation 8
Australian Council of Social Services
    115–16, 133–34
Australian Council of Superannuation
    Investors 14
Australian Defence Forces 172, *see also*
    military spending; security issues
Australian Electoral Commission 185
Australian Fair Pay Commission 103–4
Australian Greenhouse Office 63
Australian Industrial Relations
    Commission 104
Australian Industry Group 97
Australian Labor Party, *see* Labor Party
Australian Ministerial Council on
    Education Employment, Training
    and Youth Affairs 32
Australian Policy Online 194
Australian Research Alliance for

Children and Youth 113–14
Australian Research Council 150
Australian Social Attitudes Survey 24,
    34, 142
Australian Society of Authors 185
Australian Wheat Board 17, 151–52,
    167
Australian Workplace Agreements
    104–5, 210
average income 14
award conditions 104

balance of trade 101
Ban Ki-Moon 178
banking deregulation 123
Barder, Brian 158
Barker, Geoffrey 185
Bartos, Stephen 152
Beazley, Kim 165
Beecher, Eric 191–92
behavioural problems, see mental health
Behrendt, Larissa 45
Bentham, Jeremy 35
biodiversity 9, 81–84
Bishop, Julie 94
Blix Commission on Weapons of Mass
    Destruction 174
Bolton, John 159–60
Bone, Pamela 2–3
book publishing 193–94
Bougainville peacekeeping mission 170
Brain, Peter 101–2
bridging visas 132
Britain
    Commission on Urban Life and Faith
        10
    Commissioner of Appointments 201
    emissions reductions 64
    health policy 112–13
    in Iraq war 168
    poverty policy 135
Broadcasting Services Amendment Act
    2006 (Cth) 189–90
Brotherhood of St Laurence 16–17,
    32, 88
Brown, Bob 207
Browne, Peter 194

Brundtland, Gro Harlem 120
Budget 139, 186
Building Australia Fund 147
Building Better Cities 110
Building Code revisions for energy
    efficiency 67
Bush, George W 158, 161, 170, 173,
    see also United States
Business Council of Australia 10, 102

California, emissions reductions 64
Callinan, Ian 148
Canada, population density 6
capital expenditure, see infrastructure
car ownership 67–68
Carbon Capture and Storage 69
carbon dioxide 56–57, see also
    greenhouse gas emissions
carbon taxing 62, 64–66, 143
Carson, Rachel 54, 60, 85–86
Casey, Richard 164
Cassidy, John 189
casual employment 99
CCS 69
CDM 66
CEDA 142
central banks 139–40
centralised policy-making 125
Centres for Science, Engineering and
    Technology (Ireland) 154
CEOs, relative pay levels 13–14, 142
challenges 7–22
Cham, Elizabeth 202
Chandler, Jo 88–89
'Charmaine' 104
Cheney, Dick 160–61
child policies 88–90, 118, 137, 208, see
    also education
China, economic policy 43
civil liberties 3
Clark, Helen 213
clean coal technology 69
Clean Development Mechanism 66
Clear Channel, media coverage 189
Climate Action Network 71
climate change 7–8, 56–74, see also
    greenhouse gas emissions

attitudes to 206
effect on habitat 83
in Australia 61–63
major proposals 208
COAG, see Council of Australian
    Governments
coal, emissions reductions for 68–69
Cole Inquiry 17
collective bargaining 104
Collins, Hugh 35–36
Combet, Greg 150
Commission on Democracy (Sweden)
    201
Committee for the Economic
    Development of Australia 142
common good 138–41
Commonwealth Bank 108
Commonwealth Government, see
    government; Parliament
Commonwealth Low Income Health
    Cards, see health cards
Commonwealth Scientific and
    Industrial Research Organisation
    61
Communications Law Centre 190
community consultation 201
Community Development and
    Employment Program 47
Community Water Grants 76
competitiveness 92
Comprehensive Nuclear Test-Ban Treaty
    174
consumerism 31
contraception, global cost of 133
Convention on Biological Diversity 83
Convention on Refugees 131–32
Convention on the Rights of People
    with Disabilities 135
Convention on the Status of Refugees
    20
Coombs, HC 30
coral bleaching 55
corporations power 106
Costar, Brian 184–85
Costello, Peter 18, 130, 139, 145
Council for Aboriginal Reconciliation
    46

Council of Australian Governments
    mental health service funding 115
    poverty policy 135
    TAFE submission 95
    water conservation policy 75
Crikey.com 191–92
crime 17–18, 47–48
Cronulla riots 18
CSIRO 61
Cullen, Peter 78–79
current account deficit 10, 126

Darfur 168
Dawe, Bruce 11
Deane, Sir William 7
death rates 4, 15
debt
    balance of trade 101
    current account deficit 10, 126
    financial stress 12
    household debt 24, 126–27
Democracy Fund 160
Democrat Party (US) 128–29, 163,
    178
democratic deficit in international
    institutions 176–77
demographics 5–6, 130–33, 136–37
Denmark 90, 106, 117–20
dental services 115–16
Department of Families, Community
    Services and Indigenous Affairs 48
dependency ratio 137
depression, treatment of 114
deregulation 123, 139, see also liberal
    economics
desalination 80
detention 18–21
developing countries 174–77
Digital Television Act 190
disabilities, people with 16, 98,
    133–37
disincentives to work 142
Disney, Julian 108–10, 143–44
Division for Social Policy and
    Development 43–44
Dodson, Mick 47
Doomadgee, Mulrunji 17

Downer, Alexander 170
Drayton, Dean 30
drinking 16, 48
drought 9, 74–80
Dusseldorp Skills Forum 11

East Timor 169–70
Eckersley, Richard 25, 30, 35
Eckersley, Robin 62
Economic and Social Council 176
economic policy 121–52
    for growth 24
    international development 175–76
    investing in the future 211
    misguided 26–31
    new direction for 37–45
    privatisation 149–52
    values influenced by 33
    water conservation 79–80
economic rationalism 26–31, 122–30
ECOSOC 176
education
    expenditure on 149
    for Indigenous Australians 15, 47
    HECS debts 92–94
    major proposals 208–9
    participation in 9
    policy relating to 37
    preschool education 89–90, 208
    privatisation of 91, 129
    public, support for 25
    schools policies 90–97
    university funding 91–94
efficiency dividend 9–10
Electoral and Referendum Amendment
    Act 2006 (Cth) 183–84
emigration from Australia 5
emissions trading 62, 64–66, 143
employment, see also industrial
    relations; unemployment; working
    conditions
    European Union 39–40
    full employment 98
    levels of 4, 125, 138
    major proposals 209
    of Indigenous Australians 47
    underemployment 11, 97–103, 209

Employment Outlook 91
energy efficiency 66–67
Enterprise Ireland 154
Enterprise Strategy Group (Ireland)
    154
Environment Protection and Biodiversity
    Conservation Act 1999 (Cth) 83
environmental issues 54–86, see also
    greenhouse gas emissions
    appreciation of 6
    biodiversity 9, 81–84
    health effects of 113–14
    in European Union 40
    work in dealing with 102–3
equality of opportunity 12, see also
    inequality
estuarine diversity 82
European Union (EU)
    economic policy 39, 43
    emissions reductions 64
    emissions trading 65
    environmental issues 40
    ideology of 29
    poverty policy 135
    stem cell research 154
Evans, Gareth 159
exclusion from rights 133–37
exports 101, 126, 131
externalities 28
Exxon Mobil 59–60

factionalism 200
Fairer Victoria, A 89
family, central to identity 24, 44
family carers 137
federal system 147–48, see also
    government
fertility rates 130–31
financial market deregulation 139
financial stress 12, see also poverty
Finland 90, 106, 117–20
Firth, Stewart 128
Flannery, Tim 54, 57
focus groups 205
foreign aid 174–75
foreign debt 10
forest management 85

Forfás (Ireland) 153
fossil fuel industry 59–60
Fraser Coalition Government 19, 122
freedom of the press eroded 185
Freeman, Cathy 195
full employment 98
'full fee' university places 91–92
Fund for Population Activities 132–33
future directions 203–15
Future Fund 110

GDP 3–4
gender equality 118
Generation Y 2, 180–81
geosequestration 69
geothermal energy 70
Gini coefficient 13
global public goods 212
global warming, see climate change
globalisation 138, 176–77, 181
Gore, Al 59
government, see also names of
    administrations, e.g. Howard
    Coalition Government
  Commonwealth government
    bookshops 186
  democracy in 179–203
  economic policy 37–45
  federal system unbalanced 147–48
  influence on values 36
  perceptions of 181
  self-advertising 186
  tax revenue and income levels 145
Grafton, Quentin 79
Grattan, Michelle 200
Gray, Gwendolyn 111
Great Barrier Reef 55
Great Prayer of Thanksgiving 2
Green Party 26
green scenario 25
greenhouse gas emissions 7, 56, see also
    climate change
  Australian 60–72
  market failure 128
  reduction schemes 60
Gross Domestic Product 3–4
Group of Eight, emissions reductions
    64
growth scenario 25
guest workers 96

Habermas, Jürgen 160
Hancock, Keith 36
Hanover (service provider) 108
Hanson, Pauline 18
happiness measures 5, 33–37, see also
    wellbeing
Harradine, Brian 132
Harris, Stuart 165
Hawke Labor Government
  immigration policy 19
  Parliamentary committee system 198
  social democratic strategy 122–23
Heads of State and Government
    meeting 39
health cards 116
health services 110
  central to identity 44
  major proposals 210
  public, support for 25
  skills shortages 103
Heckman, James 89
HECS 92–94
Hertzberg, Hendrik 191
Hicks, David 21, 160, 166
High Court 148, 182
High Level Panel on threats, challenges
    and change 169
Higher Education Contributions
    Scheme 92–94
Highland, Gary 49
Hill, Robert 170
Ho, Mae-Wan 55
home ownership 4, 107–10, 143–44
homelessness 108
Hooker, John 6
hours worked 31, 99, see also working
    conditions
household crime 17–18, 47–48
household debt 24, 126–27
household savings 15
housing 210, see also home ownership
Housing Industry Association 108
Howard, John, on Australian culture

52–53
Howard Coalition government
  adopts One Nation policies 18
  cuts off access by environmentalists 8
  daily campaigning 207
  disabilities policy 136
  economic policy 124–25
  environmental policy 59, 73
  health insurance policy 110–17
  hostility to NGOs 187–88
  Indigenous policy 45–46, 49
  industrial relations policy 103–6,
    125
  labour market policies 99
  Liberal dissenters from 198
  National Plan for Water Security
    77–78
  partisan advertising 186
  represses dissent 28, 182–88
  tax cuts vs. infrastructure spending
    142
  threats exaggerated by 185
  undermines UN 167–70
  US alliance 164–65, 172
  vocational training policy 96–97
Howe, Brian 38
HREOC 104, 107
Hughes, Colin 184–85
human consumption 79–80
Human Development Index 4
Human Rights Act proposed 185
Human Rights and Equal Opportunity
  Commission 104, 107
Human Rights Council 160
Human security report 178
hybrid cars 68

ice-sheets, melting of 8
identity 31–33
IGCC 69
ILO 105–6
IMF 43, 176–77
immigration to Australia 18, 98, *see*
  also asylum seekers
imports 101
imprisonment 18–21, 184
income levels 3, *see also* poverty

economic focus on 26–28, 33
government revenue and 145
policy relating to 37, 138
unequal distribution 13
Inconvenient Truth, An 59–60
Indigenous Australians
  exclusion from rights 17
  involvement in land conservation 85
  life expectancy 15
  major proposals 210–11
  prisoners disenfranchised 184
  reconciliation for 45–53
  sexual abuse in Indigenous
    communities 48
  visual art 50
Indigenous populations of other
  countries 52
Industrial Development Agency
  (Ireland) 153
industrial relations 103–6, 125, *see also*
  working conditions
  High Court decision 148
  major proposals 209–10
inequality 10–15, 103–6
  between children 88
  economic policy 142
  in health 112
  in Nordic nations 117
  increases in 28
infancy 88–90, *see also* child policies
infant mortality, for Indigenous
  Australians 47
inflation 27, 138
infrastructure
  crisis in 10
  declining investment 145–47
  home ownership and 109–10
  in Ireland 154
  vs. tax cuts 23–53
Infrastructure Australia 147
inheritance tax 143–44
Innovation report 2005-06: 149–50
insecurity 15–18, *see also* security issues
Institute for Public Affairs 187
Integrated Gasification Combined
  Cycle 69
interest groups 202, *see also* non-

government organisations
interest rates 15, 140
Intergenerational Report 113
Intergovernmental Panel on Climate
    Change 56–57, 61, 63–64
International Conference on Finance
    for Development 170
International Energy Agency 69
international institutions 176–77, *see
    also* United Nations
International Labor Organization
    105–6
International Monetary Fund 43,
    176–77
international tax agency proposed 144
international travel 5
internet 4–5, 190–91
intra-party democratic deficit 200
IPCC 56–57, 61, 63–64
Ipsos Mackay 44
Iraq War 26, 157–63, 189
Ireland 152–55
irrigation 74–75, 77–78
Irwin, Steve 195

Japan, solar panels in 143
'Jenny the barmaid' 31–32
job insecurity 24
Job Network 100
joblessness 97–103
Jobs Strategy 92
Jones, Barry 29, 150
journalism 193, *see also* media industry
Jupp, James 6–7
justice 156–78, 210–11

Keating, Paul 135, 197
Keating Labor Government 19–21,
    123–24
Kelly, Jackie 107
Kelly, Norm 183
Kennedy, Paul 168–69
Kennedy, Robert 215
Ki-Moon, Ban 178
Kingston, Margo 187
Kirby, Michael 148, 182
Kirner, Joan 121

Knobel, Lance 190
knowledge investment 149
'Knowledge Nation' 91
Kohler, Alan 146
Kyoto Protocol 7
    emissions trading under 65
    major proposals 208
    need to ratify 62–63

Labor Party
    Caucus solidarity 198
    health policy 114
    infrastructure policy 147
    labour force policy 152
    resurgence of 26
    tertiary education policy 93–94
labour force 119, 126–27, 152
land clearing 73, 84–85
land rights for Indigenous Australians
    50
Law Council of Australia 183, 185
Lawrence, Carmen 16, 179, 185, 201
Layard, Richard 34
leadership 205, 214
Leading Technology Development
    Allowance 150
legitimacy of institutions 196
Leibler, Mark 48
Leigh, Andrew 13
Leunig, Michael 35
liberal economics 26–27, *see also*
    deregulation; economic rationalism
life expectancy 4, 15, 47
Lincoln, Abraham 206
'Living Murray' Programme 75
Low Emissions Technology
    Demonstration Fund 70
Lowe, Ian 8, 44
Lowy Institute poll 166
Luxembourg Income Study 13

Mabo case 50
Macfarlane, Ian 140
Mackay, Hugh 10, 23–25, 33, 182
magazines 193
Maintaining Australia's Biodiversity
    Hotspots Programme 83

major proposals 208–15
Mandatory Renewable Energy Target
    71
Mandela, Nelson 53, 175, 203–4, 214
Manne, Robert 52, 60, 189
manufacturing industry 100–102, 120,
    126
Marginson, Simon 93
marine biodiversity 82
market failure 28, 128, 151–52
market fundamentalism 26–27, 36
Marsh, Ian 201
maternity leave 106–7
mature-age workers 11
McGeough, Paul 193
McKibben, Bill 8
MDGs 44, 174–75
media industry 14, 188–94
Media Peace Awards 193
median income 3, 138
Medicare 110–17
Melbourne, gang murders in 17
Melbourne City Mission 99–100
Members of Parliament, entrenchment
    of 183
mental health 16, 114–15, 210
Menzies Coalition Government 36
micro-regulation 127
migrants, qualifications of unrecognised
    98
military spending 161, 172–73
Millennium Assembly 44
Millennium Development Goals 44,
    174–75
Minchin, Nick 68
minimum wage 129
mining sector 50–51, 150–51
ministerial staff 186–87
mitigation targets 63
monetary policy 140
Monk, Paul 167
Moorehead, Caroline 20
More secure world, A 159
Morrissey, Michael 49
MRET 71
Muland agreements 49
Mulgan, Geoff 214

multiculturalism 3, 18–22, 211
multilateral engagement 171–78
Murdoch, Rupert 189
Murray-Darling Basin Water Agreement
    75

NACCHO 46–48
NAIRU 138
National Aboriginal Community
    Controlled Health Organisation
    46–48
National Action Plan for Salinity and
    Water Quality 84–85
National Affordable Housing
    Agreement 109
National Competition Policy
    Agreement 124
National Development Plan (Ireland)
    153
National Drug Research Institute 48
national emissions trading scheme 65
national exceptionalism 161
National Framework for Energy
    Efficiency 66
National Greenhouse Gas Inventory 63
national innovation blueprint 102
National Institute of Economic and
    Industry Research 101–2
National Land and Water Resources
    Audit 75
National Native Title Tribunal 51
National Plan for Water Security
    77–78
National Reconciliation Plan (Iraq)
    160
National Security Strategy (US) 164–65
National Strategy to Sustain the
    Reconciliation Process 46
National Water Commission 75
National Water Initiative 75
National Water Summit 76
native title 50–51
natural abundance 70–71
natural heritage, *see* environmental
    issues
Natural Heritage Trust 84–85
Natural Resource Management

Ministerial Council 84
neo-liberalism, *see* economic rationalism
New Zealand 52, 64, 213
News Corp 189
Nicholson, Peter 214–15
NIEIR 101–2
NNPT 173–74
non-accelerating inflation rate of
    unemployment 138
non-government organisations 187–88,
    199–202
Nordic nations 106, 117–20
Norman, Peter 195
Norway 90, 106, 117–20
nuclear energy 72–73
Nuclear Non-Proliferation Treaty
    173–74
nuclear weapons 173–74
NWC 75
NWI 75
Nye, Joseph 196

obesity 16, 111–12
ocean energy 70
OECD 4
O'Faircheallaigh, Ciaran 51
Office for Children (Vic) 89
Office of Indigenous Policy
    Coordination 48
Olympic Games 19, 146
On Line Opinion 194
One Nation Party 18
Organisation for Economic
    Cooperation and Development 4
Orr, Graeme 184
overweight and obesity 16, 111–12
Oxfam Australia 46–48

Pacific Solution 20–21
parental leave 107
Parliament
    Budgeting Commission proposed
        199–200
    committee system 194, 198–99
    effectiveness of 197
    entitlements 183
participation income 38, 137

participatory democracy 180, 195–203
part-time work 15
Pauling, Linus 201
Peacebuilding Commission 160
pensions, *see* welfare
personal debt 24, 126–27
Perth desalination plant 80
Pittock, Barrie 8
plutocracy 14
polar bears 58
political donations 184–85
political issues
    Australian democracy 179–203
    participatory democracy 195–203
    passivity about 28–29
    political parties 200–201
    separate Indigenous representation
        52
population issues 5–6, 130–33,
    136–37
positive psychology 34
poverty
    child poverty 88
    European Union 40
    financial stress 12
    global targets for 44
    policy to combat 133–37
    relative poverty 12
    taxation contributing to 141
power, uneven distribution of 14
preschool education 89–90, 208
Press Freedom Index 185
preventive medicine 113–14
Prime Ministerial Task Group on
    Emissions Trading 65
prisoners disenfranchised 184
private education 25, 37, 91, 129, 149
private health insurance 111
privatisation 123, 125
productive diversity 19
productivism 117, 127
Productivity Commission 12
professionalisation of politics 181
profits vs. wages 14
prosperity, *see* GDP; income levels;
    quality of life
public broadcasting 192–93

public expenditure, *see* infrastructure; welfare
public housing, major proposals 210
public service 187

quality of life 25, 30, 35, 44
Question Time in Parliament 197
Quiggin, John 126, 148

racism, policy to combat 132
radioactive waste 72
Raising National Water Standards 76
reciprocity principle 35
reconciliation for Indigenous Australians 45–53
recycled water 80
refugees 19–21, 131–32, 211, *see also* immigration to Australia
Regional Assistance Mission to the Solomon Islands 170
Regional Forest Agreements 85
relative poverty 12
religious attitudes, central to identity 44
Renewable Energy (Electricity) Act 2000: 71
renewable energy sources 70–71, 118, 208
representative democracy 3
republic movement 195–203
research and development, funding for 9–10, 92, 149–50
Reserve Bank 140
retirement age 136–37
Richardson, Louise 163
risk management 37
river conservation 75
Rodenbeck, Max 161
Roosevelt, Franklin 164
Rosen, Ian 190
Rothman, Garry 108
Roy Morgan surveys 12, 79–80
Rudd, Kevin 26, 102, 181, 206–7

Sachs, Jeffrey 175
Saikal, Amin 165
Salvation Army 98

Saulwick and Miller polls 180–81
SBS 192–93
Schlesinger, Arthur 161
schools policies, *see* education
Scottish Parliament 201
sea level rises 58
Securing Australia's Energy Future 66–67, 70
Security Council, *see* United Nations
security issues 87–120, 156–78, 211–12
self-determination for Indigenous Australians 45–46
Senate Committee system 194, 198–99
Senate Community Affairs Committee 133–35
Senate Estimates Committees 183
Senate majority 183
service industries 126, 151
sexual abuse in Indigenous communities 48
sexually transmitted diseases 133
Shared Responsibility Agreements 48–49
Sheehan, Peter 145–46
Shonkoff, Jack 88–89
Shortlist of Fourteen Structural Indicators 39, 42
Simons, Margaret 192–93
single mothers 98
Skills Fund 97
skills shortages 9, 126–27
smoking 16
Social Attitudes Survey 24, 34, 142
social democracy 38–39
social dialogue 140
social disadvantage 13
social harmony 18–22, 132
social inclusion 39
social indicators, for Indigenous Australians 46–48
Social Justice Project 108–10
social partnership, in Ireland 153
social settlement 37–45
Society for Knowledge Economics 102
socioeconomic determinants of health 112–13

SOE Report 76, 81
software investment 149
Solar Cities project 70
solar panels 143
Solomon Islands 170
Sopoanga, Saufatu 58
Southeast Asia, tree planting in 73
St Vincent de Paul Society 98
Stacks, John 192
State of the Environment Report 76,
    81
Stern Review 73
Stiglitz, Joe 139–40, 161
Stoker, Gerry 200
Stokes, Kerry 194
Strategy for Incomes 138
Street, Sir Laurence 17
Stretton, Hugh 38, 108
subsidiarity principle 148
Survey of Social Attitudes 24, 34, 142
sustainability, economic policy 138–41
Sweden 106, 117–20
    child policies 90
    Commission on Democracy 201
    health policy 112–13
    knowledge investment 149
    research and development funding
        150
Switkowski, Ziggy 72–73
Sydney Morning Herald 190
symbolic measures 51–53

TAFE sector 95–96
Taiwan Strait 165
talkback radio 191
Tampa crisis 19
Tanner, Lindsay 152
tariffs 122
taxation
    cuts in v. infrastructure spending
        25–53
    economic policy 141–44
    real increase in 27
    revenue from 125
    States' powers of 148
Technical and Further Education sector
    95–96

technical schools 95–96
technological change 180, 190–91, 201
Teese, Richard 90–91
terra nullius 45, 50
terrorism
    exaggerated fear of 15–16, 185,
        191–92
    in perspective 171–72
    used to justify spending increases
        129
    'war' on 161–62
tertiary education, see education
The Age 73–74
threatened species 81–83
Trade Practices Act 191
trade unions 104, 122–23, 184–85
training, see education; vocational
    training
transportation, energy efficiency in
    67–68
Treasury department 123–24, 130
Trewin, Dennis 4
trygghet 119

UK, see Britain
underemployment 11, 97–103, 209
unemployment 11, 97–103, see also
        employment
    levels of 4
    major proposals 209
    Nordic nations 119
    retraining and 91–92
unfairness, see inequality
unions 104, 122–23, 184–85
United Kingdom, see Britain
United Nations, see also names of bodies,
        conventions and declarations
    Framework Convention on Climate
        Change 62–63
    Fund for Population Activities
        132–33
    General Assembly Special Session
        43–44
    High Commission for Refugees 21
    improvements to 171
    on Iraqi war 157–58
    support for 158–60, 166, 177–78,

211–12
US undermining of 158–60, 167–70
United Nations Association of Australia 187
United States
  Australian alliance with 163–67, 211–12
  Democrat victory of 2006: 128–29, 163, 178
  health spending 113
  interoperability with 172
  Iraqi involvement 157–63
  knowledge investment 149
  obesity in 111
  poverty in 40
  preschooling in 90
  research and development funding 150
  undermining UN 158–60, 167–70
  voter turn-out 195
Universal Declaration on Human Rights 20, 211
university funding 91–94, 150
Urquhart, Brian 161
utilitarianism 35–36

values 31–33
Victoria 78, 88–89
Vinson, Tony 13
violence 17, 47–48, see also crime
vocational training 95–96, 100, 127
voter engagement 181–82, 184, 195

wages vs. profits 14
Wallace-Crabbe, Chris 2
Walter, James 29, 181
Wanandi, Jusuf 20
'war on terrorism', see terrorism
Warren, Neil 141
Washington consensus, see economic rationalism
water conservation 58, 74–80
wealth 14, 143
welfare
  households supported by 12–13
  Nordic nations 119
  policies on 125

social security payments 137
support for 25
Welfare to Work Program 13, 98
wellbeing 33–37, 138–41, 145–48, see also happiness measures
wet tropics rainforests 82–83
White Australia policy 17, 20
Whitlam Labor Government 18, 122
'whole-of-government approach' 48
Williamson, David 195
Wilson, Shaun 142–43
wind energy 70
women
  Aboriginal, violence towards 47–48
  labour force participation rates 119
work for the dole program 99
WorkChoices Act 26, 103–6
working conditions, see also industrial relations
  hours worked 31, 99
  Howard government attacks on 127
  major proposals 209–10
  Nordic nations 117–18
  retirement age 136–37
  work–life balance 106–7
Working Nation white paper 124
work–life balance 106–7
Workplace Relations Act 1996 (Cth) 103–6
World Bank, governance 176–77
World Economic Forum 92
World Health Organization, on heat deaths 58
World Resources Institute 60
World Summit for Social Development 40–43, 135
World War II 164
Wright, Judith 6
WSAA 79

Yencken, David 201
Young, Mike 76
Young, Norman 20
youth, challenges for 16–17

Zedillo panel 176
Zelikow, Philip 196

Also published by UNSW Press

WEIGHING UP AUSTRALIAN VALUES

Brian Howe

Australia's ongoing economic and social changes over the past 30 years have left many Australians feeling their lives are freer but also more precarious, as they come to see themselves in danger of social exclusion. In *Weighing Up Australian Values*, Howe examines why so many Australians feel this greater sense of risk, and suggests that, through coordinated government economic and social policies, 'risk' can be converted to opportunity.

Howe's book is one of big ideas, as he argues for new institutional arrangements that will help people to manage difficult transitions in life. He contends that society needs to give more attention to anticipating the risks that people confront throughout their lives.

BRIAN HOWE A.M. was first elected to the federal parliament in 1977, was Deputy Prime Minister of Australia from 1991 to 1995 and served continuously in the Hawke and Keating Ministries from 1983 to 1996. Since leaving politics in 1996, he has researched and taught social policy at the University of Melbourne, where he holds the position of Professorial Associate in the Centre for Public Policy.

ISBN 978 0 86840 885 9

Also published by UNSW Press

POWER WITHOUT RESPONSIBILITY

Anne Tiernan

Over the past 30 years, ministerial staffers have become increasingly powerful, their close relationships and access to government ministers giving them substantial influence on policy processes. A challenge to the very role of the public service, ministerial staff are nevertheless able to wield significant covert power without true accountability.

In *Power without Responsibility* Anne Tiernan identifies and examines these ongoing problems with governance and accountability in Australian politics. Through examining the contemporary working environment of political staffers and the issues they face, Tiernan identifies the systemic weaknesses in their operations that pose risks to Australia's governmental systems and suggests the responses that would best address these issues.

DR ANNE TIERNAN has extensive first-hand experience in examining and managing the interface with ministerial offices, having served as a former public servant in the Commonwealth and Queensland government sectors and worked as a consultant to many commonwealth state and government agencies. She completed her PhD on ministerial staffing under the Howard Government and is now a postdoctoral fellow at Griffith University's Centre for Governance and Public Policy.

ISBN 978 0 86840 981 8

Also published by UNSW Press

AUSTRALIA FAIR

Hugh Stretton

'Today, fairness needs defenders and there is none more eloquent and compelling than Hugh Stretton.'

Clive Hamilton

Drawing on a lifetime of research and experience, Hugh Stretton makes a passionate and convincing case for doing whatever it takes to keep Australia *fair*. Rejecting easy platitudes and vague assertions, one of Australia's leading thinkers sets out an ambitious – yet fully costed – plan that encompasses every aspect of Australian life.

Australia Fair is a manifesto that makes us realise that fairness is no longer necessarily our defining characteristic. Stretton challenges prevailing opinion and shows we can get back on track.

HUGH STRETTON is one of Australia's leading intellectuals who has made a profound impact on Australian society and politics across many decades. He is the author of *Ideas for Australian Cities* (1970, reprinted numerous times); *Capitalism, Socialism and the Environment* (1976); *Political Essays* (1987); *Public Goods, Public Enterprise, Public Choice* (with Lionel Orchard, 1994) and *Economics: A new introduction* (2000).

ISBN 086840 539 6